The Unconventional Minister

The Unconventional Minister

My Life Inside New Labour

GEOFFREY ROBINSON

MICHAEL JOSEPH
LONDON

MICHAEL JOSEPH

Published by the Penguin Group
Penguin Books Ltd, 27 Wrights Lane, London w8 5tz, England
Penguin Putnam Inc., 375 Hudson Street, New York, New York 10014, USA
Penguin Books Australia Ltd, Ringwood, Victoria, Australia
Penguin Books Canada Ltd, 10 Alcorn Avenue, Toronto, Ontario, Canada m4v 3b2
Penguin Books India (P) Ltd, 11 Community Centre,
Panchsheel Park, New Delhi – 110 017, India
Penguin Books (NZ) Ltd, Cnr Rosedale and Airborne Roads,
Albany, Auckland, New Zealand
Penguin Books (South Africa) (Pty) Ltd, 5 Watkins Street,
Denver Ext 4, Johannesburg 2094, South Africa

Penguin Books Ltd, Registered Offices: Harmondsworth, Middlesex, England

First published 2000
1

Set in 12/14.75pt Monotype Bembo
Typeset by Rowland Phototypesetting Ltd,
Bury St Edmunds, Suffolk
Printed in England by Clays Ltd, St Ives plc

A CIP catalogue record for this book is available from the British Library

ISBN 0–718–14421–X

To my wife, who hates politics
and had to put up with it all.

Acknowledgements

I wish to thank my editor, Tom Weldon, and my agent, Natasha Fairweather. Both have been patient with me, and Tom angry with me as circumstances required – but not for long, since Natasha's good humour and graceful presence were invariably to hand. A special thank-you also to Sarah Day of Penguin, whose expertise and calm saw the book through its final stages.

This book has been written without reference to official papers, in the absence of which the House of Commons Library played a most helpful role. My profound thanks to all the staff I troubled with my questions. They were without fail courteous and competent.

My constituency party, through its robust support for me during my parliamentary career, made the book possible. My debts of gratitude are too numerous to personalize. But they are well known to my friends in Coventry North West and the city as a whole, and to all of them I extend my thanks.

There are two people without whom the book could not have been written: Brenda Price, who organized my personal papers; and Margaret Sims, who alone could read my handwriting, and typed intelligently to quite unreasonable deadlines.

I have discussed aspects of the book with various friends and colleagues, whom it is probably safer to acknowledge collectively – and anonymously. My thanks to them all.

Any errors are, of course, my own responsibility.

Contents

1. The Mandelson Affair   1

2. Joska Bourgeois   16

3. Brown's Team   27

4. What a Carve-up!   34

5. Life at the Treasury   46

6. 'To Tax and to Please'   66

7. Mending the Gap   84

8. Finger in the PFI   98

9. Royal Cachet   108

10. The Euro: Anatomy of a Crisis   122

11. Sky Blues   141

12. Protecting the Heartlands   150

13. Labour and the Luvvies   161

14. The ISA Man Cometh   172

15. Wings and Wheels   183

16. Resignation   209

17. An Inspector Calls   234

    Index   244

1. The Mandelson Affair

Neither a borrower, nor a lender be
  Shakespeare, *Hamlet*, I

Hamlet was one of my set plays for A level. I had an excellent teacher who advised me to learn by heart Polonius's advice to his son Laertes, not just because we could score a few examination marks, but because he thought it good advice for life. It certainly is.

But one line I did not then appreciate was Polonius's injunction 'neither a borrower, nor a lender be'. It is plain enough that being a borrower puts us under an obligation to repay the loan. But in getting my businesses up and running I've had to borrow from the bank and risk my house on it. Most people borrow for one reason or another, do not like being in debt and successfully pay off their loans. In short, we all tend to agree with Polonius on borrowing.

About being a lender I was not so sure. After all, what is wrong with lending to a friend – doing them a good turn – provided that the purpose of the loan is a reasonable one with no ulterior motive or strings attached and that you are sufficiently sure you will get your money back? Perhaps Polonius's sage counsel here really amounted to no more than parsimony? However, the Peter Mandelson episode that broke with such furious, unforgiving violence in December 1998 suggested that Polonius might have been right after all.

Many people (including colleagues in the parliamentary Labour Party) seemed surprised that I had made a loan to Peter Mandelson. I was in the Treasury working closely with Gordon Brown and *ipso facto* must be anti-Peter. In fact I had known Peter longer and in the early days better than I had known Gordon.

Our acquaintance went back to my very early years in the Commons. Soon after the 1979 election, it fell to me to be an opposition whip on what became the 1983 Transport Act – distinguished by its commitment to privatizing the docks and extending the use of road humps.

Albert Booth and John Prescott were our shadow spokesmen. While John did extremely well mastering the details and keeping our standing committee members involved, Albert had a tendency to go on too long, oblivious to the fact that our side were finding other matters outside the committee room, particularly the bar, of greater interest. Peter Mandelson was Albert's researcher at the time. Peter was concerned to increase the attention and attendance span of our members and looked to me as the whip to do this. I explained that the length of Albert's speeches, which was in inverse ratio to the attendance of Labour members, would have to be shortened if we were to stand any chance. Even Peter's powers of persuasion were not up to that task! However, I was able to assure Peter of my goodwill by helping, together with John Prescott, to sort out his financial sponsorship with the Transport and General Workers' Union and the National Union of Railwaymen. My next act of financial support for him was to be somewhat larger scale and more far-reaching in its consequences.

Peter and I stayed in touch intermittently from then on. It was not a close friendship, but it was a good relationship. He consulted me about joining television and I urged him to do that in 1982. But even then it was clear that he had an interest in coming into Parliament. Like most of us he was in despair at the Labour Party at the time. My advice, for what it was worth, was that he should get a job, as well paid as possible, for a few years and by then things would have started to change in the party. They would have to if we were to survive. At this stage Peter's great potential was obvious. But I was not sure which direction it would take, although I regarded him as Cabinet material from the start. He also sought my advice when he was considering taking the position of Labour's director of campaigns and communications in 1985 and later when he had the opportunity to run for the safe seat of Hartlepool.

His years in television are generally judged to have brought out his deep intuitive understanding of how the media work. It is precisely this instinctive understanding of what interests the media, or how they will play a story and what story will run, that provides Peter with his ability to manage the news. In due course it was in that role that he was to become notorious – feared and admired in equal measure.

Other biographies have covered the 1994 Labour leadership race fully from a Blair, Brown and Mandelson perspective. There is no need for me to go into the twists and turns of those events. But I would like to explain it as I saw it. Firstly, my own preference was for Gordon Brown, but I had no doubt at all that Tony Blair would make an outstanding leader. For his part Gordon clearly believed that he had at least an understanding with Tony that Tony would not run against him. Gordon also clearly believed that he would have the support of Peter Mandelson in his campaign. The great tragedy of John Smith's death, in May 1994, came at the worst moment from Gordon's point of view. Gordon had been shadow chancellor for two years, winning great debates against the Tories but also lecturing his colleagues about the death of tax-and-spend. Tony, on the other hand, enjoyed a very good run at the Home Office, from where he was able to build support and popularity with MPs. He was also the overwhelming favourite with the press. It was Gordon, of course, who had promoted Tony's career at all its stages to the shadow Cabinet, and to secure from John Smith the position of shadow home secretary for him.

On the two brief occasions, right at the start of the leadership race, on which I discussed options with Peter in the Members' Lobby, he seemed to me to be genuinely distressed at the choice he had to make. He spoke of Gordon's 'vast political intellect'. On the other hand, Tony had 'greater appeal'. I was surprised he should use the words 'agonizing choice between his two best friends in politics'. Peter is not known to wear his heart on his sleeve. On the contrary he deliberately portrays an image of tight personal control.

In any event the agony was not prolonged. Within four days of John Smith's death Peter had made up his mind and his feelings appear to have returned to their proper place. His letter to Gordon of 16 May 1994 offered him his services, but it stressed in tones of harsh realism that there were few grounds for Gordon's success and left the decision to him, as if he were terminating a note from a civil service official: 'Will you let me know your wishes?' There was also a touch of condescension in the letter; Peter wrote: 'Nobody is saying you are not capable/appropriate as leader, merely that the timing is not right for you, or that you have vocal enemies or that you have presentational difficulties.'

Gordon is a proud man and he will have felt let down. But it was not this calculated act of withdrawal of support by Peter in itself that still now prevents the two from cooperating to their own and their party's best advantage. The problem is that once Peter became Tony's man, the role he saw for himself in the projection of the putative prime minister – and his skills in exploiting that role – meant that press briefings on policy and personality often quite needlessly gave affront to the shadow chancellor and others. This aspect of the problem does not belong to the present account of my relations with Peter. I have tried, however, in a later chapter to illustrate how quite unnecessary and destabilizing rows in the Blair government occur, and Peter's central role in the process. Without the distressingly frequent recurrence of this problem I am quite sure Gordon could work out a lasting modus operandi with Peter. But it is Peter who must change.

The problem of the Peter–Gordon relationship came up one evening at my flat in the Grosvenor House Hotel when Anji Hunter, Sue Nye, Fraser Kemp★ and I were having dinner. Anji and Sue are two remarkable women who had lived through the crisis of the leadership battle on opposing sides and remained good friends. The Peter–Gordon problem inevitably cropped up in the conversation and Anji not totally mischievously suggested that I might be the peacemaker. While being a great believer in the Ten

★ Anji Hunter is personal assistant to the Prime Minister, Sue Nye is political secretary to the Chancellor. Fraser Kemp became Member of Parliament for Houghton and Washington East in 1997.

Commandments, I am also a realist. There were only two people who could sort it out and, if they did not, then we would all just have to live with it. I let it be known, however, that I expected to be seeing Peter at the *New Statesman* party that month and would see if he would welcome dinner with me at my flat.

Peter arrived at the *New Statesman* party, held in my flat, with the BBC director-general, Sir John Birt. Neither was best pleased to meet Charlie Whelan, Gordon's spin doctor, in the lift. But Peter was not put out for long. He expressed his surprise that I had such a presentable flat. He admired a Cayley Robinson painting and the oriental prayer rug that has featured in many newspaper stories. He did not stay long. His parting shot was to remind me that he knew me when I had nothing and was no one. Jon Sopel, at that time a political correspondent with the BBC, was within earshot and remarked, 'Typical Mandelson.'

Peter responded positively to my subsequent invitation to dinner at the flat on 23 May 1996. From the start it was clear that Peter wanted to know where I was coming from. Declaring my colours, so to speak, has never been a problem for me. Hiding them I found more difficult. I made it clear to Peter that I was working closely with the prospective Treasury team in their efforts to prepare for government and felt we were making some progress. What he wanted to hear of course was a declaration of loyalty to Tony. It was not difficult for me to say that I thought Tony 'an outstanding, brilliant young man' about whom I would not have a wrong word said. This was by way of getting over the point that being part of Gordon's team did not mean in any way that I was not also very much in support of Tony.

He relaxed and talked openly about himself and his aims in life. He said then to me what he was repeatedly to say to Tony, the press and the world, that he wanted to be seen as his own man with a real job to do. On that evening he expressed an interest in joining the Treasury team if we came to form a government. He returned to it several times and I took particular note since it seemed that this aspiration of his, whether serious or not, might have implications for my own hopes in that direction! The other ambition Peter had for the Treasury was that Charlie Whelan should never set foot in it. He confidently predicted that Gordon would dispense with Charlie's services on the day after the election. (Indeed, there was a conversation on the topic between the PM and the Chancellor on 2 May 1997 in the rose garden at No. 10. The Chancellor, however, refused to sack Charlie.)

During the early part of the evening the telephone had rung three times with calls from Tony to Peter. On each occasion it was a question of how Tony should react publicly to a difficult issue of the day. Peter was strong and straightforward. He left no reason for Tony to telephone again. Yet he rang twice more, and was given the same advice. It was clear Tony felt reassured by Peter's advice. There was a two-way dependence: Tony needed Peter's sharp reactive instincts to handling the media and Peter needed Tony and his position to deploy his unrivalled handling of these matters. I offered Peter use of the direct-line telephone in one of the bedrooms of the flat. He declined and was obviously at ease in allowing the interdependent closeness of his relationship with the leader to be displayed.

If being only an acolyte was one frustration to Peter, the other was the straitened circumstances in which he lived. I had thought that his spell in television had been more remunerative than it was. He initiated the discussion of his financial circumstances and of his flat. He told me how miserable he felt there. Until then I had no idea where he lived or how. From what he told me it was a dingy place in Wilmington Square near Farringdon Road. My memory of this part of our conversation is quite clear. What I heard from Peter was a *cri de coeur*. He dedicated himself to New Labour but the salary was modest. He worked arduous long hours and had nothing to show for it, not even a decent flat where he could relax and entertain his friends. I asked what he had in mind. He replied, 'Oh, a place in Notting Hill is what I would really like. But it's too expensive and there is no one to help me!' At this point I said that financially I was in a good position and that I might be able to assist if he wanted me to. Nothing more was said about it that evening.

My interpretation of his remark was and remains that he was

looking for a loan. I would not say that is why he had come to dinner. But, to judge from the alacrity with which he responded, I do not think I misinterpreted what he said. The very next day, 24 May, he phoned me at 9 a.m. to ask rather anxiously if I really would help him buy a house. I replied, 'Of course, if that is what you want.' People ask me all the time whether Peter asked for the loan or I offered it. What I have written above is my distinct recollection of how it happened.

Against this background, I would not have thought it worth while disinterring this aspect of the loan – and certainly would have no inclination to do so – had it not been for the account of it given by 'friends of Peter' in Donald Macintyre's biography, *Mandelson*,★ and for the way Peter handled the press over the critical period. In the Macintyre book I am reported as having said something like, 'Look, Peter, you'll be in the government and eventually you'll be in the Cabinet. You shouldn't have to worry about these things; you should have somewhere in London where you can be settled, where you can have a good home, where you can relax, where you can bring people round and have a proper base.' The strong impression given is that the whole idea of the loan was mine! For good measure, Peter's friends' account then suggests that it was my idea that Peter would need 'something substantial'.

There is little doubt that it is Peter that is speaking here. I take exception to what he says, not because I would for a minute begrudge him any of the good things in life, but because it quite clearly conveys the impression that the loan and the size of it were initiated by me. There is almost the implication that I put him up to it. I find this most objectionable. Intentionally or not, Peter has contributed to the image that certain sections of the press have tried to create of me buying influence, power or even office. For the most part, journalists do not know me well. I am simply not like that and do not operate like that in practice. I would never think to use the existence of the loan – or any contribution I made to Labour Party research or leaders' funds – to gain influence or

★ Macintyre, *Mandelson*, HarperCollins.

advancement in personal or political terms. If there are still any doubters they should ask those people who have had dealings with me. I have made many such gestures: some bigger, some smaller. Some as gifts and some as loans – all of the latter, so far, having been successfully repaid. Whatever the assistance on my part, there have never been strings attached to it of any kind. Generosity is a redemptive quality in Shakespeare's drama. Is there anything wrong in that?

Things moved quickly. Peter was evidently in a hurry. Having confirmed my willingness to help, he asked if I would advise on the purchase. I again said yes, reflecting to myself that with eight or so properties in Britain and Europe I might be well placed to do so.

Notting Hill was the only place Peter was really prepared to consider. It was clear that the more expensive properties were offering much better value for money. After being gazumped on a house in Ladbroke Grove, Peter settled on a four-storey Georgian house in Northumberland Place. The loan requirement had risen to some £370,000. It was much more than he or I had envisaged. And he was quite undaunted at the prospect of so large a burden of debt. From my point of view I had no immediate require-ment for the money, and he had reassured me that his family inheritance would more than cover the obligation. It was also a fair observation that Peter in the private sector would easily command a salary to service the interest and repay the capital. His memoirs – eventually – would probably be sufficient, too. Peter was good for the money.

He completed the purchase in October 1996. I had no more to do with it once the loan documentation was completed in that month. I later learned there was a house-warming party and felt a bit miffed that I had not been invited.

In the intervening period, before I became Paymaster General and Peter became Minister at the Cabinet Office, there was nothing but occasional contact. During this time I gave no more thought to the loan or the house, until that fateful day, Monday, 21 December 1998, when out of the blue Charlie Falconer, a minister in the Cabinet Office and known to be a close confidant of the PM, came to my office accompanied by Lance Price, a political press officer at No. 10. I had not the faintest idea why they were coming. I had not met either of them before, though I knew Gordon had formed a high opinion of Charlie Falconer. Without sitting down Charlie came straight to the point: 'The press have the details of your loan to Peter Mandelson and the *Guardian* will be breaking the story tomorrow.'

Lance Price was rather aggressive, telling me within the first minute no less than three times that No. 10 were blaming Charlie Whelan for leaking the story. Of all the things that occurred to me in those first few minutes the least important was where the story had come from. Charlie Falconer was much more sensible. He was interested in how it came about that I had made an advantageous unsecured loan to a colleague. I explained to Falconer that I had known Peter for over twenty years, that I believed him to be good for the money and that he had told me he expected to inherit family money in due course. I took the opportunity to add that I found the last consideration distasteful and that it was good enough for me that Peter was a 'sound investment prospect'. Falconer was evidently relieved at this explanation. It was, of course, precisely what Peter had said.

They both, however, still asked, with an inquisitiveness bordering on rudeness, why I should have made the loan at all, even if I was satisfied about eventual repayment. I could not quite see where they were coming from, unless it was that I had some secret purpose for having done a long-standing political colleague a good turn. It became, particularly with Lance Price's interjections, an unpleasant sort of inquisition. It seemed they thought that, given enough pressure, some hidden truth would out. At one point I felt like politely asking them to leave the room. Rather the opposite unexpectedly happened. Ed Balls, who had heard of the meeting via the Chancellor's office, had joined us. He felt I was being unfairly challenged as to my motivation and himself decided to leave the room as a sign of his disapproval. The meeting ended almost at once. As they left, I turned to Falconer and said, 'I'm not going to be done in because of this. It was a perfectly correct arrangement between Peter and me and that's an end of it.' Of course, I knew once the door closed that it was not the end. Rather, I felt it would be the end of Peter and me.

What I found unacceptable as the drama unfolded was the way it seemed that Peter would try to off-load the blame on me or to widen the story to implicate others. It was a very difficult time for all of us. This was the biggest crisis of the new government. It was No. 10's objective to save Peter if possible. And of course Peter could be counted on to do everything to save his own skin. For example, he apparently explained to his senior civil servant that he had not informed the department of the loan because 'he was honouring Robinson's request to keep it confidential'. This was a point Charlie Falconer had kept coming back to. In fact it was confidential only because we had both mutually agreed that it was a private arrangement that concerned no one else. At the time we entered into it, that is just what it was. There was no hidden agenda. When Peter became Secretary of State for Industry and was responsible for the DTI investigation of my links with Maxwell the position changed. Peter should have declared it. Why did he not? I do not think it ever occurred to him to do so. I certainly would have agreed if he had asked me – I would have recommended that he did. In my ministerial declaration of interests at the Treasury I had included loans that I had made to the *New Statesman*, a magazine which I owned. I should add for the record that we had no discussions on it at all. So it was a massive oversight on his part. Nothing more, nothing less. He should have faced up to it – not, by some irrelevant prior mutual understanding, tried to escape it and effectively blame me in doing so.

The *Guardian* duly broke the story on Tuesday, 22 December. The morning headlines were just about as bad as they could be. The *Mirror* and the *Daily Mail* somehow carried it in every edition, while all the others – *Independent*, *Times*, *Telegraph*, *Sun* and *Daily Express* – changed their front and inside pages to carry the story in their later editions.

The *Sun* turned on us, and on Peter in particular; they called it

'Tory-style sleaze' and demanded his head. The editor got his wish within forty-eight hours: the Christmas Eve edition, looking more like *Grocer's Weekly* than Britain's biggest-selling tabloid, showed Peter's head stuck on a turkey on the front page. But for the intervening twenty-four hours Peter fought for his political life. He launched a TV and radio offensive, aimed at riding out the storm by putting all the facts on the table and declaring his innocence of any wrongdoing. It was to no effect. The questioning was constantly hostile and, though commentators reported that Downing Street did not consider it a hanging offence, it was clear we would be hanged, by a press lynch mob if necessary. Peter was floored almost from the off, when he was asked by Dermot Murnaghan on ITN if he had declared the £373,000 loan on his Britannia building society application form. He could not remember. In fact, it emerged that he had not declared it. Britannia announced it would take no action and was subsequently inundated by requests from other customers for similar treatment. I am told that extra staff were temporarily required to handle the situation! For Peter the suggestion that a criminal offence might have been committed was another nail in the coffin.

During his increasingly desperate forays before the radio microphones and TV cameras, as the day wore on Peter called me an 'old friend' who had innocently helped him out in buying a house, safe in the knowledge that I would in due course get my money back. I felt really encouraged by this as it recognized the letter and the spirit of the arrangement we had entered into.

Despite Peter's vigorous and fair defence of both of us throughout the day of the twenty-second, it was clear that the press, almost uniformly, had made up its mind: Peter had to go. This was the gist of the headlines and the leaders of the press next day, 23 December, to which, curiously, the *Guardian* proved the sole exception. Their headline seemed to hint at, and by so doing lead the story on to, wider implications. It used me to drag in Gordon: 'Mandelson wounded, Blair furious, questions for Brown'. It seemed odd, to say the least. Peter was not just wounded, but fatally stricken, the Prime Minister was quite rightly furious, but Gordon

Brown had nothing to answer for. Yet he was brought into the story by the allegations that I funded his operations, in respect of which I was asked a whole series of questions. There could be nothing much more irrelevant to the main, very major, news issue of the day.

There could be only one reason why the *Guardian* was so out of step with the rest of the press and this was that there was a determined effort to shift the focus away from Peter and on to Gordon and me. Later I was told by a respected journalist that it was 'just moving the story on'. What was meant was moving on a story that had not reached its conclusion so that it would not reach its conclusion. This was the only sensible interpretation that could be put on the *Guardian* story. Subsequently it was confided to me that a journalist close to Peter had been overheard reassuring one of Peter's political aides that he would be keeping an eye on the story to ensure it got written that way.

It is sad to think Peter could have tried to shift the blame on to me by briefing his famed media network that the responsibility was mine rather than shared. It was demeaning of him and hurtful to me.

Amidst the unrelenting hounding there were shafts of humour that made me smile. The *Guardian*'s pocket cartoonist, Austin, portrayed Father Christmas, pen in hand, telling Rudolph, 'I'm writing a letter to Geoffrey Robinson.' The *Sun* presented me as an estate agent willing to finance purchases and invited its readers to apply for help. I've still got the completed application forms from those who did!

Who leaked the loan two years after the deal was made? The truth is that I still do not know. The more I delved the more it appeared like a John Le Carré thriller, with tales of manuscripts being stolen from the Commons, counter-leaks and rescue missions.

Lance Price's culprit, Charlie Whelan, was put in the frame by the *Guardian*, but the paper then declared, somewhat bizarrely given it was effectively blackening his name, that it was not Charlie. There remains much speculation as to the source of the story, including the possibility that Peter had accidentally committed political suicide by leaking it himself, fearing it would be revealed by the *Mirror*'s Paul Routledge in a hostile biography which was about to be published. If Peter did, that was a big mistake. Routledge confessed the story had been in the draft but was being taken out to protect his friend Charlie from blame, who, for good measure, was not the source. How the leak happened is, in any case, irrelevant to the dramatic events it unleashed.

Once it was clear to Peter that his pilgrimages to media shrines would not deliver his salvation, the game was up. When he recognized that, he did the right thing in the right way. From this point he behaved with great dignity. At ten o'clock on the morning of 23 December Gordon phoned, requesting that the conversation be personal, without anyone in the private office listening on the line. He told me that he had just had a very difficult conversation with Tony. The bottom line was that Peter was resigning and that Tony insisted that I should go too. Gordon indicated that he had remonstrated with Tony but to no avail. Tony was adamant. I could tell from Gordon's tone of voice that he was genuinely upset but I reassured him that I perfectly understood the situation and would offer my resignation at once. All I needed to know was the timing and the arrangements.

He explained that Peter's resignation would be announced at noon and my own would follow, probably about 2 p.m. that afternoon. I said that was fine, but did not quite understand why both statements were not to be issued at the same time. I decided not to pursue the matter. Peter would be seen as a much bigger fish. He could choose the frying order.

Gordon told me that Tony would be speaking to me soon, which he duly did. The PM did not convey any sense that he blamed me for what had happened. Rather he was annoyed and dismayed at the press reaction to the private arrangement. He made precisely the point that for me had always been the nub of the matter: 'Someone like Peter,' said Tony, 'could easily earn in the private sector a salary that would justify a house like this.' I concurred and interjected that of course Peter was good for the money.

I have always got on well with the PM, a man I like and admire. Tony said he understood I had not 'inveigled' Peter into accepting the money. I thought that was a strange term to use but did not pick him up on it. It was not the time or place. I told him how sorry I was about the situation and thanked him for his support over what had been a difficult year. He reciprocated my gratitude and asked me to agree the letter of resignation he had personally drafted with his office and faxed over to me.

The letter was, in the usual way, flatteringly appreciative of what I had done. There was only one point that I wanted to add and that concerned our reform of corporation tax. Since this was the one measure more than any other that had got public finances back into a healthy state, I felt it was important to have it included. After all, a tax measure raising £5 billion on an ongoing basis and a £20 billion cash inflow for the government in the years running up to the next general election was not to be sneezed at.

Having received the text, I rang Tony's private office in No. 10 and spoke to Jeremy Heywood, the Prime Minister's principal private secretary, who was somewhat fazed that I should want to change the letter after it had been agreed with the PM and was ready to go. I pointed out that I had not agreed it and that in fact the PM had agreed I could change it. I insisted corporation tax reform must be added to the list of important things we had done. The letter identified me as single-handedly saving the coal industry. It was true but struck me as a bit odd. Whether it was intended as a compliment or intended to stick the blame for a policy that did not exactly find favour at No. 10 I was not sure! I was content with either interpretation.

I received one more call during this morning of high drama, from Peter himself. Peter came through on the phone just before he formally quit. He was not interested in how the story had broken. I assured him I did not think it was Charlie Whelan. 'Oh, I'm well past those sorts of considerations,' he said. It was evidently a cathartic experience for him. Peter told me he was 'dreadfully sorry' about what had happened. He mused that far from being the Prince of Darkness or the reincarnation of Niccolo Machiavelli, he thought he was really rather naive. He went on to say that he had decided to sell the house and repay the loan.

It was a hurried conversation, against the background of watching the BBC's political editor Robin Oakley, posted outside No. 10, informing the country that the Paymaster General was considering his position and was thought likely to resign in the early afternoon.

As I chatted with my colleagues and my private secretary, I could not help but recall the sequel to the quotation from Polonius at the head of this chapter: 'for loan oft loses both itself and friend'. Peter sold the house – at a handsome profit – and repaid the loan, so Polonius was wrong on the first point. Peter and I have exchanged only a few words since our resignations; I hope that Polonius is not right on his second point.

2. Joska Bourgeois

I first got to know Joska Bourgeois in 1974 when I was chief executive at Jaguar, shortly before I first became a Member of Parliament; she was the importer and distributor of Jaguars for Belgium and Luxembourg.

She was an egregious figure in a small world of top European motor-car executives in the post-war decades. She was a woman for one thing and in those days of rampant male chauvinism could never be forgiven for succeeding in a man's world. She was also a person of striking allure – one of those people to whom all heads turned when she entered a room. Robert Maxwell had a similar capacity. Joska had many other gifts: a brilliant though untutored mind; a gift for repartee; and charm, when she wanted to use it, to bring the birds off the trees. Nevertheless, there were very mixed feelings about her amongst my colleagues at Jaguar.

These were the heady days after the British Leyland merger in 1968 when the BL group, combining Austin, Morris, Rover, Triumph and Jaguar, had over 40 per cent of the UK market. There was a policy to expand sales into Europe – self-evidently a sound policy. Where it went wrong was to rush ahead, buying out independent distributors and agents at huge cost before the essential rationalization and improvement of product and facilities had been carried through.

The price to be paid for these independent privately owned sales businesses was bound to be high. They were unwilling sellers. The contracts to be bought out were subject to the law of the local country, where there were often precedents protecting the indigenous company. It was a protracted, messy and expensive business for British Leyland, but a field day for the distributors who were being bought out.

Joska despised the European distributors who transferred their businesses, ready-made sales organizations, to BL's competitors and prospered. Joska would have none of that as far as her Jaguar distributorship was concerned. Her heart was in Jaguar, which she had represented in Belgium since 1947.

She was at the peak of her commercial strength when our paths crossed at Jaguar. I had been appointed chief executive in 1973. Despite her huge success with Toyota – for whom she was Belgian distributor – she was in no mood to give up on Jaguar. With my arrival as chief executive she saw her chance to reopen earlier negotiations which had ended in a short-term extension of her franchise, not a cash buyout.

Her problem was that no one at Jaguar was in favour of extending her franchise further though it was perfectly possible to do so. And certainly no one was in favour of my responding to the several requests from her that had reached my office asking for a meeting. They seemed to be afraid of her. They bristled at the mention of her name. I was intrigued that anyone should arouse such a level of feeling. It was irrational because the Belgian Motor Company, Joska's organization, had obtained a larger market share for Jaguar than any of our other European markets. When I asked why we were trying to get rid of our most successful distributor, I was told she did well only because she got the best prices from the factory. When I asked why, no one knew; and when I suggested that if she was selling twice as many in Belgium as we sold in the whole of France or Germany she perhaps deserved competitive prices, I was told she was very litigious. I asked for the legal history of our relations with her and Jaguar. There was no history. She had never instituted any legal actions at all.

It is sad to say that the motivation of some colleagues was jealousy of her personal gifts and envy of her personal possessions. It was a trait that I was to see repeated over and again in my life.

However, despite the concerted efforts of Jaguar management and head office staff, Joska contrived a meeting with me. She was accompanied by her general manager, Jacques Mounier. Joska was not her usual flamboyant self. She had dressed down, as she thought it an important meeting and I had a reputation as a serious but hardly sartorial manager. I had two suits that I wore on alternate days. Two things struck me at once: just how easy it could be to envy this woman all her success; and how important Jacques Mounier was to her success.

The meeting was pleasant enough at first, but grew tense when I raised the issue of the prices at which we sold the cars to Belgium. I told them I intended to increase the prices on the next shipment. Joska said she would cancel the shipment. We had a good row. The Jaguar management was very pleased with how things were going until I put forward the suggestion that, if the Belgian Motor Company could take the price increase and give a firm commitment to an increased volume of sales, Jaguar would look at an extension of the franchise for a further twelve months.

The row subsided and Jacques said he would look seriously at the proposition and come back to me on it. I said I was looking for a legally binding arrangement without loopholes on either side. And in any event the price increase would be put through.

The next day the old BL network went into overdrive. Tens of pages of telex piled on to my desk – all with one objective only – to kill off the proposed deal before it could be properly evaluated. I took no notice. After a tough negotiation with Jacques the deal went through. Jaguar gained on price and volume. Everyone was satisfied – except the bureaucrats at BL head office and their sales teams in Europe, who were consuming cash as if there were no tomorrow and missing sales target after sales target with impunity.

Over the next year I would see Joska at motor shows and periodic review meetings. After our initial row we got on very well. She did not bear grudges – at least not many. And the few she bore would never be allowed to get in the way of doing business. Sadly, my period as chief executive at Jaguar came to a premature halt.

In 1974 British Leyland had run out of money and turned to the government to bail it out. The DTI set up the Ryder Committee to review the situation. The ill-starred report recommended that all the car operations, Austin Morris, Triumph, Jaguar and Rover, should be amalgamated into one company and their different activities – engineering, manufacturing, sales, finance, personnel – split up functionally. Jaguar no longer existed as a company. There would be no chief executive – or indeed any other function – that related to Jaguar as an entity. I was offered a senior position in the new integrated operation. But I had already made it clear during the consultation that preceded the report that I was not interested.

I had put forward a different plan for a largely integrated specialist car division comprising Jaguar, Rover and Triumph. I still believe this could have worked, though when it was tried later under Sir Michael Edwardes it did not succeed. I do not believe the line management got it right. What I was sure about was that the Ryder plan would never work. I resigned. Others took the new jobs on higher salaries. The British-owned car industry took another lurch towards extinction.

It was a lonely resignation. I saw Harold Wilson shortly after at a reception at No. 10. He was bemoaning all the money the industry was costing and told me I had resigned at the wrong time. I simply replied that it was going to cost him a lot more money yet and would probably end in disaster. Sadly, it did, but that is another story.

On leaving Jaguar I decided never again to work for something I did not own or at least effectively control. For that reason, Joska's proposal that I should act as a consultant to her company had many attractions. They had expanded as far in motor cars, with the top-selling Toyota range, as they could expect and were considering diversification into related areas such as motorcycles, with which I had in my last few months at Jaguar become involved, at Tony Benn's request and with Donald Stokes's approval, via the Triumph Meriden Motorcycle cooperative venture.

While I was having preliminary discussions with Joska, however, in 1976, Maurice Edelman, the MP for Coventry North West, the constituency in which both major Jaguar factories were located, died quite unexpectedly. I stood for the seat and won it.

Having been elected to Parliament, I was concerned to avoid any potential conflict of interest that could arise from consultancy work. I therefore agreed to a consultant role in Joska's company, only on condition that there was a clear framework of understanding on the relationship of the consultancy to my duties as Member of Parliament. I set out my conditions in a letter I addressed to Joska in December 1976: firstly, that my availability would be subject to the overriding priority of my commitments as a Member of Parliament; and secondly, that I would not accept any advocacy role either at Westminster or in European political organizations. Joska did not much like the letter. She was used to people being at her beck and call. Later it seemed to me, however, that it was precisely because of my independence from her, and because I would argue with her, that she came to rely on me and trust me more than anyone else. It had turned out that way at Jaguar: a fine old row, followed by a difficult negotiation leading to a good deal all round. She enjoyed that way of doing business.

There was not much in our backgrounds that was similar. She shared the typical views of the circles in which she moved – very well-to-do business people who voted Conservative. Beyond that she had no interest in politics. She mainly read magazines, the glossy ones. She had no strong interest in the arts except for painting. She was a talented amateur artist and towards the end of her life she started to find time to exercise this gift. Where we had a great affinity was in both being self-made people. She had no side to her. She despised snobs and people who pretended to be what they were not. She admired people who had made their own way in life, as I had done. I was the first in my family to go to university. I had won through on scholarships at every stage. It was a relief for her to find an Englishman who spoke French and other European languages. She was curious about my background. She met both my mother and father in their own homes and came to my mother's funeral. She visited Wandsworth Common with me, where I played football and cricket; she liked driving round Balham, where I had grown up in a mainly working-class neighbourhood. There were no books at home. It was a different background to her own essentially middle-class one.

She had been born in Sterpenich, a small Belgium town situated hard by the border with Luxembourg. Her father was a middle-ranking customs official. He was sent to Iraq to establish a national customs organization. The family spent seven years there. Her mother looked after the two daughters at home. Her elder sister Micheline had a sad life, living unmarried and alone in a run-down flat in Brussels. Her father had died relatively young, at fifty-seven, and she never spoke about him. She was much closer to her mother, though she soon outgrew her mother's ambitions for her. Her mother was proud of the daughter's fabulous commercial success. But she was puzzled by the agglomeration of material goods that accompanied it. She would say, in the Luxembourg patois she had learned as a child, 'What are you doing with all these things?' Later, as her daughter's wealth grew, she would ask in exasperation, 'What is the point of a gold chain if it's to hang yourself with?' I never met her mother; Joska told me these sayings. They were not altogether lost on her, it seems, though her wealth continued to rise unabated.

But Joska was not a big spender on material goods. She had some expensive jewellery but, particularly in her later life, more frequently than not she bought copies or openly fake pieces. She invested comparatively little in furniture or paintings. She liked a bargain. She indulged herself in clothes. But very rarely would she buy from the expensive fashion houses. She had her own tailor in Paris who copied their designs for her at an attractive price. She preferred to have the money in the bank!

There was not much in her early career that marked her out openly for commercial success. Before the war she was the girlfriend of Willy Toussaint, a well-to-do casino owner in Namur. With him she learnt to know what the 'good life' was. But she was not taken in by it.

And anyway the war changed all that. Joska was proud of her war record. She worked with the resistance helping British air crews who were shot down over Belgium to escape. Willy Toussaint had a less distinguished career. He was arrested at the end of the war on suspicion of collaboration and died shortly after being released from prison.

Joska was just over thirty when the war ended. She was keen to enter business on her own account. She had some money – gold florins mainly – left her by her father. She kept it for a rainy day. She started in a cramped single-room office. The only heating was a coal fire which she lit herself. She had one employee – a part-time secretary – who would answer the phone with a standard response: 'Madame is in a conference meeting.' Many people will have had a similar experience when starting out on their own account.

After brief and small-scale involvements selling dried flowers and a version of ready-to-wear clothing, she met a retired British colonel who introduced her to Jaguar. Thus began her long association with that company and the motor industry. It was in 1947 that she signed her first contract as Jaguar importer and distributor for Belgium and Luxembourg.

Jaguars were always in short supply throughout Europe in the post-war decades. Overseas distributors did well out of the franchise. Joska's business, the Belgian Motor Company, moved into new premises in the centre of Brussels. She retained the distributorship for the next twenty-five years. She regarded her relationship with Jaguar as an old-fashioned marriage: it had its ups and downs, but divorce did not come into it. She felt horribly jilted when BL, after my resignation, unilaterally took action to terminate the relationship. Jaguar had made good money for her. But it was an affair of the heart. Toyota made big money for her; that was an affair of the head. It started like this.

In 1962, she went on a world cruise, accompanied by her husband, George Buydendyk. They were due to visit Japan. She asked for a business brief from her managing director, Jacques Mounier, who had joined her from Renault the previous year. In his brief Jacques stressed the potential importance of the Japanese motor industry. She was intrigued. In her capacity as president of the Belgian Motor Company she secured meetings for herself at a high level with both Toyota and Nissan. She returned from the cruise determined to secure the franchise of one or other of them for Belgium.

As is usually the case with the Japanese, the negotiations were long drawn out. She opted early on for Toyota, who she felt followed the GM approach to its distributors rather than Ford's –

in her view GM allowed more latitude to the selling organization; Ford tended to be more prescriptive.

Her negotiations with the Japanese for the Toyota franchise centred largely on the price at which the importer bought the car from the manufacturer. That is a fact of life in all countries and industries. Many of her colleagues felt an arrangement with the Japanese would never be found. For them, she was wasting her considerable energy. But just as it was her idea in the first place to obtain a sales agreement with the Japanese, it was her determination that saw it through to a successful conclusion.

She finally signed with Toyota in 1967. The business took off largely due to Jacques Mounier's great drive and business acumen. She had chosen well. They were very different personalities and had quite different working hours. Joska was an owl – a night bird. She might not arrive in the office until well after lunch. But she would then work till midnight, ending up on her own.

Jacques was an early bird: in the office at the crack of dawn and leaving, if he could, at a reasonable hour (which was not often). Their complementary working hours proved useful for the business. But for Joska's marriage it was not so happy an arrangement. She would usually get back home from the office after 9 p.m. Her husband, who worked in a senior executive position for Goodyear, followed the American working pattern with a 7.30 a.m. start. Often – all too often for George, it seemed – their only contact was a wave as she mounted and he descended the staircase of their flat (in a fine apartment block in Avenue Louise, the Park Lane of Brussels). George was to have one further marriage, and neither worked out. Joska did not remarry. She had two long relationships with a Greek and an Algerian, who were both much younger than herself. Perhaps predictably, neither proved a success. In fact both were, in their different ways, stormy affairs with more downs than ups.

But whatever the mixed success of her private life, her business career thrived. The Toyota distributorship progressed dramatically. Within a few years they were number one in the Belgian market, selling 40,000 cars a year. During the initial period the business continued to operate out of the old Jaguar HQ in La Cantersteen. But it soon outgrew those cramped quarters. A new site at Diegem on the road to the airport was purchased and plans were put in hand for a major new building. Joska decided that if she was to invest on this scale she needed a longer-term commitment from Toyota. She wanted to negotiate a ten-year contract to replace her then current three-year selling contract, which was the norm for the industry. No one gave her a chance. 'Don't make yourself look ridiculous, madame,' was the advice she received all round, even from Jacques Mounier. She was undeterred. The second siege of Nagoya took place in 1970. She again emerged victorious, with the ten-year contract in her handbag! She was shortly afterwards to start her charm offensive on me to retain Jaguar. The head and heart were both working well. It was her last decade in business.

The early seventies did not provide major new activities. Perhaps the most useful purpose I served was to introduce her in 1978 to the Inchcape Group, who were well-established in the UK as Toyota distributors. As it turned out they were keen to expand in Europe and made an offer to purchase the business from her and her co-shareholders. She was in her sixty-sixth year and had resigned herself to retirement. The European car industry was doing well. It was a propitious moment to sell for all concerned. The deal went through in 1979.

She divided her retirement years between Geneva, Cannes and London. She often spent Christmas and the New Year with my family in England. After the death of her sister she had no family of her own. Under any circumstances she hated to be alone and she tended more and more to be surrounded by people whom she would herself call '*pique-assiettes*' – people who associated with her for the free hospitality, or in the hope that they might inherit something in due course. Shortly after her death I received calls from 'old friends' of hers inquiring whether they had been left anything in Mme Bourgeois' will. Was there not a fur coat going spare? These were people I had not even heard of.

Her last years were in many ways sad. She would often quote the French saying, *Si jeunesse savait, si vieillesse pouvait* . . . She still wanted to do so much. Somehow she could not accept the diminution of her physical powers. She was justifiably proud of her appearance. She took every step to maintain her striking looks. She would frequent health farms in southern Spain to keep her figure. She stuck to the diet with a determination that amazed the German owners: '*Warum will sie so viel fasten?*' they would ask me, as she persevered with a minimum liquids-only regime far beyond the normal time and even beyond the point where the diminishing returns were self-evident.

In March 1994 she underwent a hip replacement operation in the American hospital in Paris. The operation went well and after a week in hospital I brought her to London, and she recuperated in a flat in the Grosvenor House. She learned to walk again round the quadrangle of corridors.

It was her intention to go to Cannes for the summer as usual. Given that she had had a major operation and that the administration of morphine under an automatic injection system had been very heavy, I thought it worth while for her to have a health check-up before leaving. As part of that she underwent a full heart examination, which she passed with flying colours. Apart from a slight enlargement of the aorta and a very slight leakage from a heart valve, there was nothing to give concern. It was a clean bill of health for a person of her age. She left in good spirits for her last visit to Cannes.

During my stay with her that summer she was not herself. She was getting more uptight than ever about things that did not matter much and over which she anyway had little control. But she had had difficult times before, and there was nothing to suggest any problem other than the wear and tear of life taking its gradual toll. She was planning to leave Cannes in the week of 10 October.

Out of the blue on Sunday evening, 9 October, I received a call from her secretary in Geneva to say that she had died from a heart attack at her desk in Cannes. She had struggled to the bedroom next door and collapsed on the bed. It was as sudden and unexpected as could be.

She had discussed her will with me intermittently over the years.

I understood that I would be charged with making the arrangements for her funeral and that I would be a co-executor. However, I also knew that testamentary dispositions are liable to sudden and dramatic changes. Perhaps surprisingly, in this case there were none, and my family and I became in due course beneficiaries of a trust fund she had decided to establish, which was later to prove a mixed blessing to me.

The funeral took place at the Eglise St-Lambert, a stereotypical grey suburban Brussels church. Jacques Mounier gave an eloquent eulogy in which he recalled Joska's many gifts and accomplishments. After much hesitation I read the parable of the talents from the gospel of St Matthew. I would hope that she finds now an esteem and peace that may not have been accorded to her during her lifetime because of her too many and great gifts.

3. Brown's Team

My involvement with Gordon Brown and the shadow Treasury team began with a chance exchange in the No Lobby on 18 October 1994. Gordon and I arrived at the tellers at the same time. I tapped him on the shoulder and said, 'You are a good man.' There was no need to say apropos of what. The leadership battle was still on everyone's mind. Gordon's standing down had eased a very difficult situation in the party. 'There was nothing else to do really,' he replied in a resigned manner. I sensed his disappointment. But he was not looking backwards at all. He added, 'This time I'd like to get you involved, too, Geoffrey.' Later I realized he meant this parting shot. But at the time I thought no more about it. I had been an MP for eighteen years and had no expectations of office in what would be a team of much younger people.

I had felt differently when I first came into the House in 1976. It was a critical by-election caused by the unexpected death of Maurice Edelman, the MP for Coventry North West. The constituency contained both Jaguar factories, employing at the time over sixteen thousand people, where I had been chief executive till I resigned over the disastrous Ryder Report in 1975. I had taken rather bold steps to deal with the confrontational labour relations that had so bedevilled the motor industry in the fifties and sixties; these found favour with the workforce and unions and, increasingly, though more slowly, with the management. When I resigned some three thousand employees came out, in their own time, in a mass demonstration at the Browns Lane factory, asking me to stay. At least some progress had been made. Demonstrations of this kind were usually held for the exact opposite purpose. There was a wider following for me in the city of Coventry, too.

My selection, as I expected, given this background and my earlier work as a researcher for the Labour Party at Transport House, was almost unanimous. The by-election was called for March 1976. It had always been my intention to get back into politics if I was successful in the industrial sphere. The opportunity had come quite unexpectedly and earlier than I planned. After my resignation from Jaguar a few months previously I had not taken a full-time position though several were offered me, so I was available when the chance came. The seat could not have been a better one from my personal position, but the timing from the point of view of winning a by-election could not have been worse. The Labour government was surviving from day to day on a majority of one, which I would be defending against the Labour government's net dissatisfaction rating of 42 per cent according to the NOP poll in January and a 5 per cent Tory lead in the Gallup poll that followed in February.

It was a critical by-election, and because the government's overall parliamentary majority was at risk it attracted a good deal of public attention. Harold Wilson sent his PPS, John Tomlinson, up no less than five times during a three-week campaign to see how we were getting on! The circumstances all pointed to a heavy government defeat.

In the event we had a good result. I won with a majority of 3,694, suffering an anomalously small adverse swing of 5 per cent.

It was a rather pleased with himself thirty-seven-year-old who took up his seat the following Tuesday in time for a crucial vote. I had got to know Harold quite well during my days as a Labour Party researcher at Transport House, and I felt there was a good chance he might give me an early opportunity of office. Certainly I hoped so; that is why I had gone back into politics. I will never know whether he would have promoted me, for he resigned exactly one week later!

It suddenly dawned on me why John Tomlinson had been sent on his fivefold mission and why Harold greeted me, when we met behind the Speaker's chair, with the words, 'I am *personally* very grateful to you for winning this election.' (The 'personal' part was heavily accentuated.) If I had lost his overall majority, it would have been more difficult for him to have gone ahead with his long-planned and carefully choreographed resignation. It would have suggested that he had quit because of the House of Commons situation.

When Harold resigned, Jim Callaghan took over. I have always admired and got on well with Jim Callaghan, but it did not surprise me that he did not bring me into the government. (If he had, my career might well have turned out differently.) He said, when questioned on this point some twenty years later, 'He was clearly one to watch but I could hardly have made a new boy a minister when many other able MPs had been around for a much longer time.'* It was an entirely valid point.

For the next few years I devoted a great deal of time and much heartache to running the Meriden cooperative. Inevitably it took me away from the Commons a lot but in the whips' view it was worth doing. Looking back I am not so sure at all that it was time well spent. I would not do it again. But that is another story.

In 1979 we began eighteen long years in opposition. Neil Kinnock gave me my chance in opposition as junior spokesman in John Smith's industry team in 1984. But despite Neil's courageous work to bring the party back to its senses, the policies we were espousing were an embarrassment for anyone wishing to engage in a serious discussion with the private sector. As the party policy statement to Conference for 1986 took shape, it was clear to me that I simply could not usefully play a role in the promotion of what was called industrial strategy. The document presented at the Blackpool Conference in due course spelled it out with awful clarity: 'Labour will acquire or maintain a strategic stake in defence industries and vital national industries such as oil, aerospace, ship-building and steel . . . key manufacturing industries including the information technologies and motors, centres of innovation, and industries supplying the public sector.'

John Smith knew I was deeply unhappy about such policies. He told me he was 'sorry about it', but had to give way in the interests of shadow Cabinet unity. He hoped I 'would stick it out' as he was certain that Neil, after the election which was almost sure to come

* *The Times*, 13 December 1997.

in 1987, would put both defence and industrial policies on a 'saner basis'. Neil achieved that and much more.

But back in 1986 I decided against 'sticking around'. Perhaps I was not suited to opposition. Certainly I got no satisfaction from the debating style of House of Commons interchanges. At this time I seriously thought of resigning my seat at the 1987 election. My local party dissuaded me. Coventry and my seat in particular had become a prime target for Militant. It was certain that a Militant candidate would win the nomination if I stood down. I decided to carry on. The new selection process for the 1987 election was a nasty fight and a close decision. But we saw them off. I won the seat for the fourth time, with an increased majority.

My resignation from the front bench in 1986 had its silver lining. Gordon Brown succeeded me on the industry team. I would often tease him later that I had given him the first leg-up which made it all possible for him!

Some eight years later, over lunch early in 1995, Gordon suggested bringing me back on to the industry team. We also talked about relations between Tony and him, which were good and relaxed. Europe cropped up; he knew I was very interested here. He was talking in relatively pro-EU tones at the time to reassure the CBI, keeping Tony 'protected' from the Murdoch press. I sensed his distance from Peter Mandelson but Gordon was not the slightest bit interested in talking about it. And on taxation there was evidently some controversy on the top rate, which Gordon thought could be 50 per cent on very high incomes without damaging our New Labour credentials. I shared his views at this time.

Perhaps what struck me as remarkable from this discussion – the earliest serious one I had had with Gordon – was, firstly, the ease with which he could operate on different time horizons, accommodating tomorrow's press and long-term strategy; secondly, the sheer breadth and depth of his knowledge of political events and ideas; and, thirdly, the passion he felt about issues of fairness and equality of opportunity. Restating these impressions in this way may seem trite, but there is nothing of that in Gordon, as those who know him can tell.

In any event there had been a dramatic sea change since 1986, when I had resigned, disenchanted with policy issues. I felt at home with the policies of New Labour. I knew I could make a contribution. And I felt keenly that I would like to, not having pulled my weight earlier as I should have done.

The Labour Party enjoyed an unprecedented 35 per cent lead in the opinion polls. Tony Blair was consistently achieving a personal approval rating of over 50 per cent – which was exceptionally high. Gordon himself had done a remarkable job as shadow Chancellor since his appointment to the post in July 1992. According to MORI's poll on the question of which party had the best policies for managing the economy, Gordon had turned a 5 per cent negative rating against the Tories into an 8 per cent plus rating over the period from the end of March 1992 to the end of May 1994. Critical for reversing Labour's traditional weakness in economic competence had been the shedding of Labour's image of tax-and-spend in favour of a rigorous control of borrowing exercised by the 'Iron Chancellor'. It needed to be done and it had worked well. On the other hand, many colleagues judge that Gordon's success here had cut him off from some of his natural support in the parliamentary party, and this had been a more significant factor than was generally appreciated in his defeat in the leadership race.

However much this may have hurt Gordon's leadership bid, the perceptions of business and the City were strongly positive. The adoption of the 'golden rule' (borrowing only for investment) and the commitment to stability in the economy and tax rates had established credibility for New Labour. Moreover, the fact that we looked increasingly likely to win meant that the industrial and financial worlds were keen to talk to us.

When I discussed with Gordon ways in which I might help, we agreed that I should help facilitate the development of links with the private sector. But I was also quite open with Gordon that I would like to do more than this and indeed it would be necessary for me to be seen to be doing more as a valid contributor, having not played an active role for some time. He suggested I should

write a series of pamphlets, starting with one on the Private Finance
Initiative (PFI). I took on one of his researchers, Peter Fanning, to
help with the preparation of what would essentially be research
documents with proposals for Labour policy in government. We
quickly put together a draft pamphlet on reorganizing the PFI,
where I already had very definite ideas for improvement. But
I decided against publication since the recommendations were
controversial.* As I became more closely involved with the work
of Gordon's team I sensed that confidentiality would be vital
in several other areas where substantial professional research was
required if our ideas were to be fit for use in government. It was all
too true that Labour governments of the past had a well-earned
reputation for having good but insufficiently well-thought-out
ideas for raising money; and then spending too much early on, only
to have to cut back later and lose the next election. That may seem
a caricature, but it was a nightmare that Gordon and Ed Balls were
determined at all costs to avoid.

We needed therefore a two-pronged approach: the tightest possible control of expenditure in the first two years; and new sources
of revenue to fund our youth-training programme and for closing
the fiscal deficit.

I dropped the idea of the pamphlets and put it to Ed that we
should commission professional research, starting with the very
concrete proposal we had at that time for a windfall tax. The
account of our progressively extensive preparations for government
unfolds in Chapters 6 and 7. For me it is a quite remarkable story
of good preparation and, in due course, good execution.

As I look back now at the four years from 1995 to 1998, I am
struck by how much was accomplished by such a small team in so
short a time. Gordon often remarked that it was a love of football
that first brought us all together. It certainly played its part; and we
all had our roles. Gordon was chairman of the club, its coach and
captain, and main striker. Ed Balls was his deputy in all roles, and
in charge of policy and tactics in his own right. Charlie Whelan

---

* They were in due course implemented in full in government.

was Nobby Stiles: he would take out an opponent – press or political – as soon as look at them. My own modest role might best be described as sweeper-cum-attacking mid-field, which in fact was where I once starred on Wandsworth Common. There were several other crucial players, notably Sue Nye and Ed Miliband. Sue's advice and influence were pervasive in the whole strategy and Ed was vital in writing speeches and coordinating with Millbank.

The key to the success of our endeavours in preparation for and in government was teamwork. We had our game plan. We had set our objectives. But achieving them required a team effort. It is something the government as a whole should remember, especially when it hits difficulties. Teamwork is vital, even more important than Gordon's golden rule.

One of our first objectives, well prepared in advance and announced to the House only days after we came into office, was a major reform of one of the great financial institutions, the Bank of England.

4. What a Carve-up!

Three days before the 1997 election, with Labour way ahead in the polls, we were ready for government. Monday 28 April was a fine evening and I had spent the day at my flat working on taxation papers. Ed Balls joined me in the early afternoon. We both felt confident about the overall state of our preparations. We were impatient to move into the Treasury.

Public attention was increasingly shifting from speculating not on *whether* we would win, but on how much we would win by and what we would do once in power. Our lead in the polls had hardened to between nineteen and twenty-one points and there seemed to be no way back for a bickering Tory Party. John Major was reeling from our attacks on his plans to privatize the state pension. Tony Blair was flying from rally to rally, looking more and more like the premier-in-waiting he actually was. That weekend Rupert Murdoch's biggest-selling tabloid, the *News of the World*, had come out for us, making it a Wapping tabloid double together with the *Sun*. We were surely home and dry.

Gordon Brown and Tony Blair warned against complacency and Gordon had coined the slogan, 'Don't hope for change, vote for change', to persuade our supporters to get to the polling stations. Yet privately he knew the contest was over and even took time out to give an interview to the *Independent on Sunday* looking back at the campaign. He admitted we had suffered a 'wobbly week' early on under sustained Tory fire over the economy, privatization and the unions. Then he went on: 'There is a settled view among a very large section of the population that they do not want another Conservative government. As someone put it to me, it's not that the Conservatives don't deserve another five years – they don't deserve another five minutes.'

After tying up some legal points, we waited for Gordon Brown, who normally phoned around 5 p.m. to let us know when we should expect him for our regular daily round-up of events and briefing on any work he wanted prepared for the next day. Unusually that Monday he did not ring: he simply turned up. He was obviously very preoccupied when he walked into the flat and came straight to the point: 'Look, it's the Bank independence,' he said. 'I've come to the conclusion that we should do it straight away. Immediately on taking office. The first thing we should do – can you get your paper out, Ed, and get it properly written up?' Ed, struggling on his lap top computer with problems of local government capital expenditure, did not look up as he replied; he simply said, 'Yes, but let me finish this first.' Gordon was clearly a bit irritated. Ed seemed unbothered.

Gordon left us within five minutes of delivering the bombshell news, just three days before the election, that straight after it he planned to grant the Bank of England independence in setting interest rates. We knew he had been mulling over the problem of when to do it; over the weekend of 26–27 April, which he spent in and around his constituency, he had focused intently on it and had finally decided to go ahead.

It was a pattern of decision taking I was to see often repeated. He was not hasty; he would listen to a lot of people; he would think it over; then he would decide, mostly on his own, and announce his decision. Gordon has great self-reliance and inner self-confidence.

On this momentous evening such a decision had been taken. No one had any inkling that it was coming. Next day Ed Miliband, Gordon's political adviser, asked me at a review meeting in Millbank, 'How did it all happen?' I explained that Gordon had thought about it over the weekend and told me his decision the previous evening. He pulled a surprised face. But Gordon was right – the only person who could take that decision was himself, and he had taken it. As Gordon left the flat that evening to return to Millbank, he said he would be back soon after 8 p.m. and would like to see the draft.

The initial work that had been done on the Bank pre-dated my involvement with the Treasury team. I knew of course that there were plans for a monetary-policy committee and that this would be set up and have a running-in period of a year or so before independence would be conferred. We had often talked about it in general terms. It was agreed the present arrangements could not continue.

Gordon was struck by how American interest-rate movements were not a political issue. He had been very impressed at our meeting on 20 February 1997 with Alan Greenspan in Washington. At this meeting Greenspan had gone so far as to say it was 'unfair' to expect elected politicians to take unpopular decisions on interest rates.

I sensed Gordon was agreeing strongly. I was not so sure about the probability of the benefits in the short term or about the now-conventional wisdom that the strategic blunders in UK economic policy were down to weak-kneed political decisions on interest rates. If the economy went wrong in the short term – Labour's nightmare scenario – the Chancellor would get the blame, whether or not the Bank was independent. If the economy went well – against all precedents – the Chancellor would be rewarded, since he would be recognized as the prime architect of victory, as Nigel Lawson was in 1987.

As far as past economic crises of Labour governments were concerned, I could not see how the 1947 or 1967 devaluations, or the IMF crisis of 1976, had been caused in any sense by monetary policy errors. On the contrary, Labour's error had been, in part at least, to trust the bankers too much. But I had not at this point reckoned with the full extent of the reforms that were embodied in Ed's detailed paper and which had been kept a closely guarded secret. It was the reforms taken as a whole that would make 'independence' a success. Putting them all into practice, however, was to give us a very bumpy ride with Eddie George (the Governor of the Bank of England) and his fellow members of court.

When Gordon had gone, I turned to Ed Balls and said, 'What paper is Gordon talking about? We'll never get it done by 8 p.m.' Ed had finished his wrestling match with local government finance and revealed: 'I've got the file in my PC. We now know he still wants to be leader.'

Ed was in effect echoing what Gordon had repeatedly said in the last months leading up to government. He felt that the external pressures would inevitably push us into Bank independence and concluded quite sensibly that if that were the case, it was surely better to take the initiative and get the political kudos associated with the move. If, in Greenspan's words, it was not fair to expect decent people who are elected politicians to take unpopular decisions, then, surely, a good politician should take credit for accepting the inevitable, protecting his own position and being seen to do the right thing. Moreover, he could be sure of Tony's whole-hearted support. It all looks so obviously right with hindsight.

Ed dug into his bag, pulled out the PC and called up the research paper. I began to read the remarkable document detailing reforms that were to be regarded as the most important changes in economic policy making in Britain since the Second World War.

The case for independence was made in the first two pages of the document. It was a good account, coupled with a hard-headed assessment of the political arguments in favour of being shot of monetary responsibilities. Then followed extremely detailed proposals for its implementation. The Bank of England should be split three ways:

- A new Monetary Policy Committee (MPC) would be created to handle interest rates;
- The Bank's regulatory functions would be hived off and combined with the various other overlapping organizations to form an integrated new supervisory agency;
- The responsibility for gilt sales to finance government debt would be removed from the Bank and given to a separate specialized agency.

Before I went further into the detail of Ed's proposals, I paused and asked him how the paper came to be written. He told me it was his idea, which he had put to Gordon in mid-1995. Gordon discussed it with Tony, who was very pro independence and it was agreed Ed should take a week off from the day-to-day political battle to write it up.

The detail was quite remarkable, particularly in respect of how the new monetary-policy arrangements should be established and made to operate. Political control would be retained by the Chancellor, whose responsibility it would continue to be to set the inflation target. The Bank – or rather the new MPC – would have the responsibility for meeting the target, i.e. the Governor would have operational independence. He would also remain chairman of the MPC. There would be two vice-chairmen, one from the Bank and one from outside; and in addition there would be four further external appointees made by the Chancellor. In short, the old Bank coterie would be replaced by a group of experts who could bring specialist knowledge to this vital area. It was also important that they should be paid. The MPC would meet monthly, announce its decisions promptly and publish a full monthly account of its deliberations and conclusions. This was all in the much-needed interests of transparency. If things started to go wrong then the corrective mechanism was already thought through: in the event of the Bank under- or overshooting its target by 1 per cent, the Governor would be required to write an open letter to the Chancellor stating the reasons for the divergence and what action he proposed should be taken. It was left open as to whether this should be a revision to the inflation target or further measures to achieve the Chancellor's original goal. There was not much left to chance – or for the Governor to argue about.

The other two proposals, which were bound to be extremely controversial with the Bank, were not dealt with in such detail. But it was stressed that if the UK was to have a central bank which was a modern specialist monetary authority, the package as a whole was necessary.

As I finished reading the paper I hardly noticed that it had not been tidily finished off. I sat back and reflected to Ed, 'That's one hell of a carve-up.' To which he replied, 'I've always wanted to sort the Bank out.' It was an auspicious piece of work for a young man of twenty-eight. I could not help but wonder what sort of compromise we might end up with as we moved to action on this and on other areas of key economic policy making where a strict framework was being worked out in advance. For example, in another economic paper drawn up by Ed there were detailed proposals for the Code of Fiscal Responsibility, including a strategy for embodying it in legislation. Most governments in my experience tried rather to avoid tying themselves down in these ways.

But to have doubted further would have been to underestimate the drive and determination of the Chancellor-designate himself. There was no time anyway. He arrived back at 8 p.m. on the dot, having confided to Charlie Whelan that he expected trouble from me. In fact it was the last thing I would do. We had covered that area some days before in his office at the House, where he said that there were bound to be areas of policy on which we would differ, to which I replied, 'I will argue with you, but you're the boss.'

Anyway, as I reflected on the proposals I warmed rapidly to them. We were speaking about operational independence only. The Chancellor retained the right to set the inflation target. That was vital, as it was also that the inflation target could move up as well as down. Moreover, I had long been in favour of a separate independent regulatory body. At the briefings I had attended at the Bank on the BCCI and Barings scandals, some of the top officials had come across as complacent amateurs.

It struck me that it was important to stress in the document the importance we would, as the Treasury team, attach to economic growth. The following phrase was added in describing the MPC's approach to its job: 'taking due account of the importance of economic growth'. It was a positive contribution to the document the Chancellor discussed with the Prime Minister at 3.30 p.m. on Friday, 2 May.

Ed returned to my flat late that same Friday evening thumping the Chancellor's red box like a cymbalist. It was a sporting trophy – New Labour had won.

I was not directly involved in the discussion on the reform of the Bank. I was quite busy at the other end of the corridor with the windfall tax, corporation tax and tax credits. But given that most evenings we went back to the flat and shared our problems, it was impossible not to be aware of most things that were going on.

The first confirmation I received of the bumpy ride I was expecting with the Bank came on the evening of Sunday, 4 May. It was about 8.30 p.m. and I had done for the day. I went down to Gordon's office to see if he was packing up too. He was not there, so I walked on the further twenty yards to the office of Sir Terence Burns, Permanent Secretary to the Treasury. He was still working away and pleased to chat. He was painfully concerned about the speed at which we were moving and at the extent of the proposed changes to the Bank's structure and functions. He was drafting a letter to Gordon to suggest a twenty-four-hour delay to the next day's meeting with Eddie George. I told him I could not see the point of writing a letter at this stage in the proceedings. If he wanted to be effective he should confront Gordon personally with his concern. But that was not Terry's style. Anyway, I remarked, what would be gained from a twenty-four-hour delay? We would be in just the same position one day later, since Gordon was utterly determined to proceed with the full reform package. Terry shrugged his shoulders and went back to his letter, which I think was also making the case for not proceeding at once with hiving off the Bank's regulatory responsibilities.

Time is very valuable to civil servants. It provides the opportunity to lobby and organize defences. Playing for time is probably the most used tactic in Whitehall. It is usually most effective from midway through a Parliament to its end. But at this stage, with a new administration, a powerful Chancellor and a majority of 179, a letter requesting a twenty-four-hour delay in a scheduled meeting between the Chancellor of the Exchequer and the Governor of the Bank of England seemed a pointless gesture. The meeting went ahead as planned.

In essence, what Terry was unhappy about was the sheer speed and scale of the changes proposed for the Bank – notably the removal of its regulatory functions. It was this that he wanted to delay, not just the next day's meeting. He was wrong, of course, but it was one of the few points on which the Permanent Secretary took a definite position. It was very much under this pressure that the original proposals embodied in a single package of reforms were divided into two separate letters from the Chancellor to the Governor. The first set out the proposals for the Bank's operational independence on monetary policy. The second letter dealt with the removal from the Bank of its other functions, most importantly, its regulatory role. The second letter was to be treated as 'confidential' – its contents were not released with the press statement handling the independence issue. Predictably, the Governor felt that since the second letter enjoyed this exempt status it was an open matter, up for consultation. This was not the Chancellor's intention.

As it happened I bumped into Eddie George as he came out of the Chancellor's office after the meeting on 5 May. He was beaming. 'It was absolutely the right thing to do,' he said. The implications of the whole package had apparently not dawned on him. But the reform as a whole package, including the removal of the Bank's regulatory responsibilities, had been spelled out to him by Gordon at their meeting, when only the Chancellor and the Governor were present. That evening in our discussions at the flat Gordon was very clear that the Governor knew the whole picture.

We all realized that to have two letters dealing with different elements of the reform was a mistake. I warned Gordon to expect a rearguard campaign against the less attractive elements of the reforms.

It was not going to be easy to recover the ground, and prospects for treating the measures as a package were reduced again when Derry Irvine, who was in control of the parliamentary timetable, made it clear that there would only be time for one Bank of England Bill in the first parliamentary session. This would naturally be the one dealing with the establishment of the Monetary Policy Committee.

At this point top official advice was even more strongly, with the exception of Steve Robson's, in favour of delay. Steve was firm in supporting the Chancellor's own instincts that delay could be fatal. Indeed, so strong was Steve in support of the Chancellor that he earned himself the inestimable rebuke of being turned away from the Governor's dining room at the Bank. His presence was not required, since the Governor was to have a private engagement over lunch with the Chancellor's economic adviser. If the Governor thought he could get any change out of Ed he was much mistaken was my comment, when I was told later in the day about this incident.

And so it proved. The power to remove its regulatory function from the Bank would be tacked on to the Bill establishing the MPC. It was hardly an elegant solution. But it would effectively settle the issue, which if left to drag on could only be the source of continuing and increasing uncertainty. In the world of financial regulation that is not a good idea. So really the Chancellor had no option but to press on despite what we knew would be a huge row.

If we were to go ahead it would be necessary to make a statement to Parliament and, as a minimum, to name a new chairman for the agency. In the usual informal way I was consulted as to who could do the job. Howard Davies was the name that kept coming to everyone's mind. He had an outstanding record: Oxford, Stanford, McKinsey, director-general of the CBI and currently deputy governor of the Bank itself. It struck me that he had not just the intellectual capability but also the managerial competence that would be required to integrate the difficult organizations. There was not a surfeit of alternative candidates, to be frank. But I argued that surely Davies was an outstanding candidate in his own right.

Gordon typically made his mind up rather late in the day. He was due to make the announcement to the House on Tuesday, 20 May, which meant he would have to see the Governor on Monday, 19 May, at the latest; this left just the weekend to contact Howard Davies and if possible to persuade him to take the job. As is so often the case, the candidate was 11,000 miles away on an official visit to Argentina. He was guest speaker at a dinner in the Sheraton Hotel in Buenos Aires on the Saturday evening and was invited to take a call from the Chancellor when already seated, as it happened, next to Carlos Menem, the president of Argentina, who was hosting the conference on international finance. He was offered the job and asked to make up his mind the same evening. After some toing and froing on the phone and profuse apologies to the president, Howard, to everyone's relief, duly accepted the job.

The meeting between the Governor and Chancellor took place on the Monday. Accounts of the meeting and of the Governor's imminent resignation appeared all over the press and generally tended to cast Gordon in a bad light. The simple facts of the situation are these: the meeting was always bound to be difficult; no amount of consultation was ever going to dissolve the resentment the top Bank officials would feel or change the conviction they held at the time that the policy was wrong. It was the Chancellor's right to decide and he did so. As he remarked with classic understatement: 'The Bank always said they wanted to keep banking regulation; it's their right to say it . . . we just had a different view.' Perhaps, so far from Gordon being high-handed, the Governor had overplayed his hand. This seemed uncharacteristic for so skilled a bridge player. Perhaps he had been encouraged to do so. That is how it seemed to me.

I do not think Eddie George ever seriously thought of resigning. The appointment of a new Governor would have made an interesting event at this stage in a new government's life. Alternatives were discussed. But with the policy agreed, the two men, though very different, learned to work together.

Eddie George has a reputation for not being easy to work with. This had its downside, as was brought home to us in the search for a deputy governor who would drive through the needed IT revolution to update the antiquated control and administrative systems in Threadneedle Street. One strong possibility was Dame Sheila Masters. She had done several jobs for the Tories, particularly for Ken Clarke. Her considered reaction was that she would very much like to do the job, but in her heart knew that Eddie would not delegate sufficient authority of action for her to be able to push the changes through. In her phrase Eddie 'ruled the place with a rod of iron'. Dame Sheila herself had a similar formidable reputation for being difficult amongst her colleagues at KPMG, the tax and financial consultants. She was not 'clubbable', it seems. For this reason she was not exactly welcomed with open arms when, at the Chancellor's insistence, she was nominated the senior member of court. Her male colleagues, who were clubbable, seemed less than pleased. For the deputy governorship we recruited an excellent candidate in David Clementi, from Deutsche Kleinwort Benson, where Peter Walker was most helpful to us. Recruitment to the MPC was not difficult. The inclusion of a Dutch professor from Cambridge and an American lady from the CIA suggested that the Chancellor was not afraid of an element of the unorthodox. By the end of the session all the key elements of the reform package were in place.*

Three things stand out for me. Firstly, that Eddie George himself subsequently admitted that, had he understood it was a package deal, he would still have accepted it. Secondly, and strangely reminiscent of Gordon's own sense of relief at relinquishing monetary responsibility, he is reputed to have confided to colleagues that another Barings crash might pre-emptorily destroy the credibility the MPC had to establish for sound money policy. Thirdly, his own view given to the House of Commons Treasury Select Committee on 26 January 1999, when he effectively endorsed the Chancellor's policy: 'We are more accountable than, I think, any other central bank in the world. I have to tell you I very, very much welcome that.' It is pleasing that the Governor should be satisfied with his new arrangements, the bottom line of which was that he gained independence and lost some control. Game, set and match to the government.

A Reflection

In retrospect my own view is that technically the Treasury would have managed the disinflationary movement of interest rates at least as successfully as the new MPC, which was at first finding its feet.

---

* On the first MPC of the Bank of England were Eddie George, Howard Davies, William Buiter, Charles Goodhart, Mervyn King, Ian Plenderleith, DeAnne Julius, Alan Budd.

We would have moved rates more decisively up and down, as Professor Buiter, the hawk on the committee, was reported as recommending.

There were, however, two considerations that weighed heavily in favour of making the Bank independent. The first reason, which was not often remarked on, is that operational independence removed one possible area of potential conflict between Nos. 10 and 11. Mrs Thatcher hated interest rate rises and squabbled with her Chancellors over them. When the Chancellor made the announcement of the Bank's independence, on Tuesday, 6 May 1997, it was agreed that it was vital for him to be seen to raise interest rates himself before handing over to the MPC. A rate increase was long overdue and Gordon had to show he was not ducking the issue. The question was how large an increase should it be? Given that Kenneth Clarke had already overruled the Governor three times by refusing to raise rates, it was imperative that a firm start be made. The Treasury view was that at least ½ per cent rise was required. My own view was that we should send a stronger message. The problem was No. 10 and Derek Scott, the PM's economic adviser, who were nervous of the markets' reaction and pushing for only a ¼ per cent rise. For the Treasury it was a clear-cut case but nonetheless and despite a lot of hassle, the bank rate was increased by just ¼ per cent. It was our first run-in with No. 10. We could do without that. And in future we would be free of it.

From that point of view it was a valuable step. But of far greater significance than that was the importance of the political signal the move sent to the City and the wider business community. It portended in the clearest possible terms that New Labour was serious. In essence it was a political decision, supremely important and perfectly timed. And it was all down to the Chancellor.

5. Life at the Treasury

To scorn delights and live laborious days.
   Milton, *Lycidas*

When Labour came to office, Gordon Brown's team moved into the Treasury building in Great George Street. The lugubrious tone of Milton's iambic pentameter probably just about sums up the outsider's idea of what life at the Treasury must be like. Those who actually work there would add 'and nights, too'.

Certainly the building contributes to the feeling. Built at the turn of the century by J. M. Brydon and Sir Henry Tanner, it is listed grade 2. It is typical of government buildings on Whitehall. It seems to have been built with scant regard to working conditions except for the fine rooms reserved for ministers. The rest of the interior is enveloped in a sort of penumbral gloom, especially the corridors. To offset this, as was the architectural practice at the time, white-glazed brick has been used for the walls of the inner courtyards. With age, they no longer have so much reflective quality. They have taken on a rather lavatorial aspect.

Other internal deficiencies in the building – after decades of inadequate maintenance – are the electric wiring, the plumbing and the fire-alarm system. All need renewing. The external fabric is in part in decay and everywhere is dilapidated. It is not difficult, then, to make a strong case for the refurbishment of the Treasury building. By the time we came to office Sir Terence Burns, the Permanent Secretary, had become obsessed with it.

There is nothing objectionable about Terry Burns. He is not a snob. He has not tried to lose his north-eastern accent, which his upbringing in a council house in the typical mining village of Hetton le Hole gave him. His father was a trade-union official at the local pit. Terry attended Houghton-le-Spring grammar school, going on to Manchester University to read politics and modern history. In his own words, he 'didn't know what economics was'* at that time. He switched later.

He still supports Sunderland Football Club, though he has transferred his more current loyalties to Queens Park Rangers, where he serves as a director and, as I learned, attends some away games too. He is a creature of habit, mostly lunching at the same Chinese restaurant. He is a modest man, which is perhaps why his knighthood meant so much to him. He is virtually a teetotaller. He is a member of the Reform and Ealing Golf Clubs. There really is then nothing objectionable about Terry Burns.

With such a background, as Sir Andrew Turnbull, Burns's successor as Permanent Secretary, remarked to me, it was as though 'Gordon and Terry had been destined to be soulmates'. Turnbull just could not understand why they had not got on like a house on fire. Perhaps Andrew knew Terry rather better than he knew Gordon at that time. He probably knows the Chancellor rather better now after working with him for over two years.

Gordon Brown is a man of fine intellect, great drive and with the highest level of ambition to break with the complacency that in the past has seemed satisfied with the UK's at-best mediocre economic performance. As the first Labour Chancellor for eighteen years, he was utterly determined to avoid the disasters of previous Labour governments: sterling crisis leading to devaluation or the intervention of the International Monetary Fund. He was equally adamant that he wanted none of the Tory crises either: boom and bust, and the ERM.

From 1994 onwards there was open speculation in the press about whether or not the new administration would retain Sir Terence as Permanent Secretary. None of this came from the shadow Chancellor's office, as I can testify from personal experience. When I raised the issue in a tentative and neutral way in late 1996, Gordon politely told me to drop it. He wanted no

* *Independent on Sunday*, 24 November 1994.

problems on that front. He could work with whomever he inherited.

I had raised the point because there would be the chance to make a change on taking office and because I felt it should at least be considered. I had had conversations with various senior civil servants, mostly retired. There was a generous personal sympathy for Terry. But everyone felt that eighteen years in the Treasury, situated on the same corridor, only ever occupying two offices just yards apart, was too long for any person. It was not as if during this long career the Treasury record had been marked by a row of successes. The monetarist experiment, of which he was a principal architect, collapsed in ruins. The grave errors of forecasting in 1987/88 unleashed the Lawson boom; and, worst of all, there was the ERM fiasco: Terry had locked himself and the British economy into an awkward embrace with the ERM. The divorce was acrimonious and extremely expensive.

The view was prevalent that the Treasury, especially in recent years, had got it wrong and that the Permanent Secretary must have been central to the serious policy and forecasting mistakes that had been made. Writing a profile of Sir Terence, based on an interview with him, in *The Times* in November 1994, Richard Thomson put it like this:

To have failed in one economic policy might seem like bad luck. To have failed with no fewer than three, begins, one might think, to look like something more than carelessness. But Sir Terence in good Civil Service style . . . is emphatically not about to shoulder the blame for his earlier mistakes.

But even with so little sense of personal responsibility, the 'laborious days' and the crises were bound to have taken their toll. Certainly by the time we took office, as far as policy was concerned, Sir Terence's contribution and even his interest were exiguous.

What seemed to have happened since 1992 was that Sir Terence had devoted his main energies to two surrogate activities: the reform of the Treasury organization and the refurbishment of its building. The first was undertaken by Jeremy Heywood, now principal private secretary to the Prime Minister. He produced a report that, despite excessive management jargon and buzzwords, did reduce costs and delegated responsibility, and this was welcomed by the more junior grades. The second project – the refurbishment – was very much Terry's own. He threw himself into it heart and soul. A modernized, attractively laid out and well furnished Treasury building was to be his legacy to the institution he had served with such dedication. Unfortunately it fell to me to deny him his last great ambition. I fear he never forgave me and that this could have been the source of the friction that arose over personal matters.

Predictably Sir Terence brought up the GOGGS project at our very first meeting. GOGGS is an acronym for Government Offices, Great George Street, which is how the Treasury building is referred to in official documents. The scheme that Terry was putting forward excluded an earlier bizarre idea to co-locate a hotel in the Treasury building. But it still had the following unacceptable aspects to it:

- It involved the Treasury in spending nearly £300 million when other departments were having to live within the Tory spending plans;
- All Treasury personnel including ministers would have to be 'rehoused' at Camelford House – some 1½ miles away in south London;
- This meant in turn the Chancellor would work out of No. 11 virtually on his own or be at the severe disadvantage of being geographically dislocated from No. 10 – each alternative was unacceptable;
- Ministers would quite likely miss votes (Michael Jack*, who is certainly no slouch, did a trial run with his Civil Service private secretary. He made it in the time allowed by the skin of his teeth. Terry Burns got wind of this story and told me he would not forget it – hinting at dire retribution for the grade seven secretary involved, who in fact was a very good chap);
- The proposed redevelopment of the east wing created 30 per

---

* Financial secretary to the Treasury, 1996–7, and Labour MP for Fylde.

cent more office space when the government was already sitting on 500,000 square feet of unused office space in London for which it was paying rent;

- The Foreign Office was expected to move into the Whitehall block. The footbridge between the Foreign Office and the present Treasury building would be reopened. The Foreign Office would acquire an enormous presence of some 300 yards along the most prestigious stretch of Whitehall, from Downing Street to Parliament Square. This would have sent a message of pretence and grandiosity quite at odds with what New Labour stood for;
- Moreover the Foreign Office, to make the PFI scheme viable, was expected to pay 30 per cent more for its office space than the Treasury. The Foreign Office, of course, had no intention of doing so.

It could be argued that any one of these issues on its own was a show-stopper. The money certainly was in its own right. I felt the same about the dislocation of No. 10 from the base of the Treasury activities. The timing alone meant it had to be shelved for a year. Meanwhile, the costs were mounting for the PFI partners while patience was wearing very thin. They wanted a decision: were we proceeding or not?

It was clear that the matter had to be resolved before the parliamentary recess in July. I just could not understand why the Permanent Secretary seemed intent on making this a major confrontation. A more modest scheme, at a more propitious time, could be considered, as I frequently suggested to him. My senior civil servant warned me I would get nowhere. He recommended that I should bring matters to a head and announce my decision. Reluctantly I agreed.

I sent a note to Gordon stating that I proposed to discontinue the GOGGS project. I did not ask his approval. The decision was mine unless he stopped it. Gordon agreed. First I had to inform Terry. I fixed the meeting in his office. It was bound to be unpleasant even though I was anxious to stress that the problems of cost, timing and the decant could be resolved, given time. But it was simply not on in the middle of a spending freeze for the Treasury to be seen to be spending money on itself. He was visibly annoyed and informed me in an admonishing tone: 'I think you're making a terrible mistake!' In fact I had rarely felt better about a decision.

It could not, of course, be the end of the matter. Sir Terence retired in June 1998. His successor, Sir Andrew Turnbull, lost no time in raising the matter with me. He told me it would greatly help his standing in the Treasury and do a lot for morale. Andrew's remarks took me rather by surprise. His standing in the Civil Service was probably second only to Sir Richard Wilson's. Indeed he had been Sir Richard's keenest challenger for the top job. We had also learned that Margaret Thatcher, whose PPS Andrew had been from 1988 to 1990, had let it be known that Gordon absolutely must have Andrew as his Permanent Secretary. As far as Treasury morale was concerned, I had already detected a much greater commitment and enthusiasm since we came to office, though there had been some high-level leaks to the contrary which went via the Cabinet Office to No. 10. That had stopped by the time of Sir Terence's resignation and I was prepared to take Andrew at his word, especially as I knew that the Camelford House proposal was disliked by the staff. We were through the spending review, so that was one obstacle out of the way. But I made it clear to Andrew that all my other objections would have to be met: there was no need for extra office space; there was no need for the extension of the Foreign Office; there was no need for flats or private-sector tenants; and above all there was no need for the decant. I also set a target for a minimum 20 per cent reduction in cost.

After some toing and froing we settled the matter just before the summer recess. The announcement of the resumption of negotiations was put out by way of a press release in August. Work on the Treasury building is now proceeding, I am pleased to say.

Doing the Business

If the going was difficult on the GOGGS front, that was certainly
not the case with the corporate tax reform package, which went
through in record time. It was the main revenue-raising measure
for the first Labour budget in eighteen years. We needed the money
to fund the Welfare to Work programme (soon to be called the
New Deal); to close the obstinate deficit in the national finances;
and for general disinflationary purposes. Both the Treasury and
Inland Revenue had assembled top-flight teams for what we knew
would be a heavy legislative programme, since all three measures
required primary legislation.

We were able to make such rapid progress because on the
Treasury side I had the great good fortune to inherit Steve Robson
as my top official. Steve had been responsible for pushing through
the whole privatization programme for the Tories. He had also,
without so much success, been at the centre of attempts to get the
PFI up and running. Whatever one's views on the merits of these
programmes, they had been got on to the statute book. For this
purpose it seemed to me that having an official like Steve Robson
on your side would be a distinct advantage. We had been warned
early by the Permanent Secretary that Steve wanted to leave to take
up a senior position in the City. From my contacts in the City I
had confirmed this and had a shrewd idea of the financial advantage
he would gain by the move. As far as Steve personally was concerned, I sensed he was apprehensive that we might fall into the
trap of thinking he was not 'one of us'. On the contrary, it was
soon evident to me that he was just the sort of man we needed.
Moreover, as we outlined the full extent of our forward thinking,
he regained his zest for government work. 'It's a pretty important
reform package you guys are embarking on. I'd like to be part
of it.'

The feeling was reciprocated. Steve would do the business for
us just as he had done for the Tories. We secured his overdue
promotion to second permanent secretary and he agreed to see us

through our first three budgets to mid-2000. We had calculated that we would have passed our major corporate tax measures by then, as well as completing the Bank of England Bill and setting up the Financial Services Authority. We also felt we would have laid the foundations for the Growth Unit, with its emphasis on removing barriers to growth and revitalizing the PFI, together with encouragement to productivity through intensifying competition policy. The Growth Unit was also the key instrument in pushing through the dramatic reductions in capital-gains tax. The overall objective of these measures was to register as a central objective the improvement in the trend rate of growth in the economy. They came together within Steve's sphere of responsibility. By mid-2000 they had been achieved and it was Sir Steve Robson, as he now is, who did the business.

Central to the effectiveness of what was achieved in, at times, very difficult circumstances, was the brilliant work of my private secretary, Steve Field. His calmness under pressure was an example to his peers, and some superiors. He had judgement beyond his years, a keen sense of political realities and of the need to get the essentials done.

A huge burden of legislative work fell on the Inland Revenue. They assembled excellent teams. Steve Matheson, the outstanding number two in the Revenue, took a close personal interest throughout. His desire to get things done and his experience in guiding us through the early days was vital. Steve was also responsible for pushing through the modernization of the vast IR computer systems and the change in approach that made the IR, in my experience, one of the more customer-friendly tax collection organizations. Michael Cayley and Michael Williams – 'the two Mikes', as we affectionately called them – steered us skilfully through the corporate tax reforms. Both were open-minded and far-sighted, which are not characteristics usually associated with the taxman. The windfall tax was principally the responsibility of Robina Dyall, another top-flight IR official. She remarked on the completion of the windfall tax that she had never raised so much money at one go before. Her self-satisfaction was irrepressible.

Trevor Evans led for the IR on the transformation of the capital-gains regime. After some initial hesitation the extent of his proposals for radical reform took us all by surprise.

Many other officials appear at different points in the book. I mention these here not just because their contribution was rather special, but to emphasize a different point: that if the Civil Service is given clear and firm direction it can deliver. And what officials want more than anything else are clear-headed and decisive ministers. Our effectiveness in this respect can be measured by the speed at which the first Finance Act proceeded through the parliamentary stages. The budget itself was presented to the Commons on 4 July 1997 – barely two months into office. We went into committee stage on 17 July. The Tories had promised, as all oppositions do, to tear the bill apart as they subjected it to a line-by-line, clause-by-clause scrutiny. Given that we were raising £5 billion on a one-off basis, £5 billion on a continuing basis and a further £20 billion over a three-year period, they were entitled to try.

As it turned out we had an easy ride on both the windfall tax and tax credits, which was handled with great skill by my colleague Helen Liddell. We had an excellent team of MPs, several of whom have since been promoted, notably Yvette Cooper in the Department of Health as Minister for Public Health and Ross Cranston as Solicitor-General. The Tories, I could see, had the makings of a balanced and talented team, but at this time they seemed more pre-occupied with the fall-out from their leadership election than with the matter in hand. Moreover, their front bench spokesman, David Heathcoat-Amory, always seemed more interested in Europe than anything else.

Under normal circumstances standing committee meetings on Finance Bills take place twice weekly on Tuesdays and Thursdays, over a period of two or three months. There are breaks for lunch and dinner and the committee does not often sit beyond 10 p.m. or the rising of the House. It is a tedious procedure and it is also extremely inconvenient for members with young families. Given that we had barely three weeks before the recess for our first Finance Bill in nearly twenty years, we could not allow ourselves such a leisurely procedure. We crammed the whole committee stage into one week.

The Finance Bill received the royal assent on 31 July – just four weeks after the budget statement to the Commons. I understand this to be a record: more money raised in less time than any comparable set of budget measures! I covered about half of this (and the next budget's) committee stage. Dawn Primarolo as Financial Secretary expertly took through a whole raft of other tax-raising measures. I was delighted to see her succeed me as Paymaster General in due course. The truly laborious job of steering the Financial Services Bill★ through subsequent committee stages fell to Alistair Darling, the Chief Secretary to the Treasury and one of the safest pairs of hands in the government.†

If I had to point to 'laborious days' in the Treasury they would be those spent in Committee Room A, where we invariably met. It was a grind and mostly boring. But then, as I would often remind myself and others, all jobs have their boring parts; and taken as a whole, one finance bill a year, even with all the necessary preparation, was not a bad deal. For the rest, I thoroughly enjoyed the Treasury.

This was in part because Gordon asked me to handle many of the day-to-day tricky problems and some of the more interesting and innovative budget proposals. In this way I became involved with energy policy, film finance, museum charges, productivity seminars, funding Tate Modern, the motor-car industry and defence restructuring, most of which are covered elsewhere in this book. I looked forward to each day in the office in anticipation of some new involvement in a different area of national affairs, and I was rarely disappointed. That is the advantage of the Treasury – it has a legitimate interest in everything.

However, while in opposition we had taken the view that if the Treasury was to exercise its proper interest across the whole domestic policy agenda, it would require a cultural change in the

---

★ This involved restructuring the Bank of England and setting up the Financial Services Authority.

† Alistair Darling is now Secretary of State for Social Security.

Treasury itself. Most Treasury officials reacted positively to the new possibilities this opened up, as I describe in the next section.

Changing the Culture

Most organizations these days are deemed to be in need of culture change. The BBC and NHS are two examples that immediately come to mind. Greg Dyke, from what one reads, is certainly having a go at it with the BBC. The PM's statement in late July 2000 promised nothing short of a revolution in attitude at the NHS.

It was not surprising, therefore, that the Treasury team, while in opposition, felt major changes would be required at the Treasury. Nothing could be done, of course, till we were in office; but once inside we needed to have clear ideas about the changes that were necessary and we would have to lead by example to bring them about.

There were three principal areas of concern: the Treasury's tendency towards optimism – especially in its forecasting – and a general fiscal and monetary laxity, especially from 1988/89 onwards; its relations with other departments; and its involvement in the national growth agenda.

The Treasury's professional reputation had declined dramatically in the nineties through a series of unforced errors: the hopelessly inaccurate forecasts of the 1988/89 budgets were due to over-optimism; the ERM entry in 1990 was a political decision at odds with the known facts of the economic situation; the repeated refusals to increase interest rates in the period 1995–7 were politically motivated to enhance the electoral prospects of the Conservative government.

At Gordon's request, Ed Balls drew up while in opposition a series of principles and policies that would prevent the avoidable mistakes of the Tories. The most important step was to grant operational independence to the Bank of England. That would eliminate electoral interference in monetary policy. The 'golden rule' – borrowing for investment only – taken together with the commitment to a stable and prudent level of national debt would introduce fiscal discipline and avoid over-optimism. This more open and responsible approach would be reinforced by the National Audit Office's being required to vet the underlying assumptions of the Treasury forecasts. The acceptance of the Tory spending plans for the first two years of office would avoid the profligacy of earlier Labour administrations. Re-entry into the ERM (or joining the EMU) would only be possible when sound public finances had been established (and the economies were convergent). Economic criteria, and not foreign-policy objectives, must be decisive.

Taken together, these measures – the Bank's independence, the acceptance of Tory spending plans, the 'golden rule', the limit on the national debt and the role of the National Audit Office – comprised a formidable package aimed at achieving caution and realism in economic matters. But they went beyond that. They were intended to insulate Treasury policy formulation and execution from governments' weakness of resolve or desire for electoral advantage; and, based on common sense, they aimed to exclude in principle any misconceived theory. In opposition they earned Gordon the sobriquet of the 'Iron Chancellor'. For my part I have to confess that before government I had my doubts at times about how our resolve would withstand the strain of office.

There was really no need for concern. The Bank was immediately granted operational independence; and Gordon right from the start made it clear to officials at all levels that he was utterly committed to making the prudent policies of opposition stick in government. The Chancellor certainly was giving the lead. It was important the Treasury should follow. That meant the Treasury had to face up to what had gone wrong in the recent past if it was to avoid a repetition of it. There was considerable resistance at the top of the Treasury, which showed how necessary some act of expiation was. After a lot of hassle, Ed secured the publication with the November 1997 pre-budget report (in itself a most useful innovation) of a document entitled 'Fiscal Policy: Lessons from the Last Economic Cycle'. The paper made the explicit point that in 1993, after the 1992 general election, the PSBR (public spending

borrowing requirement) peaked at just over 7 per cent of GDP
(£46 billion) representing a rise in the PSBR of 10 per cent over
just five years, and an error, between out-turn and the 1989–90
illustrative projection, of nearly £50 billion. There were two simple
lessons to be drawn: Lesson 1, take a prudent approach; Lesson 2,
be open and transparent.

The first lesson said do not be over-optimistic. The second
meant, in its context, keep politics out of it. Ed's proposal to do
this was to issue with the same pre-budget papers 'A Code for Fiscal
Stability'. The code made explicit the new framework for fiscal
policy based on the two strict fiscal rules which had been the
bedrock of our policy in opposition:

- Over the economic cycle, the government will only borrow to
  invest – public consumption (including the consumption of
  capital) will be paid for by taxation; and
- Over the economic cycle, the government will ensure the level
  of public debt as a proportion of national income is held at a
  stable and prudent level.

The paper established five criteria to which the government would
have regard: transparency, stability, responsibility, fairness, efficiency. In a sense, much of what was being said here had been
said before at different times and other places, not least by New
Labour when in opposition. What struck me now was that in
government there was a deadly seriousness of intent to make
the policies stick. The fiscal stability code was stark about the
government's determination:

The fact that the Government puts its reputation at stake by publishing
the Code, and publicly committing itself to it, may go a large way in this
direction. But an argument can be made for going further and enshrining
the code in legislation. This would make it more difficult for governments to ignore the provision of the code or drop it altogether. The
Government accepts this argument. It believes that legislation will
enhance the credibility-building process, allowing the gains to be realised
sooner than otherwise.

The code was laid before the House and approved by it in a virtually unchanged format on 9 December 1998.

In due course it may seem to his peers in the economic profession that the Code for Fiscal Stability was Ed Balls's major legacy to the Treasury. For the moment he is still there, now deservedly promoted to chief economic adviser, where he contemplates the continuation of the country's longest period of sustained growth in the whole post-war period. I can think of no policy or decision in which he was not centrally involved. His contribution to our economic success has been immense. But that would not be the right point at which to leave Ed Balls in this narrative. Important though his contributions were in economic terms, his deep concern on poverty, redistribution and fairness in society will be seen as of more importance in due course. Those issues are what motivate him. Getting the economics right is just the means to do something effective about them. I am sure he will have been well pleased with Peter Jay's summary of the April 2000 budget for the nine o'clock news for the BBC:

Suddenly the scene has got a lot simpler and clearer. We have a Labour government behaving like a Labour government. The things which he [the Chancellor] will spend his money on over the next few years as announced are things that would be understood by previous generations of old Labour. But Gordon Brown would make the point they were wholly unable to deliver what they wanted to do; they may have had the aspirations but they were unable to because they didn't have the independent central bank and strong pound that he has laid. The price of that is of course the burden of tax has gone up, and that has been so far used in order to turn around the Budget to repay debt. From now on it will be used to pay for the increases of public services.

As Peter Jay made clear, the outcome of Labour's first three years in office could not have been more different from the experience of previous Labour governments. It necessitated a change in Treasury culture that could only be inspired by the change in policies and politics that the Chancellor and Ed Balls insisted on implementing.

The remarkable accuracy of Treasury forecasts since 1997 reflects this new realism. At first they were not believed because of the Treasury's past performance. Some had perhaps doubted our resolve. But the results are there: inflation is down; employment is up; borrowing is down; the growth rate is up; debt is being repaid; and unparalleled public investment is being made in health and education. Not a bad effort. This part of the culture change was the indispensable prerequisite for the success.

The Treasury and the Spending Departments

It is not much of an exaggeration to describe the traditional pattern of working between the Treasury and the rest of Whitehall as follows: the spending departments bid for expenditure far in excess of their real requirement; the Treasury haggled for as long as it could and tried to concede as little as half of what was bid. The spending departments reluctantly accepted. Everyone was then secretly pleased with the outcome and there were congratulations all round. In fact not much had been achieved. No one really questioned the bid in terms of its priority. Nor was there systematic follow-up to monitor whether the objectives of the expenditure had been achieved or not. This process had become ritualized as the Annual Spending Review.

Our acceptance of the Tory spending plans for the two years 1997–9, despite the harsh discipline it imposed, gave us the opportunity to break free from this unproductive procedure. We instituted instead the Comprehensive Spending Review, an important innovation, introducing a switch to firm three-year plans. The rolling three-year programmes enable the departments to plan their revenue and capital expenditure over a longer period, as any business organization does as a matter of course. In return for this freedom – and the large increases in spending as announced in July 2000 made possible by the successful management of the economy – we introduced arguably the biggest spending reform of all: the linking of expenditure to the achievement of the purposes for which it is being spent and the concomitant accountability of the secretaries of state in doing so. This went to the heart of New Labour's approach: the right to new expenditure must be matched by the responsibility for using it well.

It followed quite logically that if the Treasury was to evaluate and monitor these long-term expenditure programmes, it should be involved in the policy-formation procedures. This also means that the Treasury will be required to coordinate the implementation of policies that cut across departmental boundaries. At various times attempts have been made to clip the Treasury's wings: to make it just a ministry of finance that limits expenditure. That is the wrong approach. The Cabinet Office, even with such effective politicians as Jack Cunningham and Mo Mowlam at the helm, is simply not equipped to monitor or enforce departmental expenditures, still less to coordinate them. It is outranked at any meeting by the Treasury and to challenge that ranking is bound to provoke a counter-challenge which the Cabinet Office is in turn bound to lose.

It is therefore much better to accept the supremacy of the Treasury and to ensure that it is a competent enabling and integrating entity. I believe this is being achieved not least because the Treasury itself has been willing to change. One of the important side benefits of relinquishing its at times all-consuming responsibility for monetary policy has been that the Treasury has been liberated to look at other important policy areas.

But progress was not easy. When the Treasury staked a claim to real involvement in designing and implementing the New Deal we ran into stiff resistance from the Department of Employment. But my enterprising private secretary combined, by some clever photocopying, the two crests, those of the Department of Employment and the Treasury, on one sheet of paper. The announcement of the launch of the scheme went out under two crests and over two signatures. What better sign of joined-up government could there be? The contribution of the Treasury team under Ruth Thompson and Stewart Taylor was soon recognized and such a subterfuge was not required again.

The Treasury has also taken a very proactive role in developing incentives to work and in the attack on child poverty. The policy work is carried out by the Work Incentives and Poverty Analysis team. It sounds wretchedly bureaucratic. It is anything but that. It also may not seem traditional Treasury territory but those involved are motivated by the ambition to eradicate child poverty and to tackle the barriers that impede economic prosperity and social justice in the real world. Such is the extent of the culture change under way at the Treasury that these are the issues on which some of the brightest people in the organization want to work.

The Treasury and the Growth Agenda

It was my personal interest to re-engage the Treasury in pursuit of that elusive goal: the improvement in our underlying rate of growth. Harold Wilson had first seriously highlighted the problem and tried to tackle it back in 1964 with the establishment of the Department of Economic Affairs. I had observed the experiment at first hand as a Labour Party researcher at Transport House. It tried to split the Treasury function but really only produced splits in Cabinet – between George Brown and Jim Callaghan – which did no good.

We decided to tackle the problem from within the Treasury. We established the Growth Unit in order to balance the power of the expenditure-control function and to promote taxation and supply-side measures that were specifically targeted at improving our economic performance. Steve Robson persuaded John Kingman to rejoin the Treasury from BP to take the lead on the new agenda. John is brilliant intellectually and also has great drive for getting things done. He soon became effectively Steve's no. 2.

The Growth Unit pushed the work forward on four major fronts: corporate and capital-gains taxes; competition policy; the new technologies and the science agenda; and public-sector enterprises.

Our work for lower taxes on companies and capital gains was prepared in opposition. But we could not have accomplished the capital-gains package as a whole, nor the further reduction in corporate taxes and the introduction on a permanent basis of fuller capital allowances, without the sustained focus on them that the Growth Unit provided.

The Treasury before the advent of the present administration had not played much of a proactive role in supply-side measures. It responded with alacrity, however, when given the opportunity to do so. On competition policy it took particular pleasure in galvanizing the DTI into action. The merger of two rather ineffectual organizations – the Monopolies and Mergers Commission and the Office of Fair Trading – into a new Competition Commission was pushed through under Treasury pressure. The Treasury itself led the way by commissioning, under Donald Cruickshank, the inquiry into bank charges. It also instigated the new commission's inquiries into supermarket and car prices. I know that many in these industries did not welcome these investigations. They also resented the sobriquet 'rip-off Britain', which they felt was demeaning of their companies and their efforts. But the plain fact is that prices throughout Britain are prevalently higher than in Europe, not to mention America – where the Chancellor every summer exercises his own private price-watch. All businesses, while subscribing to the virtue of competition, seek to avoid it. But it has never been more true that, just as the bench is the coach's best friend, so competition is the consumer's and ultimately the producer's, too.

Soon after his return I asked John Kingman to undertake a visit to Silicon Valley to see what lessons we could learn from the fantastic developments in the new technologies that were taking place over there. His report confirmed the importance of the capital-gains changes we were engaged in and the need to provide specifically for roll-over relief which would encourage reinvestment in the short term in new ventures. We duly brought that too within the reforms. The report also highlighted the little noticed but very important contribution made to the revolution in internet and related technologies by the immigration into the United States of young skilled people, mainly graduates. In Britain, we are just getting round to making some welcome changes in the same direction. The example of companies clustering around and working with universities in California inspired us to proceed in a £1 billion partnership with the Wellcome Trust involving scientific-based research and development projects linking into the universities. This was the first time the trust had entered into collaboration with a government, and the collaboration would not have taken place but for the wise guidance provided by Sir David Cooksey* to both parties. It was Sir David's idea that, as the genome mapping project neared completion, major funding would be required to ensure that the enormous potential for improvement in human life was exploited. British research is at the forefront of this work. Thanks to the partnership with Wellcome, nearly all the funds have now been dispersed to research centres throughout the country.

The successful reform of PFI and the work of the taskforce within the Treasury have contributed to a much better understanding by officials of how the private sector works. This will need to be extended as the wider scope offered by Partnerships UK, the company set up to promote PFI schemes, begins to be exploited. More engagement from the Treasury – not less – will be required as the major capital expenditure projects of the next five years get under way. Indeed, that applies to all the areas of projected increases in government spending.

But to speak of engagement by the Treasury or of the Treasury being 'proactive' does not mean the Treasury rushing around everywhere and trying to do every department's business for them. It does mean, on the other hand, that the Treasury accepts its responsibility for ensuring joined-up government and that this Treasury function is accepted by the spending departments.

It means that the very large amounts of money to be spent on the NHS will result in real improvements to the service that the NHS provides to patients. It means that children will have better classrooms and playing fields and are better taught. It means that

* Sir David Cooksey is chairman of Advent, member of court at the Bank of England since 1994 and director of the Wellcome Foundation until 1999. Sir David is generally recognized as the founding father of venture capital in the UK.

the alternatives to road travel will be properly thought through and not fanciful ideas. It means departments cooperating with the Treasury and an end to stupid turf wars.

As we move towards an objective evaluation and monitoring system for government spending, with the Treasury at the heart of it, there is a danger that the bureaucrats will go into overdrive. They could overwhelm entire spending programmes with paperwork involving complicated matrices of inputs and outputs, the only outcome of which would be that no one would know what had happened and no one would really be responsible. What is required for the evaluation of results is the establishment of a relatively few meaningful and measurable standards by which improvements can be judged.

The Treasury has done much by way of cultural change to equip itself to play this role. It has shed the incubus of monetary policy. It has faced up to its failings in the nineties and is seized of a new realism. Its work on employment incentives and the eradication of poverty is at the centre of its domestic policy agenda. The Growth Unit's supply-side measures were targeted at overcoming barriers to increased output and productivity.

While the catalyst for change was the arrival of a new administration, the response within the Treasury – after initial hesitation – has been widespread and positive.

This broadening of the Treasury's role and the new competence it has given rise to represents a fundamental break with the past. It established the Treasury as the focal point for policy reform across the government and it has ensured that staff morale is high. Moreover, the Treasury is becoming an enabling and educating department without in any way diminishing its quintessential responsibility for the country's finances. Indeed it can only be the former in so far as it is successfully the latter. There will no doubt be cynics in the Treasury and in other departments who doubt that a can-do, enabling attitude is feasible or desirable for Westminster government. To which I only reply that inertia and caution have not, over the last fifty years, provided a particularly glorious period in our history.

6. 'To Tax and to Please' (with apologies to Burke)

This tax is mythical, this windfall tax . . . It is all nonsense when you look at it, it doesn't work.

   Kenneth Clarke, July 1996

Gordon Brown is rightly credited with conceiving Labour's windfall tax idea. But to ascribe to Gordon the entire credit would not be quite fair on Sir Geoffrey Howe, who stung the banks for an extra £400 million on a one-off basis in his budget of 10 March 1981.

   The Tory windfall was in fact a very useful guide to Labour's own venture, which was to be the flagship policy in its first budget. The justification for the Tory tax was the high profits banks were making in relation to other sectors: it applied to all banks; it was levied as a single rate on a simple basis; it was applied retrospectively; and its receipts were diverted to help other parts of the economy, notably industry.

   It was a most un-Tory-like measure. But given that the Tories had no ideological hang-up about a retrospective tax on excess profits it was somewhat surprising that they did not pick up on New Labour's idea of a windfall tax on the utilities. They had cracked a very tough nut in the banks. By 1993, with the budget deficit standing at £46 billion, they could certainly have done with the money. But from the start Kenneth Clarke was against the idea and indifferent to Labour's goading: 'This tax is mythical, this windfall tax . . . It is all nonsense when you look at it, it doesn't work,' he said on Radio 4 in 1996.

   It was interesting that his objection was not one of principle but practicality. And on reflection I could see why. Gordon Brown's proposal for a tax on the excess profits of the utilities would be much more complex: there were far more companies involved, they had been privatized at different times and they comprised different industries. There could be different accounting conventions and the regulator's position would have to be accommodated.

Perhaps Clarke was right? Perhaps, too, the Treasury officials were negative about the prospects of finding a common equitable basis for taxing so disparate a group of companies and industries?

There could be no retreat for New Labour. The windfall tax grew in importance as the election approached. No speech of Gordon's was complete without reference to the utilities, their fat cats and the excess profits that would fund the youth training programme.

To me one thing was clear: if we were to have an early budget and if the youth training programme was to be a centrepiece of it, then the sooner we got on with preparing the windfall tax that was to pay for it the better. The prospect of a mad rush, once in government, with hastily concocted primary legislation subject to an endless stream of opposition amendments at committee stage – even the Liberals had come out against it – filled me with dismay. We would no doubt get the legislation through the committee stage; but we would end up getting less money than we could have raised and create the impression that it was just another Labour government with good ideas but no grasp of how to work them out in practice. This was certainly the case with some of Labour's major tax reforms in 1964–70.

It was with these thoughts in mind that I put a call through to Ed Balls one Sunday morning in late May 1996. I totted up with him the various estimates of what analysts in the City had come up with for the different utilities: £10 billion in tax was evidently on the cards and I suggested this should be our target. He concurred at once and was sure Gordon would agree, though nothing should be public. I stressed to Ed that it would be unlikely for us to raise the entire figure – we would be bound to be driven down and we had to remember that we would only get one bite of the cherry.

The major difficulty I was sure we would come up against would be the need to treat every company in exactly the same way. There could be up to twenty companies involved. It would be a tricky business. I suggested we would need a top-flight accountancy firm to work out a scheme for us. Ed saw the point at once and was sure we could get Gordon on board. We knew we were entering dangerous ground. I was not even sure we could get anyone to take it on. We saw Gordon the next day, secured his agreement and got straight down to work.

It was vital that the initial approach should be made correctly. Exercises like this can go completely off the rails if the wrong first impressions are created. For us to be taken seriously, it would be essential to go in at the right level; to emphasize the full personal support of the shadow Chancellor and to make it clear that we wanted a top-flight professional job done, for which we would be prepared to pay.

I was not aware of any party funds available for this purpose. On the other hand, I was able to afford the costs involved myself and regarded the research of sufficient importance for me to support it financially. Over the years I have in one way or another supported the political offices of Neil Kinnock, John Smith and, more recently, Tony Blair and Gordon Brown, though this was the first time I personally had commissioned research in this way.

It helped, of course, that we were widely expected to win the General Election and that, apart from the windfall tax, the mood music of New Labour was business friendly. In fact it was even my impression that amongst industrialists – who were not involved in the privatized utilities – the tax was not unpopular. There was a whiff of *schadenfreude* in the air. People felt that too many bureaucrats, some of whom had never taken a risk in their lives and had not shown much managerial talent, had become overnight millionaires thanks to a botched government privatization process. I was constantly to reassure Gordon that the windfall tax would be the only popular tax in the history of collecting government revenues! I'm not sure he ever believed it. But we were now starting the serious business of preparing for government.

My approach was to the tax consultants, Arthur Andersen, who

I knew had done some work for John Smith. The key figure here was Stephen Hailey, a Labour Party member and managing partner of the accountancy arm. We were well placed to make the approach.

Stephen responded positively. Our first meeting when just the two of us were present took place in the imposing Andersens building in Surrey Street. I explained to Stephen the commitment Gordon had made in 1993 to levy a windfall tax to pay for our youth employment programme. It was our view that the circumstances of privatization were very unsatisfactory and that there was a moral justification for the tax. I repeated my fear that unless it was worked out by professionals in sufficient detail, the idea could get derailed in government. That was why we had come to Andersens, who, without flattery, was amongst the very best in the country. Stephen stressed that he would have to clear the situation with colleagues and was most anxious to know what figure we had in mind for the tax. I came straight out with the £10 billion figure. Stephen seemed mildly discomfited that we were looking for a figure as high as this and demurred at the feasibility of achieving it. Nonetheless he would consult colleagues and get back to me.

Stephen phoned me the next day to say Andersens would take it on. He had assembled what must have been, even by their standards, an outstanding team. The central figures were Chris Wales, taxation expert, who later was to come over to the Treasury; Chris Osborne, a top auditing partner, and Chris Sanger, a brilliant accountant who was later to join Wales in the Treasury on secondment.

We had our first formal meeting on Wednesday, 12 June 1996 in my flat. It was clear from the start that there were different levels of enthusiasm for the tax at Andersens. This was hardly surprising given the £10 billion figure we had asked them to look for. I suspect Chris Osborne had his reservations of principle. But he went about the job with a cheerful acceptance and an attitude that said 'if it's going to be done, let's do it well'. It was clear that neither personal nor political opinions counted. It was a job like any other. They had the resources for it. It was a research exercise that would have been inconceivable in the cramped conditions and with the limited resources already stretched to breaking point of the shadow

Treasury team. Nor could the task in hand be done by a group of sympathetic part-timers. We needed professionals and we had some of the best.

We got straight down to business, defining a clear set of objectives for the Andersen team. These were:

- To examine the extent to which the privatized utilities might be able to bear an additional tax on a one-off basis;
- To consider the way in which such a tax might be structured;
- To estimate the potential yield from differing taxing mechanisms;
- To consider the wider implications of the windfall tax proposal.

The last point was an Andersen concern. They were quite prepared to do the work. But they also wanted to have their shout about what might be a reasonable end-result to aim at.

The work went ahead with the speed and efficiency one would expect from an organization with the professional resources that Andersens had at their disposal. The first priority was to establish a database of financial information. This in turn meant that we had to specify which companies should be included. There were in fact over 150 privatized entities, most of which in one way or another could be adjudged to have made excess profits. The Treasury team had only referred to the utilities. We decided on the most obvious candidates – those that had to be in: the water and sewerage companies (WASCs); the regional electricity companies (RECs); BT and BG; Powergen and National Power (the generators) and the Scottish electricity companies(SCOTSCOs). But where would that leave, for example, British Airports Authority, Railtrack, the rail operating service companies (ROSCOs) and the National Grid?

For our immediate purposes we decided to concentrate on the first group of obvious candidates, with the intention that once we had a basis that was workable for them we would seek to extend it to the 'borderline' cases.

The financial analysis carried out by Andersens of the companies' most recent accounts established that they had all done well since privatization, increasing profits, dividends and share prices well ahead of the FTSE all-share averages. We were on solid ground: there was a broad justification for the tax. So our problem remained to find a common and equitable system for levying it.

Andersens proposed two sets of options:

Simple solutions	Complex solutions
Tax on turnover	Tax on excess profits
Tax on assets	Tax on excess shareholder returns
Tax on profits	

The first two of the simple solutions – a tax on turnover or assets – had little merit other than their simplicity. There was no principled rationale for taxing either. Moreover, there was bound to be an uneven distribution of the tax burden, provoking challenges that it might be hard to resist with logical argument. There were limited precedents for a turnover tax – we could point to the insurance premium tax and Howe's banking deposit tax but they hardly made a compelling case for this option. For these reasons it was clear early on that a simple tax on assets or turnover could only be contemplated as a solution of last resort.

On the other hand a tax on profits had considerable attractions at first sight. There was a broad link to the underlying rationale that the companies had overall much better financial returns than the average. We could point again to Howe's banking tax, which had specifically maintained as a justification for its levy that banking profits had been higher than those in other industries. It would be a conventional approach and one that could further be presented as fair to all the companies affected. It also had the benefit of there being established calculation methodologies.

As is often the case, we soon found that the devil lay in the detail. If we were to apply the tax prospectively, i.e. to future profits, companies would be tempted into financial manipulation and the yield would be unpredictable. And given that we were looking for a large target, we could envisage situations where a 100 per cent rate of corporation tax would have to be applied. Old Labour had never got to that point, though with the 98 per cent rate in 1967 they had got quite close. The tax would have therefore to be levied retrospectively and if done on this simple basis would be open to wide resistance and criticism on the basis that the same profits were being taxed twice. We concluded that if profits were to be the basis for the tax we should have to go for the complex solution of a tax on 'excess' profits. Indeed, despite a common preference for a simple solution, we all felt that our case for the tax would be weakened in the absence of a principled rationale on which to base it. And this pointed to a more complicated option. Moreover, the 'excess'-profits concept fitted well with Gordon's fat-cat presentation of the proposal.

   At first glance the profit figures looked very promising. The pre-tax profits between the first full year of privatization and 1995 (the most recent year for which figures were available) had indeed increased very substantially: WASCs by 28 per cent; RECs by 36 per cent; generators by 43 per cent; SCOTSCOs by 42 per cent; BT by 45 per cent. However, as so often in our windfall tax exercise, there was one exasperating exception: over the same period British Gas profits had *decreased* by 8 per cent. Were we to choose excess profits as the basis for the tax, and let British Gas off any payment at all, we would certainly face legal grounds of discrimination and the tax would fall at the first hurdle.

   We were to come up against the same problem with the idea of a tax on excess shareholder returns. It had much going for it. The rationale was strong: linking the tax to excess returns made by shareholders was hitting the right target in principle. The information we had obtained showed that the shareholder returns in the RECs, generators and WASCs had on average all been way in excess of the FTSE all-share average. However, BG was again an exception, joined in this instance quite ominously by BT; dividend payouts at both companies had in the most recent years dropped below the FTSE all-share level. That scotched the excess-dividends idea.

   Our mounting frustration was not eased when at one moment it seemed that any tax on BG would bankrupt the company, such was the position of its balance sheet. Further research fortunately showed that this was due to the way BG had split its balance sheet.

They were back in the frame. But we were still without a solution that could be applied equitably to all the companies and raise the substantial sums we were looking for.

Perhaps Ken Clarke was right. Perhaps it was not do-able without such anomalies and complexities as to create the very nightmare of legislation that our careful preparation was meant to avoid. If the worst came to the worst we would have to fall back on one of the simple solutions. I was thinking in terms of a tax on turnover as being the least bad of a bad set of options.

Then in October 1996 Chris Wales had a stroke of inspiration. Chris simply turned the whole argument on its head: the problem was not that the companies had made too much profit, nor that they had paid out too much to shareholders and fat-cat directors, nor that they had been treated with kid gloves by the regulators. That was all true of course: but the genesis of the problem was that they had been sold too cheaply in the first place. Why not then, argued Chris, tax the loss to the taxpayer which arose from the sale of these companies at what was a knock-down price. As Chris summarized the proposals:

i.   Establish for each utility its market capitalization on flotation;
ii. Calculate, using an appropriate and common price/earnings ratio for each utility's profits over the first five years since its flotation, what its market capitalization should have been at flotation;
iii. Recognize the windfall element as the difference between i and ii, the difference between the price the company was actually sold at and the price its subsequent profits demonstrated it should have been sold at;
iv. Tax the utilities on the value forgone using the established principles of capital gains tax legislation.* This meant a 40 per cent tax on the difference.

---

* This point had an elegant attraction to us in opposition since it would provide a telling line of attack on the Tories, who had specifically disapplied section 179 of the 1992 Taxation of Chargeable Gains Act, in all but one of the privatizations.

The essence of Chris's new proposal was its simplicity and the universality of its application. Admittedly, as the Andersen team and others pointed out to us, we were using twenty-twenty hindsight. But from our point of view that was better than the uncertainties of any prospective arrangement.

Moreover, it was a widely recognized fact in the City that the utilities had been sold too cheaply. Applying any reasonable price/earnings ratio for the sector – or across the FTSE as a whole – the figures showed that all the utilities had been sold at a discount. Some more than others but all at a discount.

The Andersens model threw up a gross tax yield of £6 billion if a p/e ratio of 6 was used. If the ratio was increased to 8 – still well below the FTSE average and what might be expected of companies with strong balance sheets, tied customer bases and guaranteed cash flows – the yield rose to £12 billion. In terms of increased gearing, most of the utilities could absorb their share of this. But we gulped at the implications for two of the companies and scaled our ambitions back into single figures.

We had made the breakthrough; we had a clear definition for the companies to be included in the tax: those companies 'privatized by flotation'. We had a principled basis for levying the tax: the value forgone on flotation by selling the companies at a discount. We had an equitable and flexible method for calculating the tax: it would be applied to all companies in the same way and at the same rate, which in turn would be set at a level sufficient for our policies and affordable to the companies.

We met in Gordon's crowded noisy office in the bowels of the Commons in July 1996. In an elated atmosphere Ed Balls reminded us that we had not yet taken the legal advice which we knew would be necessary. We felt we were solid from a UK point of view but the danger lay in Europe, where problems could well arise from both the European Court and the European Convention on Human Rights. Although I winced at the thought of the cost, it was clear we had to take counsel's opinion. But whose?

Ed, having spoken with a friend from Oxford, was put in touch with Rabinder Singh, who was in Chambers at Grays Inn. Rabinder was only too pleased to help, but thought that we should involve Michael Beloff, who was his head of Chambers. There was no problem in welcoming Michael to our team. He was thought to be sympathetic to New Labour and had been described by Jeffrey Archer, with the flight of the modern novelist's imagination, as 'having the mind of a planet'. In fact, despite such an endorsement, Michael is widely regarded as one of the best barristers in the country.

Our first meeting was exploratory. While I had not much doubt that they would accept the job, it seemed right to talk our ideas through first before commissioning solicitors. We made it clear we would pay for the opinion, which seemed to come as a relief to our legal colleagues. It would be a joint opinion involving Michael himself and Rabinder Singh. We took as our instructing solicitors Wedlake Bell, who had handled a number of issues with the Labour Party. Work started at once.

Our decision to take legal advice was well timed. The utilities were making noises, with Eastern (an electricity generator) threatening to launch a legal challenge and Yorkshire Electricity, having already announced plans on 25 September 1996 for a third share buy-back, bringing their total cash withdrawal from the company, via this method and special dividend distributions, to £500 million. A number of the other utility companies had undertaken or were preparing similar measures, though on a relatively smaller scale. Their misguided thinking was that if they divested themselves sufficiently of cash they might escape the windfall tax. We had made our intentions crystal clear to all of them and we would not be deterred by any poison pill tactics. We now had to make sure that they could not be spiked by legal intervention.

Our instructions to Michael Beloff were as simple as the issues were, initially at any rate, to seem complex:

In this matter we are asked to advise . . . the Labour Party as to certain legal issues arising out of the Party's proposed windfall tax on the excess profits of privatized public utilities ('the Windfall Tax') arising under (1) domestic law (2) European Community ('EC') law (3) the law of the European Convention on Human Rights ('ECHR').

The opinion we were given reviewed each situation in turn. We were strongly placed on the domestic front, with the one quite startling qualification, which read as follows:

We should add that our view about the immunity of an Act of Parliament from challenge in a domestic court might change if the ECHR were to be incorporated into domestic law. We note that incorporation is the policy of the Labour Party. While it is no part of our remit to advise on the merits of that policy, it should be borne in mind in the timing of such incorporation that the Windfall Tax might be challenged under a domestic Act incorporating the ECHR. In particular, it should be noted that, if the relevant companies were not actually assessed for tax until sometime in 1998 or 1999 and the ECHR had by then been incorporated, a challenge in a domestic court might be excited.

All the more reason, I commented, to get on with the job and be ready for May 1997, the latest date at which Tony would be asked to form a government. Ed remarked that we might have to delay the incorporation of the ECHR. We might well! But I didn't think that a good planning base. We were planning a budget within three months of taking office. It was vital that the windfall tax, a central plank in it, be ready. Delay could be fatal.

As far as EC law went, the main concerns regarded Articles 52 and 58 of the Treaty of Rome, which sought to ensure principles of free movement, in particular freedom of establishment of nationals in the various member states. Having reviewed every conceivable precedent, including even the Bosman ruling,* the conclusion was quite simple: we were well placed so long as we did not discriminate between nationals or residents of the UK and

---

* *Union Royale Belge des Sociétés de Football* v *Bosman*, C-415/93 (1995). This ruling, which has had very questionable benefits for British football, allows a player total freedom of action at the expiry of his contract.

nationals or residents of other EC member states. Such discrimination was the last thing we had in mind. Quite the contrary: all eligible candidates would be included and treated equally. We would readily comply with the Scarman dictum: there would be no favourites or sacrificial lambs.

The implications of the ECHR were more complex. The principal conclusions of a general interest can be summarized as follows:

- There is a wide 'margin of appreciation' for member states of the Council of Europe in tax matters. The gallicism 'margin of appreciation' means scope for independent action by governments;
- The tax should have a clear public-interest aim;
- The means to achieve that aim must be proportionate and must achieve a fair balance between the general interest and the interests of the individual taxpayer;
- The tax must not impose an individual and excessive burden on a particular taxpayer;
- A retroactive tax does not necessarily violate the ECHR – the commission has noted indeed that this is a feature of some UK tax law.

These considerations were encouraging, but there clearly was scope within the convention for someone determined to mount a challenge to do so. By mid-October we had received advice running to over 150 pages. The draft final summary, which was all anyone would probably read, went as follows:

In our view the windfall tax:
i.   Could not even attract a challenge under domestic law;
ii. Should not attract a challenge under EC law, but, if it did, such a challenge would fail;
iii. Should withstand any challenge which may be made under the ECHR.

It was fine except for the word 'should' in the assessment of our ability to withstand challenge under the ECHR. The issues were admittedly more complex under the ECHR. Indeed, if the opinion related to a situation where the ECHR had been incorporated into UK law the conditionality implied might well be appropriate. But that was not the case.

We had asked for a summary of the opinion which would be suitable for release in the event that media pressures required it. We had our final conference to settle it on Thursday, 24 October 1996. It seemed to me that by their own argumentation Michael and Rabinder had made a sufficiently strong case to replace 'should' with 'would'. I made a final push. Rabinder made the manuscript amendment in his own hand and we had our opinion solid in itself and ready for the long-planned, much-trumpeted Tory attack.

We did not have to wait long. Aims of Industry had commissioned three barristers at Brick Court Chambers to give an adverse legal opinion on the tax, which of course they duly did. The Tories announced it, as part of an overall onslaught on the tax, in January 1997, as 'the only authoritative study of the legal background to the windfall tax. No other lawyers had produced anything remotely comparable. There is a serious risk that the tax would be bogged down in legal argument for years.'

To that, one could only reply that they were badly informed, and that the steps we had taken to secure confidentiality were unusually successful.

The opinion itself was a damp squib, reflecting not so much the quality of the lawyers involved as the fact that they had been asked to give an opinion to support its client's established view. Fair enough. He who pays the piper calls the tune. I hope they were well paid for it. But the arguments they raised on possible breaches of EC law and the ECHR had nearly all been covered in the Beloff opinion. Brick Court Chambers cannot exactly look back with comfort on its central judgement:

We feel able to predict, with some confidence, that legal challenges will ensue whatever the final form of the levy and whoever falls within its scope. This is in part because of the very large sums of money involved, but more fundamentally because of the legally sensitive nature of a tax of this kind.

Michael Heseltine led the Tory assault. The *Daily Telegraph* front-page headline of 12 January 1997 set the tone: 'We'll sue you over the windfall tax, firms tell Blair.' It was a well-coordinated campaign. The Tories were firmly on the side of the utilities. Heseltine demanded we should publish our legal opinion. We were nearly ready to do so. But Michael Beloff had intimated that he would be happy to advise specifically on the Brick Court Chambers' opinion and its reference to a challenge arising under state aids.★ In for a penny in for a pound. We went ahead for another opinion, specifically on the Tory opinion. We received the all-clear by the end of January. In February we launched our own very successful counter-attack on the legal front, making available to the press for the first time the source and basis of our judgement. The *Guardian* broke the story with a front-page headline, 'Labour windfall tax is legally watertight. Tories caught off guard as emphatic ruling blunts attack.' We published the legal advice, which reassured colleagues and put an end to opposition on that front.

One other aspect of our preparations for the windfall tax is worth recalling. We actually undertook detailed drafting of the legislation itself. We discussed it in early October and, since speed and security of getting the legislation through in government would be essential, we decided that if we could get it drafted in advance so much the better.

Our main concern was that the tax might be considered a hybrid bill. This is to say that the bill could be judged to incorporate public and private companies and as such would not be allowed to proceed as a government bill by the Speaker. The Tories had kept up a whingeing campaign about hybridity. This line of attack finally broke cover in February when solicitors who had played a prominent role in defeating the last Labour government's legislation were

★ The technical point the Brick Court lawyers were trying to make was that by penalizing the utilities we were subsidizing other companies. Since all were being treated equally, and since there was very limited competition with other companies outside the tax, there was no state aid involved.

quoted by John Jay, the *Sunday Times* city editor, as predicting a 'legal quagmire and huge parliamentary delays'. There was a danger of this and that was the case for drafting the bill in advance. On the other hand, I was aware that the Tories had done precisely this in their preparations for the reform of industrial relations in the run-up to the 1970 election. I was informed that the draft legislation was discarded when the Tories took office. The parliamentary draftsmen, whether out of pique or professionalism, did it their way. I felt sure it would be the same with us. It was. But before we could enjoy that experience we had to find someone to do the drafting for us.

I knew by chance who two of the previous principal parliamentary counsels were and made an approach. Not surprisingly, the last thing either wanted to do for all the money on earth was to draft any further legislation. In something of a desperate move, I phoned the then principal counsel and asked if he could recommend anyone. Sir Christopher Jenkins★ to whom I spoke replied with pained professional pride: 'But, Mr Robinson, if New Labour win the election we want to draft this legislation for you. That's what we are here for.' I explained our anxieties and he mentioned some leads that took us to Sir Peter Graham, himself a former principal parliamentary counsel. At the time of our approach he was working out of Gibraltar, helping various delinquent EC governments catch up with the alignment of their domestic legislation with the incessant barrage of detailed EC regulations. Spain and Greece were particular culprits.

Andersens were interested in this aspect of the work and having their in-house legal team involved seemed a mutually beneficial arrangement. Sir Peter came up with a construction for the legislation and the crucial first part of the bill was drafted in full.

The tax sped through all its parliamentary stages without a hitch. The Tories seemed more preoccupied with the fallout from their leadership election than with the Finance Bill. It seemed also they were not getting much support from their traditional friends in the

---

★ Christopher Jenkins resigned in September 1999.

City, since they could not even manage to get an amendment down for the first committee stage meeting.

However, if events in Parliament proceeded disappointingly uneventfully, there were the usual distractions elsewhere that livened things up a bit. One such was Sir Iain Vallance's persistent attempts to keep BT out of the scope of the tax. Quite how he could think BT, the primest of all prime targets, could be left out, I cannot imagine. He had been in frequent touch with No. 10 before the election, when he voted Labour, but threatened to withdraw his support the next time round if BT were included in the windfall tax. It was a threat we had to face up to. As we knew from the legal work, if we were to exempt any company that met the criteria we would blow the tax right out of the water. But Sir Iain did not give in easily. Recognizing the inevitability of BT's inclusion, he cleverly put forward the proposal that the tax should be levied on excess dividends paid to shareholders. We had visited that before too, and we knew BT would on that basis escape any liability whatsoever. In the end BT accepted that it would be the largest single contributor to the tax with a take of £500 million. Sir Iain himself remarked: 'We recognize that a figure in the order of £500 million . . . is considerably lower than earlier speculation might have suggested.' He was correct. On some scenarios it could easily have been a billion.

Sadly, our success with BT was not matched with regard to the National Grid and the rolling-stock companies (ROSCOs). Two of the ROSCO companies, Porterbrook and Eversholt Leasing, seemed to reflect in some ways what Edward Heath had called the 'unacceptable face of capitalism'. The profits made with no risk and little effort beggared belief.

Porterbrook was sold to a consortium led by its management team in January 1996 for £525 million. Barely six months later it was sold on for £827 million, yielding a profit of £300 million. For once I agreed with the *Sunday Times*, which called its exposé 'The Great Train Robbery'. The managing director was thought to have collected £30 million. The profit made in the two years from February 1995 to February 1997 on the resale of Eversholt was some £150 million. However, since none of the ROSCOs was privatized by flotation, they escaped the net. It was sad and infuriating, because no companies more deserved inclusion than Eversholt and Porterbrook.

The National Grid was an altogether different organization. It had been hived off from the power generators to become a discrete company in its own right. Like the ROSCOs, therefore, it had not been privatized by flotation as it had already been privatized as part of the generators. Moreover, we had partially taxed the profits contributed to the generators by the Grid, via the substantive contribution to the windfall tax being made by the generators. I did not mind National Grid escaping the net; they were quite a good group of people, as I learned during the coal crisis. In any case we certainly could not risk a challenge, which could have arisen had we included them.

An awkward problem of a different sort arose with British Gas. The company had split itself into two organizations: Centrica, a gas-supply company, and Transco, a transmission company. The division of the windfall tax was done according to the level of assets inherited by each company. While Transco could absorb the tax allocated to it on this basis, Centrica would be too badly affected by the £190 million hit it would incur. By good fortune it was an agreed part of our energy policy (together with reduction of VAT on fuel) to reduce the gas levy. This eased the burden to the extent of £100 million and solved that problem.

Concurrently with the drafting of the legislation we were conducting extensive negotiations with the companies and the regulators. Officials handled the companies with no involvement from myself; I handled the regulators, briefed of course by officials. It was vital that we secured the regulators' concurrence that the tax could be levied without damage to the investment and employment prospects of the companies involved. The regulators were as mixed a bunch as you could find. Donald Cruickshank stood out at Oftel as did Ian Byatt at water and particularly Clare Spottiswoode at gas. Her opposite number in electricity – Professor Stephen Littlechild – stood out more for his apparent lack of grasp; he cut no more authoritative a figure in the coal review.

The consultation with the regulators ended satisfactorily. All agreed that the companies they regulated could afford their share of the tax without harming employment or investment prospects. Each knew, of course, the amount of tax we were targeting for their sector but none knew the overall target. It was also important that in reaching their judgement they should not tell the companies concerned how much their individual share would be. Those would be published separately on budget day. The intriguing question was the level we would pitch the overall tax at. The target I came down to, and to which we secured the full agreement of the regulators, was £6 billion. For me this was a satisfactory outcome. The New Deal was costed at about £3.5 billion, which left a clear £2 billion, earmarked in equal measure for emergency spending on school buildings and hospitals. I knew we would need this and there was nowhere else to find it, since we had accepted the Tory spending limits.

It was to be the only point on which Gordon overruled me. We cut the yield back to £5 billion and gave up on the hospital programme. It was a great pity, since that billion would have been immediately available to the NHS and could have made quite a difference in the first two difficult years.

Gordon's caution – for that is what it was – came in part from pressure from No. 10 and in part from what seemed a belated realization of how much the other aspects of our corporation tax reform package would yield. One of these was the abolition of advance corporation tax (ACT) and of payable dividend tax credits, which we planned in detail in opposition and which played an important role in closing the financial deficit.

7. Mending the Gap

By the autumn of 1996 we had commissioned three major pieces of work from Arthur Andersens, which, although at different stages of development, were running concurrently. The windfall tax was largely completed before the end of October. Our other ambitious project on the reform of corporate and capital gains taxes ran right on into the new year. We were still working on the detailed proposal for changes to capital gains tax during the election campaign.

The level of the structural deficit had been worrying me for some time. I had put the point to Kenneth Clarke in an intervention to his opening speech in a debate on the economy in July 1996. I asked him how large he thought the structural deficit might be. Would he put it at £5 billion or £10 billion? Wisely he chose 'not to pluck a figure'. But implicitly he was acknowledging its existence and his answer was anything but reassuring. From New Labour's point of view this was alarming, as we had promised not to raise personal tax rates.

On the other hand, it was clear that new revenues would be required both to fund the structural deficit and as a disinflationary measure, since the economy was already by mid-1996 showing signs of overheating. Measures that would directly affect consumption would be preferable. But given the political limitation on action in the field of personal taxation, the corporate sector would have to bear the brunt of the inescapable necessity to raise taxes. That was our starting point and we set a target of increasing revenues by £5 billion per annum.

There were not many options. But at the heart of the fiendishly complex system of UK corporate taxation lay two interrelated issues: the payment by companies of advance corporation tax (ACT); and the tax credits that were allowed to shareholders on the dividends. We considered that there was scope here to find extra revenue.

After two initial meetings at which we went into great detail in this arcane area of tax law we concluded that: a thorough reform of both arrangements was the only way to meet all of our criteria; the reform should be a principled one; it should raise substantial revenue; it should simplify the system; that it should be neutral as to its effect on investment.

When first introduced in 1973, ACT was intended at least in part to reduce the double taxation that occurs when a company's profit is taxed once in the hands of the company by corporation tax and again in the hands of the shareholder on receipt of dividends.

What had happened in effect was that the original ACT scheme, well-intentioned though it was, did not in fact incorporate any fundamentally sound basis of taxation. It was a fix. As with all fixes, other fixes were needed to fix it and so complexity was built on complexity. At the end of it all, companies could be spending more time on tax planning than on running their business.

ACT was widely disliked by industry. Amongst the large multi-national corporations there was the specific problem that they did not have sufficient UK profits to cover the amount of tax that arose from their dividends. This led to a huge build-up running into nearly £5 billion of unrecovered ACT. The Tories had partially dealt with this by introducing the Foreign Income Dividends Scheme (FIDS), which was to become a thorny issue when we came to legislation.

There was moreover a major objection in principle to the consequential effects of how ACT interacted with tax credits. Throughout the seventies and eighties, as the pension and life insurance funds grew, their influence in the equities market became preponderant. By 1997 they controlled 75 per cent of all equities. The payment of tax credits on dividends had the very discernible effect that fund managers encouraged the maximum distribution by companies, often more than they should prudently afford. The intensity of competition between fund managers, the pressure of their three-monthly review meetings and the absence of any corporate guidance other than maximizing returns: all these factors encouraged companies to pay out high dividends to sustain the share price, with which the companies increasingly had to be concerned. If the share price dropped they might well be 'brought to play', or at least be tightly constrained in their ability to raise the new equity on which UK companies relied much more heavily than their US or European competitors.

We had, then, the worst of two worlds. A very complex system, that worked in a perverse, or at least unprincipled, way to encourage dividend payments rather than retained earnings and the capital growth to which they should lead. We decided to end this and committed ourselves to radical reform, which meant the abolition of ACT and withdrawal of payable dividend tax credits.

The decision in principle was clearly right. In practice, two consequential problems stood in our way. Each posed awkward political difficulties, but each also offered the promise of great financial benefit to the Treasury.

In the first place, if we were simply to get rid of ACT and leave the other existing arrangements for the payment of corporation tax in place, we would face a net loss to the exchequer in cash-flow terms of over £1 billion per year. This was unthinkable. The road to reform should take us in precisely the opposite direction: a modern system of pay-as-you-earn corporation tax which would mean tax revenues arriving earlier, not later. The UK system, apart from ACT, which only provided 15 per cent of the total yield, ensured that the bulk of UK corporate tax was paid on a very tardy basis. It was calculated on the previous year's profits and therefore paid some nine months after the year end. Most people on PAYE would like interest-free tick. New Labour was rightly very pro-business, but not indulgent to it.

The simple answer, as we decided, was to move to an instalment-based system in line with the practice of most modern industrial nations. This could be done with reference to prior-year profits or to a current-year forecast. My own preference here was rather in favour of the prior-year basis, since companies might be inclined to underestimate the first-year profits and gain a year's advantage in cash-flow terms. It was clear that either could work. We could leave the choice till we were in office. Under either approach the change to an in-year system would mean that 85 per cent of the then £36 billion corporate tax yield would be paid one year earlier – a cash-flow benefit to the government of some £25 billion. Obviously the change would have to be phased and Andersens undertook a study to see how the payments pattern would work itself through. The initial projections suggested a strong cash flow in years two, three and four, which was not unattractive in the time-scale of a five-year parliament. We were making progress.

The other 'problem' that arose with the abolition of payable tax credits was the consequential disappearance of tax benefits paid to the pension and insurance funds. This we all realized was a politically explosive issue.

It is important to stress that we are only talking in terms of the tax credit arrangements relating to ACT, not the overall tax-exempt status of pension funds. The case for that is not difficult to sustain. Pension funds represent the vehicle through which millions of people with prudent good sense and adequate means provide for their retirement. The government encourages them to do this by allowing them to make this saving out of untaxed income. It would be perverse, then, to tax the vehicle through which pension contributions are in effect profitably recycled. Those with high enough pensions pay tax in due course when they start to take receipt of them in retirement. In that way people are encouraged to save, and any element of double taxation is avoided. It is a benign system, and rightly so.

What was wrong in the tax credit arrangements was the illogical and really unjustifiable advantage that the funds derived from the tax credits payable on ACT. Even after the two reductions introduced by Norman Lamont in 1993 and 1994 the benefit of the tax credits mean that every 80p of dividends was worth £1.00 to the exempt institution.* There was no rhyme nor reason to it, let alone

* Charities would be adversely affected too. But one felt that, while this was very regrettable, generous transitional arrangements could be made and the problem could not be allowed to stand in the way of the major reform we were embarked on. There were, moreover, other important steps we could take to assist charities, which the Chancellor duly announced in his March 2000 budget.

any rational principle of taxation policy. Moreover, Andersens' initial calculations – which in the end turned out to be spot on – were that the abolition of tax credits would benefit the exchequer to the extent of approximately £5 billion per annum on an ongoing basis. We needed the money. It had to come from somewhere.

We anticipated a huge hullabaloo from all quarters. But if the target was going to be met, then tax credits had to go. While ACT was a useful move to precipitate their removal, it could not be put forward as the reason. Could the pension funds afford it? What would the effect be on the pension funds' capability to meet prospective commitments of the removal of tax credits? Would there be an overall drop in share prices?

Our timing, fortuitously, was good, since Andersens estimated that in 1996 some 70 per cent of the funds were in fact in surplus. There remained, though, the nagging worry that the disappearance of tax credits would lead to a general collapse in share prices. We needed detailed advice, for which we turned to a fellow of the Institute of Actuaries. The central judgement we received ran as follows:

It is unrealistic to expect the price of equities to remain unchanged after a change in ACT/tax credit. The value of equities to a pension scheme will be reduced depressing the price a pension scheme is willing to pay. Demand for equities from pension schemes is likely to fall by 6 per cent in line with the fall in the value of gross dividends receivable . . . Therefore the price of equities is likely to settle somewhere between the price before change and 6 per cent below that price.

We could live with that, though we felt that it was impossible to predict what would happen on the stock market. No research had been undertaken on the impact on equity values from earlier changes in ACT. Ed mischievously suggested that, so principled were the reforms, he expected the stock market to rise.

As with the pension funds, the timing for the abolition of ACT was propitious. A phased hit of £25 billion was bound to have an adverse effect on companies' cash flows. However, corporate liquidity stood at an all-time high and overall profit projections were on an upward trend. We judged that the CBI would take a positive view of these principled reforms. Moreover, the cash-flow benefit to the government would be so large that there was definitely scope to offset this with a reduction in corporation tax. It was a politically attractive prospect for an incoming New Labour government: a headline reduction of 2–3 per cent in corporation tax, taking the level to an historic low – beneath that of all our major competitors in Europe.

To be quite sure of our ground, we had to see how the phasing in of the three elements – in-year payments of corporation tax, the removal of tax benefits and the reduction in corporation tax – could be made to work to political and commercial tolerances.

Andersens as an organization did not have access to a database that could bring these three elements together. Apart from the Inland Revenue, only the National Institute of Economic and Social Research held such data. Ed negotiated us carefully into being able to gain access. It was a very delicate issue at a very sensitive time – the general election now being just a few months away. A leak in this area – especially on the pension funds – could be disastrous. We had to take the risk. By the end of March Andersens had run the third version of their projections on the National Institute computer. In all, we ran eight different scenarios. The bottom line was that if we coupled the abolition measures with a 2 or 3 per cent reduction in corporation tax we could secure a £20 billion cash flow to the Exchequer and, over a three- to four-year transitional phase, an ongoing £5 billion improvement in the public finances.

There was an exquisite symmetry about this combination of measures. Each was right in principle. Each complemented the other. The overall result benefited the public purse. Taken together, it was a package we felt we could sell in due course both to the CBI and the City. We were ready for government now in two main areas.

We lodged the corporate tax plans securely with those for the windfall tax in the same safe at the Grosvenor House. However, while documents can be held in safes, mouths are not so easily padlocked. In the very week of the election, a loose conversation between someone very close to the plans with Sir Peter Davis, the chairman of the Pru, came to the attention of the *Guardian*. We were fortunate that, despite this incident, there was no leaking of the major elements in the reform package, including the abolition of payable tax credits. Our security held, but only just.

The corporate tax plans, together with the detailed back-up projections, were collected from the safe by Ed Balls, together with those for the windfall tax, on 2 May 1997.

The early meetings at the Treasury on our programme of taxation were attended by about thirty people. The Chancellor's is a large office – perhaps 60 × 20 feet – but there was literally standing room only. We tabled the most recent of the Andersen figures with the proviso that they were calculated on the NIESR model and were subject to the Inland Revenue's confirmation or otherwise.

Unlike the windfall tax, neither the Treasury nor the Inland Revenue knew anything about these plans before the election. They were something of a bombshell dropped on officials. The Treasury Permanent Secretary remarked by way of initial reaction to the Andersen calculations that he saw 'some big numbers'; he advised caution. I sensed that we had caught the Inland Revenue off their guard. They were negative. I could see that we would not make progress in so large and unwieldy a meeting and suggested therefore that after the full meeting the IR corporate tax team should regroup in my office for a working session. Michael Cayley led the discussion for the Inland Revenue, reiterating much to my disappointment that the IR had looked at the proposals before and that the Andersen estimates were much too high. I reflected that perhaps there was a touch of the 'not invented here' syndrome in the IR reaction. On the other hand, supposing they were right, where on earth would we get the money from then?

There was no time to be lost. I insisted that Andersens' work be evaluated and that we reconvene within a week for a review meeting. I have never known such a change of atmosphere. Michael Cayley came to the next meeting beaming. The Andersen numbers were right. We might expect even more, since corporate profits were expected to remain high – provided, as always, we avoided a recession. He then confessed, 'This is something I have wanted to do all my life!' and pronounced his blessing: 'Brilliant Chancellor! Brilliant Paymaster!' There were others equally or more deserving of his praise present at the meeting. We all basked in the warm glow of the goodwill at the IR that our proposals had generated. The officials could not get started quickly enough.

The pace of work was frantic and we were making sound progress. But it became clear that we risked botching the legislation if we attempted the abolition of both dividend tax credits and ACT in the July budget, which was by now just a few weeks away.

I therefore decided to split the package and to proceed first only with the removal of tax credits. It was an important decision ensuring sound legislation. But it was not without its complications. One of these concerned British-based companies with the majority of their earnings overseas. As they were unable to recover the excess ACT they paid, they utilized the Tory-devised FIDS (Foreign Income Dividends Scheme) to enable them to do this at least in part. The abolition of tax dividend credits would automatically put an end to FIDS, and thus re-create the ACT problem for these companies.

We knew that we would be proceeding with the replacement of ACT with an in-year corporate tax payment system. The problem posed by the removal of tax credits was a temporary one. But for Billiton, a South African mining group about to change its listing from Johannesburg to the London Stock Exchange, it was an immediate obstacle that might involve them in a decision to pull the listing. Billiton was the first of a series of moves planned by Robert Fleming, the investment bank, to make London the centre of South African mining stocks. If Billiton were pulled the knock-on effects would be considerable and our credibility as an industry-friendly government badly dented. It was an early test of our resolve.

The meeting took place in my office on 5 July – the day after the budget announcing the end of tax credits. Billiton had wasted no time. Their top brass had arrived on an overnight flight. They were accompanied by Roddie Fleming and Robin Renwick, the UK advisers. Everyone was in a positive frame of mind. I could not be specific about our next legislative step but assured them that in the next budget of March 1998 we would pass measures that would obviate the worst effects of their inability to reclaim ACT. I was surprised at the confidence with which they seized on my verbal reassurance. Robin, an experienced Whitehall hand, requested that it be put in writing. Steve Robson obliged in his own handwriting on simple Treasury-headed notepaper. This seemed to do the trick, though I doubt that many such letters are written without further clearance in Whitehall. The Billiton team, who had obviously feared a protracted negotiation, were delighted. The chairman, Brian Gilbertson, wrote to me the next day:

Dear Minister,

I write to thank you for seeing me and my colleagues so early yesterday morning. No one – particularly a newcomer – could have asked for a more sympathetic hearing, nor a more constructive response. We shall proceed with the Billiton roadshow on Monday morning. I can but hope that you will consider a successful flotation of Billiton on the LSE – with the positive message that it will hold for other multinationals – some small return on the effort that you have made on our behalf.

The incident did us a lot of good in the City. We were indeed a pro-business administration whose word could be trusted.

We found pretty much the same reaction in our discussions with the CBI. Adair Turner, who was then the director-general, was attracted by the modernization theme of the corporate reform. He was ex-McKinseys and had no time for antiquated attitudes or procedures. The telling point was, of course, the 2 per cent reduction in corporation tax. Calculated in real terms this was worth some £6 billion to the corporate sector. We were able to make great play of this especially and for the first time ever that I could remember we backdated the reduction, to 1 April 1997. For the government the £20 billion plus in cash we could expect over the next three or four years was cash in hand. The CBI were on board. The Tories were still not in sight – which was just as well since the abolition of tax credits was the most contentious and politically sensitive issue of all.

The budget was announced on 2 July. It was the first Labour budget in nearly twenty years. Gordon rose to his feet to loud Labour cheers. He sat down to even louder ones. It was a moment nearly as important as when Tony took his first Prime Minister's Question Time. One person who did not let his feelings show too much was Ed Balls. During the budget speech he was tracking the FTSE to see what impact, if any, the announcement of the abolition of tax credits would have on the stock market. As we predicted the market barely moved. It finished six points up on the day.

Capital Gains Tax

Our third target for reform was capital gains tax. As we saw with ACT – probably even more so – complexities and anomalies had crept into the system of capital gains taxation. Simplification and modernization were then, as ever, required. This in a way had been attempted by Nigel Lawson in his major tax-reforming budget of 1984. Personal income tax rates were filleted to just two with the top rate tumbling from 60 to 40 per cent. Curiously, a single rate of capital gains tax was introduced at the same 40 per cent level. It was quite a high rate and it was puzzling the Tories should have settled at it. I asked around later in the Treasury about the reason for the linking of the two rates in this way. No one really had an answer. It had simplified the rate without tackling the underlying complexities and, more importantly, it had set a rate so high that payment of it was resented and as far as possible avoided.

Our approach, on the other hand, was to embody the principle of a differentiation between short- and long-term capital gains, i.e. a lower rate for long-term and a higher rate for short-term gains. Intrinsically this meant a measure of complexity. There would be two (or more) rates instead of one. On the other hand if we could get rid of 'indexation' there would be a massive simplification of the computational intricacies in which the tax had become ensnared.

We went through these various points with Andersens in a couple of preliminary meetings. Then, in the procedure which had by this time become streamlined between us, Andersens got down to work.

Their final paper was dated 23 April 1997, the last week of the campaign. This was my sixth parliamentary campaign. With the goodwill of my constituency officers I was able to spend much more time than usual outside Coventry. Ed Balls was not too heavily engaged in the activities at Millbank. This meant we could continue working with Andersens right through the campaign.

It was interesting to note how seriously the Andersen team was by now taking the responsibility they had amorphously assumed for advising on what became an extensive and bold set of taxation reforms over four budgets. The last paper we received from them was entitled 'Request for Official Advice'. There was no identification tag on the paper at all. This was at our request, the idea being that if there was a lapse in security we would be able to say that the 'official advice' had been commissioned by the government.

By now we were short of time and could not get into such detail as we were able to on windfall tax and ACT and tax credits. But that did not weaken our drive for fundamental change. The capital-gains package as a whole was quite revolutionary:

- The taxation as income of all short-term gains;
- The consequent abolition of the annual exempt amount;
- The introduction of a tapering relief in respect of gains realized by individuals on assets held for more than three years (i.e. long-term gains);
- The consequent abolition of retirement relief.

The main objective of this section of the reform package was to encourage and reward long-term investment by the portfolio investor and more importantly by the entrepreneur. The extent and speed of the taper would be decisions for us once in government.

There were two further recommendations in the Andersen package:

- The abolition of the indexation allowance;
- The rebasing of the capital-gains system to March 1992.

The two went hand in glove each with the other and both complemented the other proposals above. The political difficulties here were self-evident. Moreover we were running late, and in the final phase of the election campaign the last thing anyone wanted to bother with was capital-gains reform. Indeed for me it was an eerie experience. I had spent seven general elections either at party headquarters or on the hustings in Coventry. Now I was working on detailed tax changes from my flat in London. Ed had moved in a few weeks earlier. We all met there daily. It was as much a working office as Millbank itself. There was no time to store the capital-gains plans with the others in the safe. The ink was hardly dry on the page of our first unofficial official advice when Ed, having retrieved the other documents, marched behind Gordon triumphally up the famous Treasury staircase.

We decided not to tackle capital-gains legislation in the first (July) budget but to target it for the March 1998 budget. There were two reasons for this: the July budget was already crowded out with the other measures; and we were not so well prepared on capital gains. We had the principles for the reform but not enough of the detailed back-up research.

The Inland Revenue were not at first keen on reform. The tax raised £1,200 million in 1995/96, which they felt would be needlessly surrendered if we were to adopt the taper and the progressively much lower rates that ensued. My own view was that the £1,200 million was in fact a small yield and that with a lower rate we would probably raise more in total. Finding I could not convince them, I told them that it was an indispensable element in our growth agenda and that we were going to do it. They sprang into action. The proposals they came forward with were startlingly radical. They had taken on board all the Andersen proposals and added some of their own: all reliefs – retirement, the annual exempt amount – were abolished, indexation was discontinued and all calculations rebased to 1992. There would be a five-year paper with a 10 per cent rate at the end of it.

In most other circumstances one would have feared a try-on: look, if this is what you want to do, these are the consequences, so why not forget it? The consequences were politically very sensitive. At one end of the spectrum we would, by abolition of indexation, be providing windfall capital gains running into many millions for successful entrepreneurs and at the other end we would be depriving small business people of their retirement relief. It was an almost exact rerun of the £50,000 limit on the ISAs. The withdrawal of the annual exempt amount – that is the first £6,500 of capital gain which is tax free – compounded the impression that we would be penalizing the 'little man' and enriching the rich. This was neither New nor old Labour.

The trouble is that whenever you make a major change in personal taxation there are going to be winners and losers. The IR from its detailed database can give quite precise estimates on the outcome of any proposed change. The numbers for capital gains were not encouraging: far too many losers, many of whom would have voted New Labour, and relatively few winners, but very big ones, who would excite envy and resentment in many sections of the community.

I took the view from the beginning that retirement relief should be phased out over as long a period as possible. The aim would be to protect those who would soon retire and enable those who were five or more years away from retirement to benefit from the paper. As far as the annual exempt amount was concerned, my view was rather different. We had no clear profile of those that would be affected. But I felt they would be different from the PEP investors, whose interests anyway we had already properly taken care of by removing the £50,000 limit. The annual exempt limit was a perk, an allowance that copied the allowance for income tax but really had no justification in principle. It could go. It should be phased out over a few years.

The real stumbling block was the abolition of indexation and the windfall winners this gave rise to. So far from trying it on with us, the IR were serious. They had had enough of all the complex computations, fiddles and clever schemes. Do it, get it over with and move on.

I gulped. We had not built up support with No. 10 as we had done on the other corporate reforms. We had not worked through all the political implications. I was not even sure Gordon had taken on board what was involved. He was prepared to go for it, but warned me Tony might not buy the whole package. I explained that we had a fall-back position, the usual compromise which would preserve the annual allowance for the time being, extend the taper to ten years and in effect retain indexation for the next five years to avoid windfall gains to the lucky few. No. 10 agreed to this more limited package.

We took it through the March 1998 budget along those lines. The Tories were ineffectual and the act constituted a major step forward in creating an enterprise culture which the Tories had talked a lot about but done nothing so dramatic to achieve.

The capital-gains changes marked the first major impact of the Growth Unit in the Treasury. We had got halfway there. The budget of 2000 completed the journey. Indexation has all but gone and the taper to 10 per cent is reached within four years.

It will seem remarkable to everyone and wrong to some that it should be a Labour administration that dramatically reduced both the tax rate on capital gains and the period of time over which the tax would be payable. Such a short taper to such a low tax rate may appear to some and probably to most of my old Labour friends as short-termism. But the rate of technological change, and the speed of company growth, is such that investment and reinvestment occur and recur much more quickly than in the past. Under the new arrangements entrepreneurs will have incentives to invest and re-invest. The UK is the most attractive place to build, sell and rebuild. The industries of the new information-based technologies that are developing across the country will be a major source of growth in the economy.

8. Finger in the PFI

When we took office the PFI had become something of a laughing stock. It was distrusted by top management and by trade-union leaders in equal measure. The TUC at its annual conference in September 1996 had gone so far as to pass a resolution calling for its abandonment.

Both parties had legitimate complaints to support their platform rhetoric. Companies were fed up with the large abortive tendering costs they incurred in quoting for a whole raft of projects, many of which it was doubtful that the government had any intention of proceeding with. Some complained that valuable know-how incorporated into their bids had been made available to their competitors for no consideration. But above all it was the sheer length and complexity of the PFI process that had first frustrated and then disillusioned the business community.

Some trade unions disliked the principle of public–private partnership. It posed for those trade unions representing the public-sector workforce a serious threat to membership levels and to the terms and conditions they had negotiated for the employees.

By 1997 no one had a good word to say for the PFI. It was a shambles.

In opposition Gordon had asked me to look at the situation. He had suggested in mid-1995 that I should write a pamphlet on how the PFI could be improved. It was an area I had followed with some interest from its launch by Norman Lamont in 1992. Lamont stressed that PFI projects would be additional to the planned level of government capital expenditure. We could expect, therefore, a badly needed increase in expenditure on infrastructure projects in particular. There would also be the benefit of private-sector management expertise, which would give better value for money. In due course this should rub off on to the public sector too.

The idea was good. But the process was soon bogged down by departmental bureaucrats who distrusted the private sector and operated, under the pretext of accountability, to protect their control of expenditure. In fact, it was not really their overall control of projects that was being challenged. Nothing would go ahead without a department's consent. It was the day-to-day running of projects that was being taken away. Having agreed a detailed specification for a proposal, the whole idea of the PFI was that the private sector should be left to get on with it. It was a freedom brimming with danger for an organization trained to be risk averse.

The Tories wanted the initiative to work. In desperation they introduced the system of universal testing. Under this draconian arrangement, any public capital-expenditure programme could only proceed as a publicly funded one provided it had been tested for PFI and found unsuitable. It was a win–win for the Treasury: public and PFI expenditure plans both got bogged down. Capital expenditure was further reduced. Universal testing had created universal chaos. It was clear to me in opposition that universal testing would have to go.

There were two other aspects of the organization set up by the Tories to run the PFI that on the evidence of performance could not be considered effective. These were the private finance panel of advisers and its executive.

Any pamphlet I wrote would be bound to deal with these sensitive issues. It would easily be taken personally by those involved. On balance I thought discretion was the better part of valour. This is not often the case with me. But it was clear that having a row in opposition by implying criticism of distinguished City and industrial figures was not the best way forward. I decided against a pamphlet. I had clear ideas and chose to bide my time, in the hope that I could implement them if I was given the chance in office. I also had a clear idea of the person I would like to push them through.

Malcolm Bates came to see me at the Treasury on Thursday, 8 May 1997. He was my first choice to carry out a wholesale review of PFI. He brought to the job a rare combination of qualities and experience. He had worked closely with Lord Weinstock for nearly thirty years at GEC. Anyone who could withstand the rigour of Weinstock's personality and intellect had to be very strong himself in both departments. Malcolm was. He was also decisive, not given to fudging issues. In addition to this, he had been one of the panel of advisers on the PFI in the period 1992–5 and had had direct experience of negotiating a major PFI deal for GEC. His abiding memory of the negotiation was the three-feet high pile of legal documents that concluded it. I knew we would get a set of practical proposals from him aimed at simplifying the whole process. We agreed he would complete his report within six weeks and carry out widespread consultation in doing so. It was a quite unreasonable timescale. But Malcolm took it on with good humour and delivered on time.

With his agreement, we took certain preliminary decisions while he was completing his review. These were the abandonment of universal testing; the establishment of a limited number of key priority areas for PFI which each spending department would concentrate on; and the disbandment of the advisory panel. Malcolm endorsed all these steps, which he felt would send an early signal to the private sector that we meant business.

We made an inauspicious start in disbanding the panel. Alastair Ross Goobey, the chairman of the panel, took the matter of his resignation very personally. Try as he might, Steve Robson could not persuade him to stand down voluntarily. I spoke to him and he insisted that I sack him and be seen to sack him. Well, if that was what he wanted, I was pleased to oblige. After my confrontation with Mr Ross Goobey I was apprehensive of the attitude of Dame Sheila Masters, another figure who had prospered in public-sector appointments under the Tories and enjoyed a formidable reputation. 'Quite right!' she expostulated, although I had barely begun my account of the reasons for my decision to get rid of the panel. 'It serves no purpose', she added, thus concluding her concurrence. I hung up, feeling this was a person New Labour could work with. The other panel members also agreed without difficulty. Some, I felt, were quite pleased to be spared the bother of polite exchanges with high-ranking officials in the spending departments who would outwardly be all in favour of PFI while inwardly doubting the validity of the whole idea.

The proposition that each minister should establish his own order of priorities was well received. The PFI had spawned hundreds of possible projects, only a handful of which could be proceeded with. Elimination and prioritization of projects by spending departments was urgently required. It would fall to the Treasury to decide which department's projects ranked highest in government priorities and to facilitate their implementation. This meant any new PFI unit should be part of the Treasury and working within our building.

Malcolm took this view very strongly from the beginning and it was a central recommendation of the report which he presented in July 1997, exactly six weeks from his undertaking it. There were over thirty recommendations in all. The report called for the replacement of the forty-strong executive team which was located in offices in Victoria Street by a much smaller unit comprising a half-dozen or so people based in the Treasury. The new unit was to be headed by a prominent City figure experienced in negotiating large-scale capital projects. The team supporting him would have complementary skills relevant to the same area of expertise.

One of the Bates's recommendations that I thought would prove controversial in Whitehall was that compensation costs should be paid to the private sector when a project was abandoned because of a change in government policy. Derry Irvine rather surprisingly joined the debate on this point. He was concerned that the government would be unnecessarily exposing itself to private-sector claims. The matter was presumably solved at official level as I heard no more about it.

In the event, largely because Malcolm had involved the Treasury PFI team at every stage and because he had consulted widely, his report was welcomed by the business community and by Whitehall. Moreover, by the end of November 1997 we had implemented all its recommendations. The Tories were mounting an attack by then on the numerous reviews set up by the government. I resisted a smug satisfaction that we had completed and implemented our review before most departments had got theirs under way.

It was a pity about the PFI executive team. They were able and bright people, but they had no clear definition of aims. I hate the phrase 'mission statement' but it was certainly what was lacking here. It rather reminded me of the rumps of initiatives that cluttered up some parts of the Cabinet Office. I made the announcement of the closure personally and stressed to the employees that they were free to apply to join the new team we were establishing in the Treasury. One of them did do so and made a significant contribution to getting our schools refurbishment programme under way.

We had cleared the ground for a fresh start. It was vital that we made the right appointment as chief executive of the new unit. We turned again to Malcolm Bates for advice. We were anxious to avoid the cost and long-drawn-out process that headhunters would involve us in. And we were still able to make an appointment without the complicated procedures that the Nolan Committee on standards in public life was about to bequeath us. Malcolm, drawing on his wide network of City contacts, put together a shortlist of three outstanding candidates, any one of whom could have done a good job for us. Malcolm did an astonishing job in putting the list together in a matter of ten days.

We came down in favour of Adrian Montague, who was the head of the capital projects team at Kleinwort Benson. (We later returned to fish in the same pond for a deputy governor for the Bank of England.) Adrian brought with him several outstanding qualities. He had a first-class degree in law from Cambridge. He had infinite patience, which, if he was not born with it, he had acquired as chief legal counsel in the negotiations on the Channel Tunnel. His expertise lay in exactly the area we wanted: finding a basis for agreement on complex projects where conflicting interests between the public and private sectors and within the private sector itself were contending for a settlement on terms favourable to themselves. Adrian had all this. But it was perhaps what he did not have that counted just as much in his favour. He brought no baggage with him. He had no share options. He took a halving of his salary without demur. He required no exceptional arrangements for his pension. He settled happily into a pretty dingy office on the ground floor of the Treasury and brought together there a very able team around him. His only demands, so to speak, concerned myself. These were that he should have direct and ready access to me as the minister in charge; and that he should not be held up for too long on decisions. The first I met, to the best of my knowledge, completely. The second I met as best I could, given the circuitous route by which most important government decisions are taken.

Under the new leadership and organization, the PFI fairly steamed ahead once we had pushed through the necessary legislation enabling health trusts to participate in joint financial investments with the private sector. This had been botched twice under the Tories by an excess of official caution. The excellent local government minister, Hilary Armstrong, steered it through for us.

Our priorities for the PFI were clear: hospitals, schools and transport. By the end of 1999 over £3 billion had been committed to the new hospital programme, £1 billion to a new schools programme and £8 billion on other infrastructure projects, notably transport. The new investment in hospitals is the largest construction programme since the NHS was established in 1947. Such a programme of school building as we have embarked on has not been seen since compulsory education was introduced in 1892.

It was a good achievement in such a relatively short time and owed much to the expertise of Adrian and his team. They had simplified the process and built up confidence in departments and with private-sector companies. But from the beginning Steve Robson, Adrian Montague and myself were all quite clear that the task force's job should be completed within two or, at the maximum, three years. The last thing any of us wanted was to create another layer of bureaucracy within government. Unless we were very careful the task force would itself develop an interest in self-perpetuation. It happens all the time in the public and private sectors, especially in the public.

For that reason, on receipt of the Bates report in July 1997 we insisted that there would be a review of the task force in July 1999 in order to see what, if any, continuing role there was for it. By the time of my resignation at the end of 1998 most of the objectives of the task force had been completed. Most departments had prioritized their projects and had developed their own tendering and control procedures. There was no need for the task force at its present size to continue as part of the government machine itself.

It had also become clear, however, that there was a certain category of major public–private projects, often involving two or more departments and several private-sector companies, where there was a tendency for things to go wrong. Two prime examples of these were the Channel Tunnel rail link (CTRL) and the Post Office–Benefits Agency project for the development of a new credit card for the payment of benefits through the nationwide network of local post offices. This was commonly called the POCOL project. Both of these, I was told, were championed by Michael Heseltine. There were good reasons for each in principle. The CTRL would upgrade the railway line from King's Cross/St Pancras to Ashford. It would cut thirty minutes off the time of the rail journey from London to Paris and rid us of the embarrassment of users of the system imagining, as they surfaced from the tunnel in England, that they were turning the clock back some fifty years or more.

Both were good ideas in themselves. They were both large-scale public–private partnerships. But each lacked commercial reality and an effective integrator of the public and private interests involved. Commercial considerations were forced to fit the wider political objective, and that never works.

In the CTRL case the government willed the end but not the means. It wanted the rail link extended and longed to be rid of the embarrassing contrast to the superb French system just twenty miles away across the Channel. But on no account would it put up any cash. Instead it gifted hundreds of millions of pounds' worth of land, buildings and rolling stock to a consortium that was underfunded from the start. The consortium comprised eight parties; the intelligent ones, the consulting engineers and financial advisers, took their money out in fees before the underpowered train stuttered into the buffers. The consortium was from the start in need of refinancing. But so badly did it come unstuck, despite the government's munificence, that no one in the City wanted to know. Inevitably, as always, the problems came back to the government, who not only had gifted huge assets but also had underwritten the operation of the line to the extent of £400 million per annum by way of operating subsidy for years ahead!

It was not difficult to demonstrate that it was more expensive to continue with the CTRL project than to close it down. It was a hopeless mess. To get the show back on the rails the government put up guarantees of £2 billion. Quite how that did not score as spending in the year, I am not sure. It was a decision for the chief secretary to the Treasury and his officials, who can be quite adept at solving problems when they want to, especially when they are of their own making.

The POCOL misadventure was no less instructive. The Royal Mail had privatized many of its rural and urban post offices. In many cases the management had become owners and invested relatively heavily in the process. Most of these businesses depended, however, for their profits on the continuing right to pay out benefits over the counter to claimants who wished to obtain them in that way. In the age of bank accounts, computerized systems and smart cards this was self-evidently an expensive way of administering the benefits system.

The obvious solution would have been for the post offices to link up with an established banking organization and to install progressively an automatic transfer system of payments. Instead, with what can only be called a neo-Luddite decision, the Royal Mail won DTI approval to develop a smart card customized for the use of the post offices and their customers. There would be no other use for it. The contract to develop the highly complicated software and integration systems required was won by ICL, a subsidiary of Fujitsu, the Japanese computer giant. Needless to say, there were interminable wrangles about the specification. The project ran late and way over budget. The DSS/Benefits Agency, which had always opposed it, was at every stage opportunistically obstructive. As the costs soared the savings of £400 million per

annum disappeared over a continually receding horizon. The project's profile, by contrast, grew to the point of being raised with
Tony Blair by the Japanese Prime Minister on Tony's official visit
to that country in January 1998. It was another fine old mess and
an expensive one too. The project was finally put out of its misery
in May 1999.

There were no winners. The Benefits Agency obtained its savings
later and more gradually than it hoped; ICL suffered a heavy loss
in terms of finance and company prestige. Its flotation on the
London Stock Exchange was called off; the post offices did not get
the protective system they wanted; and the DTI was left picking
up the pieces with a statement made by the Secretary of State in
June 2000 that no pensioner would be obliged to change to an
automatic transfer system if they did not want to. The effect on the
Post Office is uncertain. It has posted its first operating loss for 1999
of £264 million, which may be indicative; it has had to set aside
£570 million to cover the losses caused by the fiasco.

The point of analysing critically these two major public–private
partnerships is not to ridicule the previous government's ineptitude
or the incompetence of the private-sector companies involved. Less
still is it to harp on about the Civil Service and its lack of contact
with the real commercial world. The point is simply that both
projects were flawed not in the original concept but in execution;
and that the wrong financial, commercial and management
decisions were arrived at largely because each party was looking to
the protection of its own interests – whether commercial or official
– and not to the success of the project itself.

Those were my thoughts as I returned to the office after the
summer break in 1998. I discussed them with Steve Robson in my
private office. We shared one conclusion: there was a need for an
organization in the private sector, backed by some public capital,
but managed commercially and independently, that could balance
and integrate the different interests involved. It would be essential
that there would be a majority of private-sector directors on the
board of the organization and that they would be prepared to tell
the government of the day what would or would not work. All

governments have an inbuilt capacity to take the easy option, the one that seems to cost less. As we saw with CTRL and POCOL, however, it often ends up costing more. So the purpose of any new arrangement must in large part be to say no; or yes, but only on realistic conditions.

For this reason it is essential that the new organization, Partnerships UK, announced by the Treasury in the March 2000 budget, is established on a commercial basis. There will be wider ventures involving public–private partnerships where the tight contractual relationships established for PFI projects are no longer sufficient in themselves – they too often become adversarial at the first whiff of trouble such as any large-scale capital project can be expected to run into. The tying of individual interests to the success of the total project will be a precondition for the wider ventures that the major capital expenditure programmes announced in July 2000 will make possible. This in turn means establishing Partnerships UK with a capital structure that enables it to undertake a range of financing initiatives including, for example, equity and mezzanine funding.

No one imagines that finding the right balance between public and private interests and subjecting both to the commercial disciplines of the market are easy. They are not. Much will depend on the people in charge. An excellent team has been established: Derek Higgs, ex-Warburgs and Pru Capital, is chairman; Adrian Montague will move over to be deputy chairman and James Stewart has been recruited as chief executive from Newcourt Capital.

With such a team Partnerships UK will be firmly rooted in the private sector, with the ability to pay and incentivize its staff accordingly. The public sector needs access to their expertise. But they will know, too, that the organization can only survive on its merits. If it fails to produce successful and profitable projects it will die. Personally, I think that it will succeed. Everyone should wish it well.

9. Royal Cachet

'The cachet is the thing. You must preserve the cachet.' Sir Robin Butler was insistent on 'the cachet' as we left a meeting in the Ministry of Defence. It occurred to me that we might well have been talking about any luxury item: Gucci shoes, a Rolex watch, a Chanel dress, a Rolls-Royce. In fact we were talking about the ultimate in luxuries, the royal yacht *Britannia*.

As the Treasury minister responsible for the Private Finance Initiative, I had been asked by Gordon Brown to attend a meeting in the Permanent Secretary's office at Defence in June 1997. The aim was to see whether a new yacht to replace *Britannia* could be built using private funds.

Apart from the Cabinet Secretary, Sir Robin Butler, and the MoD Permanent Secretary, Sir Richard Mottram, there were present only the Queen's principal private secretary, Sir Robert Fellowes, and myself as Paymaster General. We each had our own starting point.

For Sir Robin, unless we kept 'the cachet' there would be no point in replacing *Britannia*: so no cachet equalled no new royal yacht. Sir Robert Fellowes was at pains to make clear right from the outset that the Queen was making no request for a *Britannia II*. It was entirely up to HMG, he stressed. She would consider whatever PFI proposition was put to her but, he cautioned, we must not take her approval for granted. Sir Richard, as accounting officer for the Ministry of Defence, was concerned about his £20 billion budget. The royal yacht's £10 million a year running costs may have been a drop in his ocean, just one two-thousandth of the department's resources. Yet he was in the throes of a very tough comprehensive spending review. Any saving helped. If the Treasury private finance team wanted to undertake the project, then the capital and running costs must not come out of his budget.

There did not seem much room for manoeuvre here. And anyway what on earth was a New Labour government doing, after barely two months in office, trying to find a way of building a new royal yacht? To so many in the country it was a symbol of wasteful elitist expenditure.

Ruling out the use of taxpayers' money to build a replacement for ageing *Britannia*, steaming to retirement in December 1997, was a welcome election pledge. In the January before our May triumph, the Tory Defence Secretary, Michael Portillo, had tried to wrong-foot us by announcing a £50 million replacement. Tony Blair had been worried about opposing it and Alastair Campbell was initially unsure about how it would play with the public. But Gordon guessed taking a stand would be popular as well as right and within days we had made our position crystal-clear. Nothing got a bigger cheer at election rallies. A phone poll reported in the *Mirror* found a phenomenal 21 to 1 majority of callers backing us. A more scientific ICM survey for the *Guardian* found a 3 to 1 majority in our favour. Taxpayers would not be paying for *Britannia II*.

Yet the question of the royal yacht remained unfinished business when we arrived in government. At Gordon's request, I agreed to look at alternative ways of funding a replacement. Before the MoD meeting broke up, I laid it on the line: if this was to be a public–private partnership, it could only be sold to private investors if there was a return on the capital. That meant it had to generate income, which in turn meant the boat would have to be as intensively used as possible for private occasions involving sales, promotions and spon-sorships. Would the Queen accept that? And what would she say to use of the royal apartments, a question that was bound to crop up.

The point I was making was that if there was to be any chance of getting a private-sector initiative off the ground it would require a wholly different way of looking at *Britannia* and of using it. As I walked across Whitehall back to the Treasury I reflected that Sir Robin was right. The 'cachet' of the royal yacht is what would sell it to the private sector. Lose that and we had nothing to sell. To keep the cachet it would be essential for the new boat to be known as the royal yacht and that the Queen and senior members of the royal family would wish to continue to use it. The Queen, then, had the whip hand. If she disassociated herself from the project it would not succeed. We would just have another luxury yacht available for charter.

I discovered from a briefing that *Britannia* had had its fair share of unusual, sad and historic moments. She was built after the Second World War because King George VI felt he would require a sea-going royal yacht to carry out his worldwide role as King and Head of the Commonwealth. Sadly the King died in 1952 before even the keel was laid down.

Both the Queen and Prince Philip subsequently took a personal interest in the building of the vessel. An important early decision was to commission Sir Hugh Casson, president of the Royal Academy of Arts, to undertake the interior design and decoration of the rooms. They remain classics today, with many of the fittings salvaged from *Britannia*'s elderly predecessor, the *Victoria & Albert*. The economy of the *Britannia*'s origins struck me as remarkable even for the time. Built by the John Brown yard on the Clyde, which also launched the *Queen Mary*, the *Queen Elizabeth* and QE2, she cost £21 million. The entire cost of furnishings came to only £78,000, with £9,000 being spent on carpets; the bedlinen first used on the new yacht had belonged to Queen Victoria and was sixty years old! Even uprated to today's prices *Britannia* was quite a bargain.

The yacht was launched in April 1953. Princess Margaret and Antony Armstrong-Jones used her for their honeymoon voyage. Undeterred by the unhappy outcome of that union, Charles and Diana followed suit in 1981. I wondered whether the ship had a jinx.

In the original concept for *Britannia* the royal apartments were designed so that they could be converted within twenty-four hours into hospital quarters with wards for two hundred patients, but *Britannia* was never put to use as a hospital ship. Indeed, when it was considered sending her to the Falklands it was discovered she used the wrong type of fuel★ and would thus be hard to replenish

★ She ran on Furness fuel oil before being converted after the 1982 conflict to the diesel used by the rest of the Royal Navy.

in the south Atlantic. At the time I remember thinking it sounded like British Rail's wrong type of snow!

Back in the Treasury I asked Adrian Montague, our recently appointed PFI supremo, to come to see me about *Britannia*. At the mere mention of the name he winced. 'I'd rather stick to hospitals and schools,' said Adrian. I noted to myself that we had made a good choice here and did not want to divert him from Labour's priorities. This would be one I would have to do myself. I asked him if he could give me any pointers as to where I might start, on what would probably turn out to be a wild-goose chase. He suggested the shipping giant P&O, and even thought it would be a project they could take over in its entirety if they felt so inclined.

The P&O chairman, Jeffrey Sterling, made a peer by the Tories for his unflagging support, readily accepted my invitation to discuss the project. Jeffrey had been a very important adviser to Margaret Thatcher and was also very patriotic, once using the tannoy on a British Airways jet carrying Tony Blair home from China to criticize the airline for removing the Union Jack colours on its tail fin!

As far as Jeffrey was concerned, a private initiative on the royal yacht was not as important as the looming abolition of duty-free goods within Europe. His company, P&O, was locked in a fierce cross-Channel battle, along with Eurostar and other ferry operators who relied on cut-price alcohol and tobacco sales to keep profits up. That it was very profitable business could be judged from the persistence with which he pursued the matter in the context of our discussions on *Britannia*. Repeatedly I explained to him that the long-established Treasury policy on duty-free goods was that it was anachronistic and anti-competitive and should be abolished. Responsibility in the Treasury lay with the Financial Secretary, my colleague Dawn Primarolo, whose office was just round the corridor on the same floor as mine. I told him if he wanted to put his case about duty free he should pop down there and I was sure Dawn would be very pleased to discuss it with him. I offered to arrange a meeting for him on several occasions. He declined to take it up, no doubt being a realist and seeing little chance of changing the Treasury's official line.

However, I was anxious to show willing on duty free in order to secure a positive contribution from him on *Britannia*. I suggested therefore that he talk to the Deputy Prime Minister, John Prescott, who had responsibility under his transport brief for the ferry trade. I knew that John was anxious about the adverse impact on jobs the abolition of duty free could have. Jeffrey with typical assiduousness had already been to see John. He was trying to win the Treasury over and found a sympathetic ear both from me and at No. 10. Indeed, the Prime Minister did launch a rearguard action to save duty free and assembled, as he put it, a 'mighty coalition' with the French and Germans at the June 1999 European summit. But the Dutch and Danes refused to give way, sinking cheap alcohol and cigarette sales within Europe.

I was finding it more difficult to get much of a sympathetic hearing out of him, however, for a public–private partnership to build the replacement yacht. Jeffrey's view was simple. The royal yacht was of immense value to the UK both commercially and as a symbol of national prestige. So a new one should be commissioned by the MoD, paid for by government and subsequently crewed by the Royal Navy. Nothing else would do and we should face up to it instead of seeking private-sector involvement.

There was no way New Labour could go down that route. As to a public–private partnership, he was deeply and, I think, genuinely sceptical that it could be made to work. Such a project, in his view, would be bound to prejudice the cachet and would not generate the income to provide the commercial return that the private sector would be looking for. When I asked directly if P&O would take it on, he replied that he had to look after the profitability of P&O. I had got that message from his concerns on duty free.

Jeffrey Sterling's views were fair ones. But they hardly broke new ground. Flair and imagination beyond the commonplace were needed if we were to find a way of keeping a royal yacht sailing.

Sir Donald Gosling brought these qualities to the party. He wrote asking if he could come to see me. I knew of him as the founder, together with Ron Hobson, of the NCP empire. They had had the inspired idea back in 1948 of converting bomb-sites into car parks. It was a fabulous success. We met in June soon after I received his letter.

I took to Donald at once. He was a real entrepreneur with a strong public-sector ethos. He was also, as they referred to him in the MoD, a 'sea-buff' with his own fine yacht, usually moored at Antibes on the French Riviera.

His proposal was innovative and practical. A new yacht would cost too much. His view was that the £50 million price tag put on a replacement for *Britannia* was quite unrealistic. A modern boat built to the specification required to maintain the cachet and justify the chartering fee he had in mind would cost at least the best part of £100 million. The Sultan of Brunei's new yacht had cost £250 million.

Quite apart from these comparisons, which suggested that a new yacht costing £50 million would be a very poor relation, Donald, with his keen eye for elegance at sea, considered a new design produced by the Admiralty team in Bath to be an unhappy compromise. It was meant to look like *Britannia* and yet be a modern yacht. It was neither one nor the other. It was bland, lacking in inspiration and to be done on the cheap. It looked second class. It would have been much better to take up an idea of Maldwin Drummond, commodore of the Royal Yacht Squadron, for a new sailing ship which could double as a training centre for youngsters.

Donald, unlike Jeffrey Sterling, readily understood the political reality that the Treasury could not countenance spending £50 million, let alone £100 million or £150 million, on a new royal yacht while holding back on health and education. The Tories had quite cynically committed the government to building the replacement knowing that they would not have responsibility of carrying it through; Michael Portillo, when he made the announcement on 22 January 1997, knew the Conservatives were heading for defeat at the election. Perhaps he was goaded by John Redwood, his great right-wing rival, who during the Tory leadership contest in June 1996 had issued the clarion call: 'Tories keep royal yachts, not scrap them.' Redwood lost that battle, Portillo lost his seat and the Tories the election of May 1997. We were opposed to using taxpayer's money, though not opposed in principle to the royal yacht.

Donald came to see me because he felt he had a way out of our dilemma.

He saw that the present yacht was a classic with a line and style that no modern yacht could match. It would never again be built like that. The sense of dramatic presence it created at sea was an essential part of the cachet, as was Casson's interior design, right down to the light and bathroom fittings. What could be, indeed had to be, changed were the engines, electrics and plumbing. As Donald outlined his proposals I remembered General Schwarz-kopf's* remark on being shown the immaculately polished silver and brass of *Britannia*'s steam turbines: 'Great museum, now where's the engine room!'

Donald's inspired idea was the exact opposite of what in the motor industry was called a facelift. I had done one very successfully at Jaguar in conjunction with Pinin Farina in Turin, which gave us the Series III XJ6. They involve delicate operations affecting the style of the car, but not the engine or suspension. Everything under the bonnet remains the same yet the outside is restyled. The plan for *Britannia* was to keep the outside but change the inside.

Donald's proposal on *Britannia* was to rip out the guts of the yacht – a 'rebuild' rather than a refit. It would be major surgery costing between £45 million and £50 million. He suggested the Devonport Royal Dockyard at Plymouth should be our next port of call. They would best be able to advise on the cost and practicality of refurbishment.

Tony Pryor, Devonport's chairman, stepped on deck. The company had serviced *Britannia* and carried out the major refit, including new teak flooring, in 1987. It was not the most modern or best equipped of yards. Devonport could not match the facilities at Bremen/Hamburg in Germany, the Fedship facilities in Holland

*Commander of the operation, Desert Storm, to free Kuwait in 1991.

nor Italy's La Spezia. Devonport was different from these modern shipbuilders, who were responsible for some vulgar and vastly expensive 'floating gin palaces'. But it did not really matter that Devonport could not compete with these modern builders in terms of capital equipment or that it had no chance to break into their market. It had a dedicated and highly skilled workforce that knew how to create 'cachet' – the unique selling point in the adman's lingo and also in Sir Robin Butler's mind.

Devonport had completed a refurbishment of John Getty's 250 foot yacht, *Tabitha G*, which had been built in 1929. It was twenty-five years older than *Britannia* and a classic in its own right. They had done a brilliant job. Ironically, the Duke of Edinburgh was to use it for Cowes after *Britannia* retired in 1997.

Tony Pryor came well prepared for the meeting. The refurbishment of *Tabitha* had cost less than £50 million. The initial estimates suggested that that sum would be adequate for *Britannia* too. He knew *Britannia* well from the 1987 refit. They were familiar with the internal mechanics in some detail. However, before he went firm on a quotation he would need to inspect her.

The MoD's permission to do so was required. I was not sure what response we would get. They had been very cagey throughout the search for a solution. We needed to see if we had a set of proposals that would justify moving to this deeper level of examination. By now we had been looking at the problem for some six weeks. I took stock of the progress. A set of ideas had emerged which could provide the basis for a technically and financially viable project:

i.   The proposals for a new yacht would be scrapped;
ii.   The present *Britannia* would be refurbished with state-of-the-art British equipment, especially communications and satellite technology. New diesels, probably German, would be fitted. Essentially it would be a flagship for advanced British maritime technology;
iii. A tight but realistic budget in the region of £50 million would be fixed for this work;

iv.   The yacht would continue to carry the name of Royal Yacht
      Britannia;
v.   The Queen would use the yacht as previously for state
      occasions and for personal holidays, such as for Cowes week
      in June and for the annual royal family cruise around the
      Western Isles;
vi.   The refurbished *Britannia* would be available for chartering
      to suitable private-sector organizations;
vii. The daily rate for hiring *Britannia* would be in the order of
      £70,000, and it would have to be hired for at least six
      months every year;
viii. *Britannia* would continue to be crewed by the Royal Navy;
ix.   MoD would continue from its budget to contribute £5
      million per annum to the running costs;
x.   The crew would be augmented by a crew of sea cadets aged
      between sixteen and twenty-one from Commonwealth
      countries.

All in all, I felt there were many attractions in these ideas, most of
which came from Donald Gosling. In particular, the force of
Commonwealth cadets training at sea under the Royal Navy was
very dear to Donald's heart and it was he who had put the idea
forward.

Three important questions were posed by the proposals. Firstly,
would the Queen accept the principle of regular private usage of
Britannia? On this point we were clear that there would be apartments reserved for the use of the royal family. Sir Robert Fellowes,
who was the model of correctness and good sense when I spoke to
him about these matters, confined his replies to stating the Queen's
position: she was not requesting a new yacht. She would look at
proposals that were put to her.

The second question was whether the MoD would continue to
contribute £5 million of their budget to *Britannia*; and, more
importantly, under what arrangements would it be possible for the
Royal Navy to service private-sector organizations and individuals?
There were protocol considerations such as saluting; and more

general ones relating to what could be considered a suitable organization and person. I did not see so much of a problem here. On the limited number of occasions that *Britannia* had been used for commercial purposes – the ceremonial signing of large export contracts that had already been clinched – the arrangements had worked very well. A vetting procedure would be required. It seemed to me that our national gift for administration made us rather good at this sort of thing. There would only be a problem if MoD wanted there to be one. And from our discussions it certainly seemed they did. It was becoming clear that they were none too keen on the plan for a refurbished *Britannia* and were determined to sink it.

We discussed with the MoD the tricky question of 'sponsors' displaying their brand names on the vessel. Banners in the rigging were ruled out for obvious reasons. Discreet plaques were not. There was clearly a way around the problem to avoid it becoming a floating advertising hoarding.

The third problem concerned me much more. Would there be sufficient demand from the private sector to hire the boat at £70,000 per day for the six months a year that were required to make the project pay? I asked for the recent history of *Britannia*'s use to be made available to me. That might give us a clue as to what likely demand there would be from the private sector and which organizations might provide it.

Britannia's log book made very sad reading. In the seven years to 1997 the yacht had been used for only sixty-three days to promote British exports and attract inward investment – just nine days on average per annum! Over the same period its longest uses were two fifteen-day trips comprising Cowes week and the royal family's holiday sailing round the Western Isles. In the last two years of *Britannia*'s life, the Queen used the yacht on only five nights on foreign trips. In the twilight of her career *Britannia*'s steam turbines tended to vibrate even at modest speeds. It seems the Queen suffered from mild sea-sickness and found it difficult to sleep aboard. *Britannia* would reduce speed to alleviate royal insomnia.

I shared these usage figures with the MoD. Their reaction was predictable. This showed only one thing. To them the private sector was not much interested in using *Britannia* – even when it was free! Who in their right mind could think they would use it if they had to pay for it? I did not think too much of the MoD's understanding of human nature or the private sector. Donald, on the other hand, dismissed the past history of *Britannia* as totally irrelevant. The real point was that it had never been marketed. Its use was probably more discouraged than encouraged, which might well explain the minimal involvement with the private sector.

Donald pursued his argument further. It would be necessary, if a public–private partnership was to succeed, for an agency to be put in charge of marketing the yacht at commercial rates with the salaries of those responsible relying heavily on incentives. The agency would report to an advisory board of the great and the good, whose job it would be to vet prospective customers.

The MoD did not like this proposal at all. They were losing control and still being asked to crew the ship and contribute to its running costs. The complement of crew required would fall from 250 to 100 after modernization. But it was hard to make ends meet without the £5 million that from the beginning I had insisted would be needed; the MoD's involvement remained vital.

From my point of view, while there were many merits to the proposal, including valuable contracts for the Devonport yard and our high-tech companies, I could not recommend a project that did not have a firm commercial footing. We were still lacking a bankable commitment from the private sector to charter the boat on commercial terms.

Here Donald played his trump card. He told me in early August that he would personally underwrite seventy days a year at a very attractive rate of £75,000 per day – a total of £5.25 million for a minimum of five years.

He confirmed this later in writing on 27 August in a three-page letter with a covering note showing a cartoon of a businessman jumping from a jetty towards *Britannia* captioned 'Don't miss the boat'. In his letter he made the bold commitment to guarantee private-sector involvement. If enough private firms failed to come forward, he would pick up the tab. Donald, unlike most others, had put his money where his mouth was. What a good man! '*Britannia*'s profile is classic, unmatched and recognized worldwide. This would continue under this option as her profile would remain unchanged,' he wrote. Later he added, 'It is difficult to quantify the value to our exporters and bankers of the high quality of audiences that attend solely because of the unique and mystic privilege of being invited to the royal yacht.' In all honesty, one could not say that of the past. But here was someone prepared to make it happen in the future.

I rang a senior official at the MoD to tell him of the private sector's important commitment. His response was quintessential Civil Service. He said: 'Interesting.' In translation from Whitehall-speak to plain English he meant, 'Mad.' I smiled and concluded we now had the MoD on the run.

In broad terms, Donald's calculations for the running costs for a refurbished *Britannia* envisaged a reduction from £10–12 million to a figure in the order of £5 million. No one doubted that substantial reductions could be made with new technology, and in particular with the installation of modern turbine engines. The maintenance and repair costs to *Britannia*'s antiquated steam set-up were horrendous! I felt it important to keep Jeffrey Sterling involved and asked him to have Donald's assumptions reviewed by his finance staff at P&O. Predictably, P&O took a jaundiced view of the projections.

Meanwhile the MoD was making it difficult for Royal Devonport's chairman, Tony Pryor, to have access to *Britannia* to confirm his costs, and their experts in Bath were doing their best to rubbish them. Understandably, the naval establishment in Bath were keen to design a new yacht. It was a point of pride for them as well as the sort of creative challenge every architect dreams of. They saw little value in rebuilding *Britannia*. Their estimate was that it would cost at least £20 million more than Devonport's initial estimate. P&O similarly adjudged running costs to be 20 per cent higher than Donald's estimate. We were in the politics of statistics.

This was the situation towards the end of July, just prior to the parliamentary recess of 1997 and the end of Labour's first few months in power. In a review of outstanding business in the Chancellor's office, I took the opportunity to brief Gordon on the progress we had made. Instinctively, he did not have much enthusiasm for the project, being keenly aware of the adverse political fallout that could come from it. On the other hand, there were elements that appealed to him, particularly the corps of Commonwealth sea cadets, which offered hope to hundreds of young people and fitted in with the New Deal ethos. Under the proposals the 'new' *Britannia* would be ready in 2000 or 2001, ahead of the Queen's golden jubilee. We decided to test public reaction.

Gordon's spin doctor Charlie Whelan briefed five Sunday news-papers that *Britannia* could be given a new lease of life by a refit paid for by private companies that would use her when the royal family were not on board. The briefing did not go well. Fears were raised about logos being plastered on the ship, while the Treasury and the MoD were portrayed as being at war over the proposals.

In Gordon's words the story 'spiralled out of control'. It annoyed Tony, who had not been told about it. Peter Mandelson seemed peeved about it and began counter-briefing over the weekend, suggesting that it was he and his close friend Prince Charles who were responsible for the plans. The Prince of Wales, like Peter Mandelson, was not involved. The royal link was Sir Robert Fellowes. The project was left on this discordant note as the House went into recess.

During the summer recess I visited Gordon, who was on holiday in Cape Cod. We returned via Boston, where we met up with friends of his. We were having a drink in the lobby of the hotel. It was midnight, the last day of August. Out of the blue an American visitor to the hotel, hearing our British accents, informed us 'that princess of yours has just died in an automobile crash'. We, like everyone else, were nonplussed. We hurried up to Gordon's room and turned on the TV. Every channel was running with it.

The impact of Princess Diana's death touched every part of British life, not least the monarchy itself. A new royal yacht, a refurbishment of *Britannia* or whatever, did not seem to fit the post-Diana atmosphere. Back in Whitehall I told Gordon that we should let the project drop. He agreed at once. I telephoned the MoD. They responded with unrecognizable alacrity that that had been their view all along, as I knew. When I phoned him, Sir Robert Fellowes said the Palace felt the same way.

It only remained to inform our two worthy protagonists of the change in thinking. Both Sir Donald Gosling and Tony Pryor were naturally disappointed. I think they still feel that way. For them it was a great opportunity missed.

I formally dropped the project in the middle of September 1997. The decision was briefed to the *Independent* for 27 September, the Saturday before Labour's annual conference in Brighton. The Defence Secretary, George Robertson, made an official announcement on 10 October. He stressed that the Queen had made clear that the yacht was not required for royal travel and that the substantial annual subsidy could not be justified from public funds.

Whether Diana's death was just a convenient moment to move on and away from the project, I am not sure. There was always something odd about the Treasury, even with its PFI responsibility, being in the lead on the project. But I felt sad and am pleased the Duke of Edinburgh's preference to scuttle *Britannia* at sea did not find favour. She sits very nicely for the moment in Leith docks in Edinburgh and will no doubt, ironically, give pleasure to many more people in retirement than she did in her seafaring days.

10. The Euro: Anatomy of a Crisis

Europe: we don't have to chase every headline.
  Tony Blair, June 2000 (speech to the Women's Institute)

A *Times* leader at the height of the October 1997 government shambles over Europe, headed 'Ins and Outs', concluded that 'Mr Blair will continue to be dogged, like every other post-war Prime Minister, by questions about Europe.' It seems a sound judgement. Such were the embarrassing contortions performed by Harold Wilson on this issue that he was accused by one of his own backbenchers of conducting political 'coitus interruptus'. Was Wilson in or out? Harold Macmillan was humiliated by De Gaulle and in large part Europe was instrumental in Margaret Thatcher's downfall. For John Major, Europe, at whose centre he wished to be, developed such centrifugal force that it brought his government to the point of disintegration. Even Ted Heath had had his problems. With fifteen of his own party against him he had to rely on the votes of five Liberal MPs to get the European Communities Bill through Parliament. For Blair, the issue was a live one from day one; within seven months of its election the government had to decide whether to join the EMU in the first wave, or delay.

Against this background it would have been surprising indeed if the Blair government could get through a whole parliament without problems on Europe. The remarkable thing about the crisis on the euro in October 1997 was that it was to a large extent a crisis of the government's making. Too much spin by too many people? Probably yes; but also one headline that was not spun enough.

By way of background to the high drama and low farce that led to the statement to the House of Commons by the Chancellor on 27 October 1997, perhaps I can review my involvement on the issue with the leadership. In the first place I should make clear that I have never discussed Europe with Tony Blair. My judgements emerge from what I have heard at second hand from those close to him and from the press. As far as Gordon is concerned, it was never a central topic in our policy discussions. But it did inevitably obtrude. I recall three distinct occasions when this was the case.

The first occasion was over lunch back in 1994, when we were testing out ideas to see if we could work together. My own Euro-sceptic views were known, though less well advertised than Gordon's pro-Europe views. He had been a quite strong supporter of membership of the ERM. I raised the issue in this context and wondered how his thinking had moved since we had been forced out. Gordon said in quite a matter-of-fact way that he was pragmatic about relations with Europe. For him it was not, as with John Smith, a matter of principle. It was a question of what was in our national economic interests. I noted the accentuated distinction of his position, which accorded with my own, and felt reassured.

The occasion for our next conversation arose from the increasing difficulties John Major was having with the sceptics in his Cabinet, who were pursuing him to commit the government to a referendum before entry into EMU. It seemed to me obvious and inevitable that there would have to be a referendum before any government could take us in. Why not, I urged Gordon, make a virtue of necessity, take the initiative and propose a referendum? We could, I pointed out in passing, wrong-foot the Tories in the process. The important point would be that Gordon must be seen to be controlling events, not reacting to them. Gordon mulled it over in his usual way for a few weeks. Then, after close consultation with Tony Blair and with his full agreement, Gordon took the opportunity of an interview on the 'Breakfast with Frost' programme on 17 November 1996 to give the referendum commitment. The Sunday papers had been briefed beforehand. Paul Routledge, the then political editor of the *Independent on Sunday*, summed it up: 'Labour promises referendum on single European currency'. The *Observer* called it: 'Labour's dramatic switch on currency'. Although some of the papers thought we were only 'matching Tory policy', we had in fact stolen a march on the government. In the debate on the EU that took place barely a month later (18 December), Gordon challenged Kenneth Clarke to follow Labour's example and 'consult the public', but Clarke did not accept the challenge.

It was a wide-ranging policy discussion on our economic strategy that provided the third occasion at which Gordon, Ed and I went more specifically into the economics of the EMU entry. Ed was known to be cautious. When he was working at the *FT*, he had written a pamphlet★ which put the economic case against UK entry in the economic circumstances of 1990–92. As we discussed it, Ed's thinking was that if you could take a twenty-year view and if all went well he was sure a common currency in Europe could bring benefits in terms of growth, employment and living standards. The problem lay in the condition 'if all went well'. There were bound to be unforeseeable shocks and crises on the way. Could the system itself withstand these; and even if the integrity of the system held, would the UK economy within it be strong enough to ride out the shocks and reap the benefits? Ed felt it would be too risky in the early stage of a Labour administration. We needed to re-establish economic stability first.

I agreed with Ed and I also took him up on this point about the 'shocks and crises' and doubted that there was sufficient flexibility in the system to cope. Gordon listened for the most part. He could see the obvious political attractions of being in the EMU; but it was clear, too, that he saw the real dangers of premature entry. The discussion of EMU rather petered out and we turned to other areas where we knew what we wanted to do.

The impression of this last indeterminate conversation was still fresh in my mind in September 1997 when an article by Robert Peston, the political editor of the *Financial Times*, precipitated the first major crisis of the Blair government. The Peston article appeared on 26 September as a front-page scoop. Peston, on the

---

★ *Euro-Monetarism: Why Britain was Ensnared and How It Should Escape*, Fabian Society, December 1992.

basis of conversations with ministers, made the following claims with regard to the government's attitude on EMU: that there was a big shift from the government's previous negative tone; that Gordon Brown and Robin Cook had reconciled their differences and were now at one in favour of entry; and that the Cabinet itself had moved towards entry soon after the planned EMU launch in 1999.

The article caused alarm bells to ring everywhere. There were the usual mutual and futile recriminations about who said what to whom and why. No one of course admitted saying anything. But there were a lot of people with a lot of opinions involved.

The dramatis personae lined up as follows: the Prime Minister, who was politically in favour of EMU, was at pains to preserve a sceptic stance to reassure the Murdoch press and the *Mail* group. He did not want the euro to spoil the prospects of a second term; but he did want to be in the common currency. The Chancellor wanted first and foremost to do what was right for the UK economy. That meant staying out in 1999, a decision which in his judgement meant staying out for a whole parliament. But neither the PM nor the Chancellor wanted to say that, or not just yet. It would not play well with the leadership of the CBI, who were in favour of the earliest possible entry. To the Chancellor fell the role of keeping the support of the pro-euro CBI, while the PM took care of the anti-euro press. It was a double act that to some extent reversed roles. But given the intellectual contortions all politicians go through on Europe, there was nothing particularly objectionable about that. The real question was whether the inherently contradictory position could be held. Peter Mandelson was always a major player on the presentation of the big issues. He also had strong views on EMU. He was pro and did not want to rule out entry for a parliament. At the Foreign Office Robin Cook, who in opposition had been anti, was coming under the influence of his office and its officials, and moving to a pro position. At No. 10 Derek Scott, the PM's economic adviser, was on economic grounds strongly opposed to early entry, as was Ed Balls in the Treasury. Of the spin doctors Alastair Campbell was against entry while Charlie Whelan was in favour. Charlie got fed up changing currency when he travelled abroad. The officials at the Treasury, scarred by the ERM experience, were strongly against early entry.

The situation had all the elements of a major drama: a big story – the euro; a deadline – the end of the year for a decision; all the key players holding strong and conflicting views; the press deeply committed and divided on the politics. When the crisis came in the wake of the Peston article it did not disappoint.

At first there was an agreed view in government that the Peston article was an inaccurate minor nuisance that would blow over. Peston himself had backed off by letting it be known that two paragraphs giving anti-euro opinions had been cut from his article. The story was denied by the Treasury: there was no shift in government policy, which was that entry in 1999 or soon thereafter was 'most unlikely'.

This line could probably have been held – at least till the end-of-the-year statement – and the story would have died, had Peter Mandelson not reignited the fire by informing Irish radio in early October 1997 that Britain 'had not ruled out joining EMU in the first wave'. There really was no need for this. It sparked a frenzy of buying in the City, one of whose leading figures called the government's policy a 'saga of leak, comment and denial which is rapidly becoming a farce'.

Whenever Peter Mandelson intervened in a major issue of this kind, outside his area of responsibility, the questions arose: was it an unguarded remark; was it a calculated remark made off his own bat; or was it a calculated remark made in tacit agreement with No. 10? In interpreting the situation from the Treasury it was safest to presume the third scenario. We usually did.

The erratic pattern of statements was unsettling the markets. The Treasury again stressed the line that early entry was 'very unlikely'. But it was pretty clear by now that the euro issue would not go away until a final point of clarity on the date of entry had been reached by the government. That was some way off yet.

The press knew they had the government on the run and were not about to give up. The story burst back into life in a big way on

13 October 1997 in a major front-page story in the *Daily Mail* by Paul Eastham, the paper's political editor. The article took the Peston line much further. Ministers were now reported to have told Eastham that the PM would announce to EU leaders in Luxembourg on 21 November that 'Britain will join the single European currency as soon as possible after its 1999 launch.' This 'bombshell', as Eastham called it, caused major shock waves at No. 10.

On the day the article appeared, as it happened, Gordon Brown and his Treasury team were attending an EU finance ministers meeting in Luxembourg. Ed Balls was contacted on the runway by an angry Alastair Campbell, who wanted to know what the hell was going on. Ed was as nonplussed as Campbell. If the Treasury were going to place a story about EMU the place would not be the *Daily Mail*, nor would the implication be in favour of early entry. That No. 10 was not satisfied was all too evident the next day when a major piece appeared in the *Independent* under the name of Anthony Bevins, the newspaper's political editor. Bevins was a well-known conduit for stories coming from No. 10 and the article on 16 October seemed to emerge from that source.

Bevins, a senior and respected journalist, could normally be relied on to get the tone and balance right. On this occasion the tactic backfired spectacularly. The briefing, aimed principally at killing off the continued press speculation about early entry, turned into a story of a major rift – in personal and policy terms – between the Prime Minister and his Chancellor. It was given the full front-page treatment. The headline ran 'Blair–Brown clash on the biggest issue of all'. The charge, levelled directly, and in terms personally quite offensive, at the Chancellor himself was that he 'was over-reaching himself and trying to bounce the Prime Minister into a single currency'. Nothing, of course, could be further from the truth or more hurtful to the Chancellor. He was against premature entry and trying to hold that line. Nor was there at this time any policy difference between him and the PM. Though, as agreed between them, each would talk with different emphasis on the issue, they were essentially united on the policy. Tony did not want a running debate on the euro or a referendum to spoil the build-up for the second election and Gordon did not want to see early entry put at risk the sound economic strategy he was putting into place to win that election. That was the reality. So quite how the Bevins article could emerge as it did on the back of a No. 10 briefing is a mystery, unless given the most sinister interpretation.

Following the *Mail* and *Independent* stories the whole press went berserk and the markets were in turmoil. By now it was evident to everyone involved that briefings had got out of control. And really the government had only got itself to blame. The Blair/Brown double act and role reversal, the rivalry in the camps, the different emphases in the government's position, repeatedly highlighted by Mandelson, were playing right into the hands of a press that possessed an incomparable capacity for hype, misrepresentation and mischief. It was high time for everyone to shut up and let the Chancellor bring forward a considered statement of final clarity. And indeed that was the position of No. 10 and No. 11, and of Peter, too, who wanted the issue 'shut down'.

The strategy to achieve this was devised with the full involvement and agreement of the PM during the Wednesday and Thursday, 15 and 16 October 1997. It was that the Chancellor would issue a carefully worded statement backed with an interview to a selected journalist. In the light of all the recent problems with the press this seemed in retrospect something of a quixotic venture. However, it went ahead. The journalist selected was Philip Webster, political editor of *The Times*. Webster is a fine journalist and no politician's poodle. But when, as was the case here with the government's position on EMU, he is given the opportunity of an important statement and interview on a major policy he could be relied on to get it right. By 'getting it right' in this context I mean quite simply reporting accurately what the government wants to say. If the government's statement is to achieve the right perception it can be necessary to discuss with the journalist both the position in the paper that the article will occupy and, most importantly, as far as possible what the topline will be. The headline proper is not decided by the journalist but by sub-editors and agreement on it cannot be guaranteed. Therein was to lie our problem.

Given the normal state of trench warfare between journalists and politicians, such civilized arrangements on occasions seem reasonable to me. The charge of news manipulation can be made. But the rest of the papers are the ones to make the charge and to do the carping.

Webster had been fully briefed and had completed the interview with the Chancellor by Friday, 17 October. The article would appear the next day and would be picked up in positive tones in the Sunday papers, if all went well. However, even in the best-planned operations of this kind there is a danger of things going wrong. This one went badly wrong.

The objectives of the exercise were to kill off the reports of a rift between the PM and Chancellor, to rule out early entry and to hint strongly that we would stay out for the entire parliament. The problem lay in the 'hinting'. Webster in the topline and in the text of his article reported the agreed wording accurately: 'Gordon Brown is *on the verge of* ruling out British membership of a European single currency before the next election.' But the headline had not been agreed. It left out the key words 'on the verge of' and stated categorically: 'Brown rules out single currency for the lifetime of this parliament.'

The use of the words 'on the verge of' was important, since it made clear that a formal statement to the House of Commons had not been pre-empted and it respected the position of the Cabinet, CBI, TUC and our partners in Europe, who might otherwise feel they had been ignored in the key phase of decision making.

It may have been too fine a point to spin on. The story might have unravelled even if the headline had included the key words. But when Charlie Whelan was overheard on Friday, 17 October, spinning the story to other journalists in his favourite pub, the Red Lion, situated just across the road from the Treasury in Whitehall, the cat was well and truly out of the bag. The eavesdropper was a Lib Dem press officer, who tipped off Malcolm Bruce, their Treasury spokesman. Bruce rushed into the 'Newsnight' studios, where the story was already up and running.

Inevitably the point of contention was the headline. Had the decision – to stay out for the whole parliament – been taken and if so why had Parliament itself not been informed? Peter Mandelson saw the early editions, took great exception to the headline and felt he had not been informed. Sadly, some other people, too, had not been informed. The Treasury press office still maintained there was no change to government policy, as did an unbriefed Frank Dobson (then the health secretary) who told the 'Breakfast with Frost' programme: 'We may join in 1999 but we will keep our options open after that.'

It was not our finest hour at the Treasury. We had formulated the statement, chosen the journalist and the newspaper, conducted the interview and done the briefing. It was all, of course, agreed with the PM and the press office at No. 10. Indeed, when the calls came for Charlie's head, Alastair Campbell was man enough to take his share of the blame: 'If Charlie goes, I go.' It was a show of solidarity the more remarkable because it was so exceptional, almost unique. But the solidarity was not total. It was evident that at least one senior minister was continuing to resist strongly what had quite clearly by now become our only viable position: namely that we should move from 'highly unlikely' and 'on the verge of' to the unequivocal position of the headline. We were staying out for this parliament.

Peter Mandelson did not want to accept the inevitable. He gave the *New Statesman* an extensive briefing, on the basis of which the magazine predicted that the government would not rule out membership in the lifetime of the parliament – which was totally at odds with the agreed line from No. 10 and No. 11. The *New Statesman* then put forward the quite absurd idea promoted by Peter that the government would review the state of convergence with the rest of Europe 'on a regular, perhaps annual basis'. Peter had clearly still not given up on keeping open our options for early entry, which his own strong pro-European sympathies inclined him towards.

There was again no excuse to reopen the issue for a second time, though by now little more harm could be done. The point had been reached where the Speaker had let it be known with her characteristic forthrightness that a statement to Parliament was required as soon as it reassembled on the following Monday, 27 October.

At last we should have to get a settled view. The Treasury went into overdrive. It is at its best in a crisis when small teams are established to work on specific areas. We were particularly fortunate to have in charge Sir Nigel Wicks, the second permanent secretary. Nigel is a man of innate wisdom, great experience and sufficient patience. He was immensely respected by his colleagues in the Treasury. He was of great help to the Chancellor in the early Ecofin and IMF conferences, where his standing was second to none. Indeed he had been chosen by his EU colleagues to chair the management committee charged with making preparations for the introduction of the EMU. It is an irony that the successful introduction of the EMU was due to British diplomacy: Sir Nigel Wicks was the senior EU official at the working-party level; the UK held the presidency of the EU and Tony Blair brokered the final deals in 1998 at Cardiff that enabled the seven countries to proceed in January 1999.

The immediate task of the Treasury teams was to complete their assessment of the key economic criteria that would have to be met for UK entry to be a feasible proposition in terms of compatibility with the other economics. Though a few members of the government would willingly have chanced entry in January 1999, there was a more general view that the risks were too great: the economic situation in the UK was too divergent from that in continental Europe. That was the strong view of Nigel Wicks and Treasury officials, too. The work was put in hand to test the judgement in economic terms.

In opposition, Ed Balls had already established the five criteria against which the feasibility of British entry into the EMU would be evaluated. It was his job now to coordinate the Treasury teams in this exercise that would determine whether 'a clear and unambiguous case' could be established for entry. The criteria were set out in the Chancellor's statement to the Commons of 27 October 1997. They were posed as a series of questions:

i.   Can there be sustainable convergence between Britain and the economies of the single currency?
ii. Is there sufficient flexibility to cope with economic change?
iii. Will the effect on investment be positive?
iv. Will the impact on our financial services generally be positive?
v.   Will it be good for employment?

The answers given in the Chancellor's statement to questions i, ii, iii and v boiled down to this: there are potential benefits but we should not be able to realize them without convergence, the first crucial criterion on which the seminal judgement was issued: 'To demonstrate sustainable convergence will take a period of years.'★ That meant entry was out for this parliament.

The Treasury research work was finished by about Friday, 24 October. The issues then became the tone and balance of the Chancellor's speech and the context in which to place the bottom-line Treasury judgement that on economic grounds entry was ruled out for the parliament.

At the Chancellor's request, I joined the final drafting sessions on the speech over the weekend of 25 and 26 October. The PM was in Edinburgh, with Alastair Campbell, attending the Commonwealth summit. His other staff who were closely involved were working out of No. 10. Peter Mandelson and Derry Irvine at the PM's request were also to be consulted. Each and every one was to test each nuance in so far as the political and electoral implications were concerned. It made an already difficult speech more tricky. But in the end nothing of significance was changed.

Apart from the detailed economic passages, Gordon Brown writes his own speeches. But he likes to have a group of people involved. The first draft will be bashed out by Gordon himself on his word processor. What emerges is a series of ideas encapsulated in the best words he can find at the moment. These phrases are

★ As far as the fourth question was concerned, the Treasury view was that our financial services industry would prosper better in EMU than outside. In fact it had done very well indeed outside.

then honed and polished and repeated out loud until Gordon is satisfied with them.

Bob Shrum, an American pollster and speech-writer, tells me that President Clinton works in a somewhat similar fashion. The President has two teleprompter screens in the theatre room of the White House. At any one time there will be no more than five or six lines on the screen with two or three words per line. He will on and off keep trying out the phrases – changing them until he is entirely at ease with them, not just in terms of the message but also from a verbal delivery point of view.

On the occasion of the EMU speech – perhaps the most important the Chancellor would make in the parliament and certainly one of the most important in his career – a new and not altogether helpful element was introduced into the preparations. At the PM's request, John Holmes,* his principal private secretary, spent most of the Saturday rewriting the Chancellor's current draft. This was not without its comic aspects. But by the evening Nigel Wicks had had enough of it and exploded over the phone that he was not having No. 10 rewriting the Chancellor's speech. At this point No. 10 desisted. In fairness, Holmes was not trying to change the speech. He was searching for a more sequential structure, longer and more precisely parsed sentences. It was a futile pursuit. Gordon's speeches are Gordon's speeches.

The points of contention in the draft were essentially two: whether or not the Chancellor should apologize to the Speaker for having given the *Times* interview before making his statement to the House; and whether or not to leave a chink of light through the door for possible early entry before the next general election.

The insistence on an apology came from No. 10 via Alastair Campbell. This was rather surprising, since No. 10 had been fully in agreement with the *Times* briefing. What was even more surprising was the grovelling terms in which the draft for the apology was sent over. One would have thought the Chancellor had proposed

* Sir John Holmes is currently ambassador to Portugal.

the abolition of Parliament itself. Gordon and all of us were adamant there was no need for an apology. It seemed to us that pushing for an apology risked demoralizing the Chancellor when he most needed support.

The final wording on the loophole – no more than a chink of light – ran as follows: 'Making a decision to join this parliament is not realistic – *barring some fundamental or unforeseen change in economic circumstances.*' None of the Treasury team – particularly Nigel Wicks and myself – was happy about this. The one thing we wanted was a final point of clarity. We were not going in during this parliament and that was an end to it. We did not want to leave the slightest chance that the issue could be reopened and bedevil us the way it had the Major government and indeed as it had destabilized our own government over the previous six weeks. The Chancellor and Ed shared our view, but since there was no moving No. 10 on the point we would have to live with it.

The final draft was ready by about 9 p.m. on Sunday evening. We were in the Chancellor's office grouped around the end of the large table – just in front of the fireplace around which the tattered sofa and armchairs are grouped. Nigel formally classified the speech 'SECRET' and thought it was time to bring in the Treasury press officer. Peter Curwen, chief press officer, was standing by, of course, and Malcolm Graves, my own excellent press officer, happened to be on duty that evening. Both of them reacted very negatively to the loophole phrase. Charlie Whelan was also vociferously of this view. It threatened, they all felt, to become the story: that early entry was still on the cards, exactly the opposite message to what we wanted to convey. Nigel tentatively asked me if I could have a word with No. 10. I explained to him that I had no influence whatsoever in matters of this kind. Gordon, as I understood it, had tried without success.

I could see, too, that Gordon and Ed felt the problem was a manageable one, especially given that in all major respects the speech was what the Treasury wanted. We called it a day about 11 p.m. The Chancellor had worked away at the speech solidly for the last forty-eight hours, honing it down, using the inflections that suited his delivery. He was – given that he will never be fully satisfied – at ease with the speech.

There were two further reasons why this was so. He did not want the speech to be seen as anti-European. He wanted to take the pro-Europe argument forward: in particular he wanted a positive declaration in favour of entry if the economic conditions were met; and he wanted to dispense once and for all with the constitutional arguments against entry. The speech did both; and it also set up a working group under Sir Colin (now Lord) Marshall to ensure that adequate preparations for entry were undertaken by the private sector. Remarkably, all these points were not added until the Saturday. They were Gordon's ideas and contributed significantly to the success of the speech with the CBI and most industrialists. It was a balanced, rational policy that all but the extremists on either side could support. It was a package clearly consistent with any objective assessment of our national interest.

Desperately tired though he was, Gordon put in a storming performance in the Commons on Monday, 27 October. The Tories helped with an inept response.

Most TV and radio news bulletins led on the evening of the speech with the message that entry was out for this parliament. The Treasury briefing was strongly to that effect, though the other important aspects of the speech were not ignored. The press were also briefed on a similar basis, with predictably mixed success. The *Independent, Guardian, Financial Times* and *Observer*, all of whom are in favour of entry, acknowledged the good sense of the Treasury position in the light of its economic assessment. At the other end of the spectrum the *Telegraph* and *Mail* were the most dissatisfied of the anti-Euro papers. The *Mail* leading article took a funereal tone with the headline 'Slow march towards the pound's burial'. The Chancellor's speech 'marked a sombre date in the annals of these islands'. The *Daily Telegraph* leader, by contrast, though equally dissatisfied with the Chancellor, could at least produce a witty parody of his proposals: 'It is as though Gordon Brown were saying to his fiancée: "I definitely intend to marry you, but I shan't do so for the next five years – and possibly not after that. Oh, and we can't marry except in a number of circumstances that have never existed before, and may not come about." '

The Times was its ambivalent self, but remarked quite ominously, 'The government's position provides the Conservatives with an opportunity to make entry into the single currency a central issue at the next election.' William Hague has been trying to do so ever since. Unbelievably, some senior colleagues in government have started yet again to lend him a helping hand in recent months.

Perhaps it is surprising that the truce amongst government ministers on Europe held up as well as it did, given how strongly individuals feel about it. But the Chancellor's statement to Parliament of 27 October 1997 on Europe lasted as well as it did because it provided and still does provide a coherent policy and establishes unassailable reasons why EMU need not and should not be a general-election issue.

The inescapable and justifiable logic of the government's position is that nothing can be decided until the convergence test has been established one way or the other. There is therefore no need, in the national interest or in the interests of the electoral prospects of the Labour Party, to make EMU a live issue for the general election.

This claim needs amplifying. From the national point of view it is essential that an issue, described by the Chancellor himself as 'probably the most important question that this country is likely to face in our generation', should be decided in a single-issue referendum. It is a great national issue: it transcends party politics and does not belong to a general election, where the result could easily depend on the popularity of the government or opposition parties and not on the merits of the issue. Roy Jenkins, writing in the *Independent* in June 2000, said a 'referendum campaign must be fought on a cross-party basis'. I agree, and I say the government should allow a free vote for members. That would create the right atmosphere. Jenkins speaks of the 1975 referendum as a liberating experience. He is right, but when he asserts: 'A euro referendum must not be long delayed after the coming election,' he is putting politics ahead of economics. Well, if you want to court the same disaster as the ERM, then you go in at the wrong time and at the wrong rate – except that this time it could be the wrong interest rate as well as the wrong exchange rate. We cannot allow the politics to override the economics. Which means that some semblance of sustainable convergence must be demonstrable and the Euro economies must show greater flexibility than they have so far. That may or may not be possible soon after the general election, the date of which is uncertain in any case.

The case as I have outlined it for a referendum on the euro is a principled one and widely accepted. That the euro entry need not be a major issue in the forthcoming general election follows from that, and it is as plain as a pikestaff why on electoral grounds the Labour Party should not seek to make it one.

Nevertheless, certain colleagues speaking for their departmental interests – principally the Foreign Office for political reasons and the DTI for investment and trade reasons – continue to put the pro-euro case, usually carefully worded, however, to respect the government's position that the economic conditions must be met. That can be understood and accommodated within what even under the present Prime Minister is a relatively forgiving system.

What I cannot understand is why Peter Mandelson has to interfere. Looking back over the euro-crisis of October 1997, it is hard to escape the conclusion that it was Peter who ignited the row in the first place and then reignited it after the crucial *Times* interview. So perhaps it should not be surprising that Peter has returned to it now. In his speech to the GMB on 16 May 2000 he made this statement: 'The fact is that, as long as we are outside the euro, there is little we can do to protect industry against destabilizing swings in the value of sterling as they affect Europe – the largest market we have to earn our living.'

It was not an off-the-cuff remark. It was a considered statement that we are led to believe was not cleared with No. 10. It was obviously not cleared with No. 11. Peter will have known precisely the effect of his words, how the press would pick on them and reopen the euro issue and the wounds in his relationship with the Chancellor. He will have known that the PM would get dragged into the story and that a full-blown row would ensue. It did. The question cannot be ducked: why did he do it?

I admire Peter's administrative and marketing skills and his deep understanding of how the media work and can be made to work. I am delighted to see him back in government. With all those positive aspects to his personality, why is it that he is so frequently a destabilizing element in the government and in particular in the crucial relationship between the PM and the Chancellor? The continuing euro-crisis shows in sharp relief this negative aspect of Peter's personality and of his manner of operating. My loan to Peter is discussed elsewhere in this book, but this is an appropriate point to consider Peter Mandelson's role in the government.

All governments have their tensions. This is inevitably so where women and men of huge ability and matching egos clash on policies about which they care passionately. It is not surprising therefore that the Blair government has its fair share of tensions. What past history shows – with both Conservative and Labour governments – is that it is imperative to settle policy and personality feuds to the maximum extent possible in private. Once in the press, the stories feed on themselves, become hyped and distorted. The combatants eventually retire wounded from the field of conflict. Some more – the resignees; some less – the eventual willing or unwilling retirees. But nobody really wins. The government as a whole is the loser. Its capacity to affect the administration of the country is impaired and its standing with the public is diminished. The public hates to see politicians squabbling and punishes divided governments and opposition parties alike. The press, of course, love it and encourage it. They also, and not entirely sanctimoniously, believe they have an obligation to bring out the inner conflicts and underlying tensions of the government of the day as a matter of public interest. At present they are concentrating very hard on three people in the Labour government: the PM, the Chancellor and Peter Mandelson.

Let me start with the PM and the Chancellor. In my view the Labour Party, uniquely in its history, is blessed in Tony Blair and Gordon Brown with two outstanding politicians who complement each other and can work together to great effect. The Wilson

Cabinets of 1964 and 1966 had a galaxy of talent and intellectual brilliance, but they did not realize their full potential as an administration. There was not the teamwork at the apex that characterizes the Blair–Brown relationship when it is working even in middle gear. There is, of course, rivalry between the camps but this must be put into perspective. The Prime Minister rightly has a much larger staff, including the policy unit.

And since the departure of Charlie Whelan there has been no one to match Alastair Campbell. Hurtful things have been said in the Chancellor's direction. No doubt he was disappointed at losing the leadership campaign race. But he has never in my presence questioned the pre-eminence of the Prime Minister's position. And he wants nothing more than the success of the government and its Prime Minister. We have, then, two men at the height of their complementary powers, reconcilable and able to work together. Sadly, this is the cue for Peter Mandelson's entry on stage.

Peter by his own admission is not a deeply philosophical politician. He does not have behind him the wealth of reading and study of political ideas that inform Gordon Brown's intellectual horizons. But Peter has a few clear-cut strategic policies. They are momentously important and, in my opinion, momentously wrong. They are set out with disarming clarity in a book he co-authored with Roger Liddle, entitled *The Blair Revolution: Can New Labour Deliver?* The book has no great literary or intellectual merit. It reads rather like a primer for sixth-formers. But the ideas it recommends would entail historic changes for the Labour Party and the country. The message is that the Labour government should:

- Adopt proportional representation for general elections;
- Enter into a permanent pact with the Liberal Democrats;
- Push strongly the integrational agenda in Europe, starting now with entry into the euro.

My objections to each can be simply stated. With considerable risk of oversimplification, they are: that proportional representation makes for weak government; that the Liberal Democrats are at best unreliable partners; and that the present conditional euro policy is better than just plunging straight in.

I am sure that the strong majority of the Labour Party shares my view on proportional representation and a pact with the Liberals. But Peter wishes to win them over. His aim is to engage the heart, mind and office of the Prime Minister in this battle. And it is at this point that the battle becomes wider, inevitably involving the Chancellor, who does not, I believe, support either cause.

No one, of course, can ask of Peter that he should not pursue his own ambitious agenda, which he believes to be in the best interests of his party and country. But he must do it openly and in his own right and within the limits of collective responsibility accepted by his colleagues. He cannot plead some sort of political version of a public immunity certificate for briefings and leaks to the press, for these cause him to become a destabilizing influence between the Prime Minister and his Chancellor.

My own judgement is that on his own he will not make much progress in winning the Labour Party over to his ideas. Moreover, if they did become official policy, I fear we would face a split in the party on the scale of 1931 and 1983. But that is not the point here. Peter has often told me and many others he wants to be his own man with his own department and his own defined set of responsibilities. He now once more has those; and if he bends his talents to the job in hand the extent of them will assuredly increase. Indeed he could well become an even more significant figure in a future Labour administration than his grandfather, Herbert Morrison, was in the Attlee government.

Peter 'going on being Peter' in Tony Blair's words, is not good enough. He must 'become his own man'. And the Prime Minister should help him do so.

11. Sky Blues

What ultimately is the point of Coventry City?
  Daily Telegraph, 13 February 1995

Every MP will tell you that with the constituency comes its football team. It was my good fortune to inherit Coventry City Football Club. Coventry is no ordinary team. It is the fourth longest survivor in the First and Premier Divisions, where it has perilously clung on for the last thirty-three years. Only Arsenal, Liverpool and Everton have survived longer. Even Manchester United in 1974 suffered the ignominy of relegation that it has been Coventry's Houdini-esque capability to escape. It is no small achievement to avoid the drop in the last game of the season no fewer than ten times in thirty seasons, as Coventry have done. It makes for interesting times for supporters, in the words of the Chinese curse.

In my first season (1977) as an MP supporter we played fellow strugglers Bristol City at home in our all-too-familiar predicament: there was only one point between the bottom five teams. Both Bristol City and Coventry needed to win but each could survive with a draw if Sunderland lost. Our game had started fifteen minutes late and with five minutes to go it was a draw. Coventry were under heavy pressure and looked likely to concede a winner when the word came through to the directors' box that Sunderland had lost at Everton. From that point both teams kicked the ball from one side of the field to the other and back again. A draw was enough.

It was Jimmy Hill who as manager had put Coventry on the map in the sixties. In five years of unbroken success to 1967 he had taken us from the Third to the First Division – today's Premier League. In that promotion season we went twenty-five games unbeaten, and to clinch the Second Division title we beat Wolves at home in front of a record crowd of 51,455. No one knows how things might have worked out had the chairman, Derrick Robins, acceded to Hill's request for a ten-year contract. As it was, Jimmy resigned and, rarely for Coventry City, the news was carried prominently on the national TV channels. Sadly, and probably quite unfairly, Jimmy's return to Coventry as chairman in 1983 ended with him being booed out of office by the fans.

Coventry's long spell in the First and Premier Leagues has seen two high points for the club. In 1970 we finished sixth and qualified for Europe, where unfortunately we crashed to a second-round 6–1 defeat by Bayern Munich, a team graced with Beckenbauer, Maier and Muller. It remains the heaviest defeat of an English team in continental football. We did, however, win the second, by 2–1 at Highfield Road.

By contrast on 16 May 1987 Coventry beat Spurs and won the FA Cup. Spurs, who had not been beaten in seven previous cup finals, were strong favourites for the trophy, even though *Old Moore's Almanac* predicted that a team in blue stripes would win.

Normal service resumed soon after the Wembley triumph when we lost to Sutton, a team from the Vauxhall conference, in the FA Cup third round – not even two years since the trophy was paraded through Coventry. I was in the welcoming party that Sunday afternoon. It was a moving experience. The crowd was huge. Our gates had rocketed as the season and Coventry progressed. It brought home how much a soccer team means to a city. People do care and success is important.

It was still early days for TransTec, the small high-tech company I had started. But I resolved on that Sunday afternoon that if it were a success and if I had the capital to spare I would put it into the club to secure it a position amongst the top half-dozen teams in the country.

To this end, I met Bryan Richardson, chairman of Coventry City, in November 1995. He had readily acceded to my suggestions of a meeting after I had asked Graham Hover, the club's excellent secretary, whom I had known since he joined in 1984, to effect an introduction.

It was at once clear to me that Bryan was not the stereotype of a football club chairman. He cared about the game and, though traditionally an Arsenal supporter, he had thrown himself into Coventry's cause. He came from a family of sportsmen. All three brothers played in first-class cricket. Peter and Dick Richardson played for England, Worcestershire and Kent. Bryan opened the batting for Warwickshire. He was also a talented striker on the football pitch.

We met for lunch at the Grosvenor House. I explained the background to my thinking. My interest was purely football. Coventry had started the season disastrously despite a rash of signings by Ron Atkinson, whom Bryan had brought in at the end of the 1995 season to replace Phil Neal. In December Coventry was bottom of the league.

The plan I put to Bryan was simple, though I stressed to him that the decision would not be mine but the trustees of my family trust. The deal I would put to them was that up to £10 million could be invested in the club. This would be £5 million straight away and a further £5 million in the course of the season. The first £5 million could be interest-free for the first year, the equivalent of a £½ million donation to the club. The other would incur a modest interest charge of bank rate plus 1 per cent. In exchange for what I thought the trustees might think was a generous offer I suggested as part of the deal that he also try to secure a sizeable block of shares for the trust and invite me to join the board and become joint deputy chairman with Michael McGinnity, whom Bryan had brought on board the previous year. The club's accounts showed it had borrowed up to its limits: all I could see for the trust by way of security was a second charge, after the bank, on its assets and a prior charge on the players that were bought with the money.

He understandably asked what price might the trust be prepared to pay for the equity. I explained the trust situation and said that I doubted they would be prepared to pay a high premium. In the event Bryan was able to locate 27 per cent of the equity for which the trust agreed a price of £1.2 million.

I had already discussed the opportunity with the trustees. Taken together, the loan and the equity were a package I thought they might find interesting. One trustee hated football. The other was fortunately a long-standing Spurs fan with a better idea than any of us as to where football was heading. His view that it could be a good investment prevailed. He might even yet be proved right.

It may look a reasonable investment now. That was not so in the dog days of December 1995. Football was not awash with money. With £10 million backing, both Bryan and I agreed it was not unreasonable to expect Coventry to be in the top half of the Premier League and to qualify for Europe in a good year. Those were our ambitions. Thus began a period of quite remarkably productive cooperation between Bryan Richardson and myself. He and I have never had cross words. We agreed that I would not interfere in team matters nor brief the press, and I happily went along with both. (He really went for the *Telegraph* when it printed the notoriously rude article about us, and our press continues to improve. We no doubt still have some way to go.) Bryan has an easy and confident manner in dealing with the press and on radio and TV. I was pleased enough to let him get on with it.

The arrangements Bryan proposed for the trust to take a charge on the players were already in place at Coventry. A local charity had loaned the club £2.5 million. Quite naturally it had taken the available security on the part of the playing squad at the time it made the funds available. The trust's security would be on the new players we bought with their loan. When the first purchase with the trust loan was Noel Whelan from Leeds for £2 million, I felt we were in good shape. He scored three goals in the first five matches and kept us up for the 1996 season, but not before we had to settle the survival issue yet again in the last match of the season. This was disappointing, as we had beaten Wimbledon away in the last-but-one fixture, only to learn that Southampton and Manchester City had both won as well! Gordon Brown, who came to the Wimbledon match with Ed Balls and Yvette Cooper, remarked we had it all to do the next weekend. We held Leeds to a scrappy draw at Highfield Road and survived on goal difference. Like so many others before me, I vowed 'never again'. The trust came forward with the next £5 million.

This bought us amongst others Darren Huckerby in 1997 – again the money was clearly well spent. Perhaps I ought to explain exactly how the loans were secured on the players. There was no up-side: there was no share of the 'profits' if a player moved on at a profit – as Huckerby did in 1999, turning £1 million into £5 million with his move to Leeds. All that happened there was that the trust's £5 million, secured in part on Huckerby, was transferred to Robbie Keane, who has proven to be an even better investment for the club. He scored three goals in his first two matches. So the trust's money looked safe straight away, but there is a snag: you cannot get it back without actually selling the player and retaining the money. That was never the trust's idea. For the investment to be successful, Coventry must remain a premier-league club. In the last two years we have had comfortable mid-league positions. But it was not like that when Bryan first took over.

Ron Atkinson was seen as a great coup when Bryan appointed him manager in February 1995 to lift our game. He put five thousand on the gate for one thing. He had been in the game at the highest level – winning the FA Cup in two seasons out of four when managing Manchester United. But in his first full season we were again at the foot of the table by the end of October 1996. He had improved our attendance, but not our performance on the pitch. There was talk of sloppy training sessions. My disquiet was shared by the board but Bryan seemed reluctant to act. Perhaps he just did not like being pressurized. I decided to force the issue at the November board meeting. Bryan reluctantly agreed to do the necessary, pushing Ron upstairs as director of football and making Gordon Strachan team manager.

Charlie Whelan, who seems to have a personal dislike of Ron, ran a story about my role in Ron's removal in the sports columns of the *Daily Mirror*. I think the hand of the then *Mirror*'s distinguished political correspondent, Kevin Maguire, was behind it. Quite how Charlie got to know of my involvement, I am not sure. But I was embarrassed by the leak and apologized to Bryan, since it was not in line with our understanding. He brushed it aside as a matter of no consequence but, like myself, was puzzled when later Charlie resuscitated the story as part of his post-Treasury fantasies under the headline 'How I sacked Big Ron'. It was not one of his most helpful forays into print!

It became clear to Bryan and myself soon after our cooperation started that a sounder financial base for the club was required if we were ever to secure a decent position in the league and lay the basis for paying back the trust money. Since we had embarked on the enterprise together in 1995 the economics of the sport had changed dramatically. Post Bosman,★ the players were taking more and more out of it and Sky was putting more and more into it. The £10 million that went into Coventry soon seemed small beer when Alan Shearer was sold to Newcastle for £15 million. We may have clung on to a place in the Premier League in footballing terms, but we were being pushed out of it in financial terms.

Bryan and I both felt the need to strengthen the board. At our invitation Derek Higgs joined us as director in July 1997. Derek is a highly respected City figure. He had been head of corporate finance at Warburgs, and then he moved to be chairman of the Prudential's portfolio management and a member of its main board. Moreover, his family had long-standing links to the city and he was a football fan. Derek was tailor-made for us and as the election approached I was keen to bring him in as a shareholder, too.

The occasion to do this came early in 1997, when the opportunity arose for me to bring to the trust's attention another large block of shares owned by Derrick Robins, who had been chairman for a long spell until 1973. There were mixed views about the extent of his real commitment to the club, which were not enhanced when he departed for South Africa, taking with him his 15 per cent holding in the club's shares.

It was mentioned to me that he was considering disposing of these shares. I made contact with him in Cape Town to see if we

★ See footnote on p. 76.

could agree a price. It was at once clear that price was not really the issue at all. What he was concerned about was that 'his' shares, as he repeatedly called them, should not be sold on to Bryan Richardson. Quite what caused his ill-feeling towards Bryan I am not sure. Robins's attitude seemed a silly one for a grown man to take up. I did not and do not feel bad about the way the purchase was transacted. He took a different view when later contacted about it by the press. No one seemed to bother much. It was soon after this that Derek Higgs joined the Board, which represented a tremendous strengthening of the club in all respects. We all three recognized that a recapitalization of the club was required to put it on a firmer financial footing. Bryan and Derek conducted serious negotiations with several financial organizations but they came to nothing. However, one avenue of development turned out to be a real winner. This was the building of a new stadium.

It was well known that for years Coventry council had wanted to develop the ten-acre site at Highfield Road for housing. It was a cramped site for a football stadium and the traffic congestion on a Saturday was a continuous source of complaint. I was also aware of the disused gas works on a huge derelict site in north-east Coventry, in the heart of Bob Ainsworth's constituency, and for years had discussed with the council possible development, including a new football stadium. Of course I had nothing to do with the planning application while I was at the Treasury. The Council's team, driven along by John McGuigan, together with Bryan's vision and drive, have brought the city a dramatic development plan.

Some sixty acres of polluted and despoiled city landscape will be made over into a convention centre with hotel and sports facilities, a new football stadium doubling as an arena for staging major entertainment and commercial events, and a large retail investment by Tescos. It will be by far the single most important development in Coventry since the blitzed centre was rebuilt in the immediate post-war years. There was from the start everything going for it, including the enthusiastic support of the city council. The Department of the Environment decided not to call in the project, for which it granted outline planning permission in November 1998. Even here the Tories could not leave well alone. Gillian Shephard tried to circulate an Early Day Motion linking my position as Paymaster to the DETR decision and implying incorrect practice. It was a risible gesture and was refused by the Speaker's office.

The new football stadium with retractable roof and pitch will be the first of its kind in Britain and only the second in the world – the other being in Arnhem, home of Vitesse FC. Ireland are building their national stadium in Dublin on the same principle as Coventry's, as are the German football club Schalke 04. One of my golden rules in business is never to build the first of anything. I am comforted by the fact that Arnhem have pioneered the way. There are two compelling reasons for a retractable pitch: the grass has problems growing within the confines of a bowl-shaped stadium. These are compounded when the roof is closed. And in any case the pitch has to be removed to allow other events to be staged in the arena. At the new Millennium Stadium in Cardiff, which was completed only a couple of years ago, the pitch is removable but not retractable in one piece. It is made up of removable pallets, and moving it represents a substantial cost.

Under the Arnhem/Coventry system the whole pitch retracts – all 13,000 tonnes of it! It is supported by a concrete slab, beneath which are located concrete cubes finished with Teflon pads. There are no wheels involved. The pitch is pushed by four enormous hydraulic rams and slides along ceramic-coated steel rails. Moving the pitch the 120 metres required takes six hours at a speed of 20 metres per hour, which is virtually imperceptible to the human eye.

The Football Association advertised the new Coventry stadium as part of its marketing activity to bring the World Cup to England in 2006. For a variety of reasons England was unsuccessful in its bid. But Coventry City Football Club will be working in its new stadium from 2002 onwards for league and cup honours and a place in Europe. No visiting team, however distinguished, will be able to blame pitch conditions for their defeat. Nor can home or away fans blame lack of facilities for not turning up.

So what ultimately is the point of Coventry City Football Club? It represents, embodies and enhances its city. It is also playing good football — on which note I'll leave the last word to Lynne Truss, sportswriter on *The Times*: 'Coventry were gorgeous on Saturday, and that's a sentence I thought I would never write!' — her verdict in January 2000, a new start for Coventry in the new millennium.

12. Protecting the Heartlands

Six months into Government, we faced another crisis for which we were quite unprepared. The largest privatized coal company, R. J. Budge, announced a programme of pit closures in November 1997, and this potential disaster was being presented in the press as a virility test for Tony Blair and New Labour. It was as if we were being set up. Close down pits is New Labour; support for coal is old Labour. The *Independent on Sunday* of 23 November wrote, 'Labour prepare to spin away 5,000 miners' jobs'. The article took it as given that coal was finished. The DTI's role appeared to be confined to spinning its demise as part of a damage-limitation exercise.

At a personal level I felt deeply that mining communities had suffered gravely over the last two decades from the abrupt closures. The catastrophic consequences to whole areas dependent upon coal mining were obvious for all to see. A complex social and economic infrastructure had fallen apart overnight. The Major government's *coup de grâce*, following the savage bullfight between Thatcher and the miners in 1984–5, was to privatize the remaining industry by selling 90 per cent to one company, R. J. Budge Engineering. As an inducement to Richard Budge, the Tories gave this company a five-year contract for the supply of coal at a fixed high price to the power generators. The coal problem – high prices in a changing energy market – was neatly shelved till after the next election, when the contract would have to be renegotiated at much more commercial prices.

Labour's manifesto commitment was to have 'secure and diverse energy supplies'. However, we had no agreed policy as to what that commitment would constitute and we were now faced with pit closures. My reaction was that the least a Labour government could do was to have a programme for regeneration. There was nothing in place. And getting the money – the bare necessity for a renewal programme – would have been very difficult in this period of extreme financial stringency. We had accepted and were sticking with Tory spending plans which nobody thought the Tories themselves would be able to achieve.

On the policy issue we had done no research while in opposition. But what I heard from colleagues and from Tony Cooper, the general secretary of the Engineers' and Managers' Association, was that the 'pool' which secured electricity supply for the whole country did not operate a really competitive market and indeed was weighted against coal. Gas was being brought into the market under favoured conditions.

I took my concerns to Gordon. In his heart he agreed with me. He came from Fife, a coal-mining region that had gone through the trauma of closures without any real support to ease the social hardships involved. On the other hand, he disliked the idea of New Labour subsidizing a traditional extractive industry. I understood and shared this point of view. It was certain that Tony would feel the same. Gordon listened carefully to my reservations concerning the terms on which gas was being brought into the market and the lack of competition. I think he had heard much the same as I had about distortions in the market. What we needed was a breathing space to review the problem objectively, with the aim of achieving a coherent energy strategy based, if possible, on the manifesto commitment to diverse and secure energy suppliers. Anything would be better than blundering through a crisis that had no further point to it than closing at least half the remaining pits, and with the danger of more being closed as a result of a precipitate financial collapse.

The immediate problem was to gain the necessary time to take stock of the situation. The only way we could do this was to break the deadlock between Budge and the generators – as was entirely predictable, they could not agree on the price for the new supply contracts. I convened a meeting with Budge and the generators to see if we could thrash out a holding position for up to six months while we could evaluate energy policy and the role of coal, if any, in it. It was a gamble, but we had nothing to lose since there was no alternative available.

Gordon agreed I should take some soundings in the parliamentary party and with ministerial colleagues, and to see how we would gain time for the review.

The parliamentary Labour Party was still surprisingly sympathetic to the miners. The miners group itself was well informed about the pool arrangements. Amongst ministerial colleagues Margaret Beckett, who held direct responsibility for energy, was deeply unhappy with the policy. She said she would be 'delighted' for me to become involved. John Prescott, who would have a key role to play both on emissions and regional policy, was staunchly in support of a review before embarking on a major pit-closure programme. John nominated Richard Caborn as his link man; he was supportive throughout.

There was then much goodwill for the miners despite all the damage done by Arthur Scargill. It would not be going too far to say that there was a widespread distaste for what was about to happen to what remained of the mines and a belief that it was not in fact inescapable. The government had its first industrial crisis and was being bounced by anti-coal civil servants: that was the message from the parliamentary party. There was therefore good reason to try for a holding position, obtaining an interim agreement between Budge and the generators. I convened a meeting to this end at short notice between them in my office. From experience I knew it could rapidly erupt into a shouting match – the usual argy-bargy. I kept tight control to avoid that. The key figure to win over amongst the generators was Powergen's Ed Wallis. Wallis was the one driving the hardest bargain against Budge; and a large order for coal from him would buy us the time we needed. I asked Wallis if he and I could adjourn to our tearoom next door. Wallis got straight down to business. He recognized that the government was in an unacceptable position. If Budge would come down to a reasonable figure he would do a deal. We reached agreement quite quickly, almost exactly on the halfway line between the two sides.

Tony Blair used Prime Minister's Questions that week to announce the deal and the review. We had averted a potentially wretched situation. Some colleagues expressed admiration of my negotiating skills in securing the agreement. I got something of a fixer's reputation on account of it, about which I was not best pleased. Nor did it serve me well. In fact this was the easy bit. Getting the right policy from the review to be carried out by a Cabinet subcommittee would be much more difficult. It would be a rough ride.

If there was any doubt at all about the officials' position, it was dispelled at the pre-meeting to the first Cabinet subcommittee meeting. This took place in the Chancellor's office with the only people present being Gordon, myself and the influential head of the Cabinet Office's important economic secretariat, Robin Young.* The Cabinet Office spelled out in stark terms what we were up against. There had earlier been a meeting of officials of those departments represented on the Cabinet subcommittee, and every single official, we were assured by Robin Young, quite uniquely in his experience of Whitehall, held the same view. There had been an immediate and unanimous view: coal as an energy fuel was finished. It was just a question of how quickly it could be run down. Euthanasia with a not-altogether human face.

Although I expected this, I was still pretty taken aback. Perhaps we should just let officials have their way: present the rundown as best we could and stump up some money to cushion the social consequences? I imagine the same thoughts must have crossed Gordon's mind too. But I did not like giving in without testing the strength of the arguments in the case. So much agreement amongst officials seemed odd. I resisted the official arguments on grounds that they prejudged the review, which had to evaluate whether conditions for effective competition between fuels existed and, if not, what should be the policy on coal until a level playing field could be achieved. This was labelled a 'political decision'. The pre-meeting ended on this discordant note, just in time for us to get to the Cabinet Office for the first meeting at ministerial level of the subcommittee.

Although Gordon and I had no time to coordinate our positions

---

* Now permanent secretary at the Department of Heritage.

following the briefing from the Cabinet Office, the discussion at the ministerial meeting was going quite well until somehow the idea of the introduction of greater competition became equated with the inevitable demise of coal. And in the inchoate way in which policy sometimes develops at ministerial meetings, a fixed three-year period for its total rundown was being agreed on.

The situation was getting out of hand and the discussion was bad-tempered at times. I was desperate to close the meeting – and rather keen there should not be another one. We were attempting to make policy, but this was what the review had been set up to do. I suggested, therefore, that we ask officials to minute the meeting and draw up terms of reference for the review in the light of the discussion that had taken place. At my request Gordon mercifully closed the meeting and I felt great relief that at least we lived to fight another day.

The last thing I wanted was to see an official record of the discussion and in fact I do not recall seeing an agreed minute of that meeting, though there must be one somewhere. My immediate concerns were to avoid another meeting of the ministerial subcommittee and to repair the damage of the alleged breach in Treasury policy over coal.

This was being hyped around Whitehall. Cabinet Office sources were gleefully putting it around that Gordon had 'savaged' me. Peter Mandelson, who had turned up at the subcommittee meeting, mischievously asked me afterwards, 'What was that Treasury in-fighting all about?' It would be helpful if I could get on with the job without the frequent or formal involvement of the Cabinet Office.

It was a stroke of good fortune that Anna Walker was assigned to lead the review for the DTI, the responsible department. Anna was the daughter of Jack and Doris Butterworth, two good friends of mine from Coventry; Jack had done an absolutely outstanding job as vice-chancellor in building Warwick University from scratch into one of the best in the UK. Anna was a feisty woman with whom I knew we could do business. We were also lucky in the junior DTI official, who actually understood how the pool worked, which was of great value to us, since no one else seemed to – or, if they did, they did not want to tell us.

With the joint Treasury/DTI teams in place we proceeded to commission the consultants to provide professional assessments on the case for diversity; the UK coal reserves; the UK gas reserves; world gas reserves and their security of supply; and the system security of the UK's national energy supply given the preponderant dependence on gas. It was the usual consultants' field day. And I felt pretty sure that it would not tell us much we did not know already. I found out later that a similar exercise had been carried out at the time of the Heseltine review in 1993. As far as I could make out no one had taken any action on it then or looked at it since.

While this seemed likely to be the destiny of the expensive advice we had ourselves commissioned, there were three points on which it was essential that positive views should be formed if there was to be a justifiable future role for coal:

- That the criterion of diversity in energy supply should be endorsed;
- That UK coal supplies could be maintained at present levels without the requirement to sink new pits for the next decade;
- That the existing coal-fired power stations were also good for the same period, given routine service and maintenance.

As the review progressed it seemed that these three points could realistically be demonstrated. Why was it then that gas was enjoying such a boom? The question always came back to the role of the pool.

Any explanation of this arcane subject tends to get technical and boring. It was often suggested to me at meetings that I should not involve myself in the details. The problem was that the more I involved myself in the technical details of the pool,★ the more I learned and the more I disliked what I learned. Suffice to say that the pool operated by the National Grid had kept the lights on

---

★ There is an appendix setting out the role and pricing procedures of the pool at the end of the chapter.

during the privatization process, but did so by using an operating and pricing system that was not competitive and was weighted against coal. Gas was being brought on to the market with a guaranteed off-take and fixed high prices. The pool arrangements that were meant to be temporary had become permanent.

I felt irked at times that it had taken some relentless probing to get to the bottom of the problem. But the essential point was that, as the anti-competitive and anti-coal ramifications of the pool became evident, so their reformation became recognized by the review team as preconditions for a rational and balanced energy policy. That in turn inevitably meant a moratorium on further consents for gas-powered energy until the new arrangements were in place. It was the turning point in the whole review.

There were still formidable obstacles to be overcome. But as all seasoned observers of the Civil Service will have noticed, once a clear and definable position has been established and the will of the government unmistakably demonstrated, it can work with a quite ruthless efficiency to push a policy through.

The multinationals were our major problem. While the threatening letters arrived at the Treasury, most lobbying seemed to be taking place at No. 10. Perhaps they got a more sympathetic hearing there. We took advice on each case, using both Treasury counsel and the DTI lawyers. There were some tricky issues and on one difficult one our chances were not put at better than fifty-fifty. As with the windfall tax, though, I doubted that when push came to shove any of the companies would sue the government. But this was a risk we would have to take since there could be no exceptions. In the event none took legal action against us.

By the end of May 1998 the key elements of the review were in place and all the main problems resolved. The manifesto commitment to a balanced and diverse policy was vindicated and the need for a halt to the consents policy for more gas-fired plants followed from that. The UK's coal mines were adjudged to have up to ten years' life without major investment in sinking new mines; the existing power stations were good for another ten years plus, given routine service and maintenance; we could face, with an acceptable level of confidence, legal action from the multinationals; coal prices were expected to fall, with increased efficiency and competition. We expected to see a further reduction of 10 per cent, in addition to the already agreed 9 per cent, in electricity prices to the consumer; the regulator was prepared to go along with the policy subject to the shortest possible halt to the consents policy; the DETR judged we could meet our international obligations on emissions; two small pits could be rationalized, which would show that the pain was being spread around.

We had one last hurdle – reservations at No. 10, which came out right at the last moment and after a prolonged silence. These emerged when Margaret Beckett's draft statement embodying all the above points of the new energy policy was sent over at the beginning of June for approval. It was not a particularly elegant statement. Everyone working on it was tired. It had been a long and complicated haul. The statement was stodgy and rather defensive, and did not put across the real story we had to tell. The presentation was poor.

But the problems at No. 10 and the Cabinet Office were not about style or presentation, but about substance. What seemed to be disturbing No. 10 was the fact that several energy multinationals were still angry and unsettled, and that there were no closures to speak of in the mining industry. Moreover, Peter Riddell in *The Times* had just written an article renewing the attempt to make the coal issue a litmus test for New Labour, and this made Downing Street even more nervous. It was even suggested to me by one senior official at No. 10 that we might have to change policy because of the Riddell article. The upshot of the disquiet was that the Prime Minister asked the Cabinet Office for an objective review of the situation.

A document of some fifteen pages arrived very soon. On the whole it was a good piece of analysis, a cut above much of what else I had seen. Though it did not bring out the worst aspects of the pool's operations, it did not duck the issue that it was rigged against coal. Having said that, it was still rather difficult to understand why the Prime Minister should react enthusiastically to it as 'excellent'. I wondered if he had read it? He was chairing the EU heads of government meeting in Cardiff on 15–16 June and had plenty to do the following week at a G8 meeting in Birmingham. There was nothing at all new in the Cabinet Office paper, described further to its excellence as a 'good start'. We had been working on the policy for six months!

With the benefit of hindsight, I think we were at fault in not keeping No. 10 more fully in the picture. On the other hand, it is in the nature of the Civil Service machine that all too often it only reacts when a crisis occurs or when a statement has to go out. The main objective of the Cabinet Office rearguard action was that all existing proposals for new gas plants should be allowed to go ahead even if full consent had not been obtained. This would have taken us back to square one. Half the pits would have to close and how could you stabilize the industry in the situation of the financial collapse of a publicly quoted company? The DTI stood firm to the policy. There really was no practical alternative.

A redrafted, more upbeat and better presented statement with no change of substance was adjudged an acceptable outcome by No. 10. Margaret Beckett made the announcement on 25 June 1998. I had already moved on to other pressing problems, notably the looming reshuffle.

Appendix: the Pool

The pool had two principal roles to play:

- To decide which generators to call up to deliver power;
- To provide a mechanism by which prices were set for power supplied at different times during the day.

In a normal market the cheapest suppliers would get called up first. But that is not at all how the pool worked. On the contrary the priority for call-up to supply electricity was based on the following principles:

- Nuclear power was on baseload, i.e. was guaranteed to be run at full capacity. This applied to the French interconnector as well, even though we were not sure the electricity was produced by atomic energy;
- All new gas stations coming on stream were put on baseload – i.e. they enjoyed the same status as nuclear power: guaranteed 100 per cent offtake of the power they produced;
- Coal was treated as the marginal fuel – brought in at times of peak requirement.

These supply arrangements did not reflect any commercial reality based on market forces. They were established by the National Grid and reflected the old CEGB 'order of merit' whereby the newest were called up first and the oldest last – nuclear for obvious safety reasons being left to run continuously. In a wholly state-owned generating system such a policy made good sense. But there was no element of competition in it and when transposed to different companies under different ownership in the private sector it was bound to have the perverse effect of being anti-competitive. New gas plants had the huge advantage of pre-selling their entire output. Motor-car plants would rather like that arrangement.

What was worse was that gas was also assured prices that were immune to any related competitive pressures.

The pricing system had been established as follows: there would be a pool selling price (PSP) determined by the price bid on a half-hourly basis throughout the day by those generators wanting to meet the marginal supply requirements, which were by definition at those periods of peak demand not covered by the baseload operators. Given that nuclear and gas power suppliers were covered by a baseload guarantee, it was clear that they had no interest in bidding. They would bid zero or a very low figure to sustain the sham of competition while the price was set by at first two, then three, of the coal-fired generators. It was a no-win system from the competition point of view. When Powergen and National Power divested capacity and Eastern joined the price-setting club, the new entrant bid the highest prices. The point was that with new gas stations coming in on baseload they had a shrinking market share to bid for – not exactly the best market conditions in which to introduce more suppliers and expect them to behave competitively. Moreover, all coal-fired generators also had gas stations and gas stations, irrespective of the price they bid, received the full pool selling price as determined by the coal-fired stations. There was therefore a perverse incentive to keep prices high. There was one further twist to this perverse system, called 'capacity uplift'. This was an additional price paid to the coal-fired generators for keeping spare capacity available for emergency situations. For some incomprehensible reason it was paid to gas and nuclear suppliers as well, though they were on baseload and had no spare capacity anyway.

13. Labour and the Luvvies

Museums

The arts enjoyed much the same reputation at the Treasury as the film industry did with the Inland Revenue. There was a pretty negative response, therefore, when the Heritage Department brought to our attention the fact that the Tate was at an advanced stage of introducing admission charges: detailed drawings had been made for the installation of turnstiles which would be required for the administration of the new payment arrangements. If the Tate went ahead, three major national museums – the British Museum, the National Gallery and the National Portrait Gallery – would all follow suit.★ Gordon asked me to have a look to see if I could find a solution that would avoid charging for admission, which I sensed he was instinctively against – as I was.

It was a tricky problem, rather like the Vauxhall Motors one (see Chapter 15): how to find money without spending any. Fortunately, as I was again to find out after stubborn refusal to accept no for an answer, government accounting is a flexible as well as a complex procedure. But first I had to meet the Tate's chairman and directors to gauge the extent of their difficulties and just how likely it really was that in the absence of any support from the Treasury they would go ahead with charging. It became clear from my first meeting with the Tate that they were serious about the matter. They were not crying wolf; and if they went ahead the others would follow. That much was clear. But what struck me even more was how little money we were talking about – just two million pounds could make the difference – and what an

★ We later added to the list of major national galleries the fine Wallace Gallery, which opened its elegant courtyard extension in June 2000.

enterprising bunch for the most part the museum directors were. They had certainly not been given credit for that. They felt unloved and had some reason to do so. The problem lay not in the Thatcher decade but in the Major years. Under Thatcher, in fact, the museums had done rather well. Their funding had increased in real terms just slightly, but enough for them to keep their heads above water. Under Major, on the contrary, this support from the government had been reduced for some museums. They deserved better, since they were on the whole doing a good job.

As in most walks of life it was the people that mattered. Mention the Tate and you think of Nick Serota, now an internationally recognized figure in the world of museums. Many people may not like his taste in modern art – I do not appreciate all of it myself – but the glittering success he has made of the Tate cannot be gainsaid. Television made Lord Clark – of 'Civilization', as he came to be known – a national icon. Neil MacGregor's recent tour de force 'Seeing Salvation' (BBC 2) is likely to do the same for him. Neil has served as the director of the National Gallery since 1988; Philip Hughes is chairman of the trustees. Philip is a skilful colourist himself, working mainly in watercolours. The National Portrait Gallery has truly blossomed under Henry Keswick, its chairman, and Charles Saumarez Smith, its director. Henry is a great entrepreneur who has tapped rich sources of support to ensure that the remarkable expansion of the gallery goes hand in hand with the high level of scholarship maintained by Charles and his team of experts. The British Museum Great Court development is on a scale comparable with what the Louvre did nearly a decade ago; the new Tate Modern has proved to be the greatest success of the millennium year in London.

It is probably fair to say that the British Museum has further to go than the others in making the change to an outward-looking entrepreneurial culture. The monastic roots of pure scholasticism run deep in Great Russell Street.

Lord Armstrong, the chairman of the Victoria and Albert Museum, came to see me at the Treasury during this consultation period on the museums with one purpose in mind: to make sure that the British Museum received no additional support. He emphasized that it was only with the greatest reluctance that the V&A had embarked on entrance fees. He and his board would regard it as 'monstrous unfairness' if the Treasury were to lend a helping hand to others, particularly the British Museum, who out of pusillanimity had avoided this harsh decision. I made no comment on that since I already had the glimmer of a solution and since anyway I was more interested in talking to him about the Thatcher years, which he brought up. He had been Cabinet Secretary to Mrs Thatcher from 1979 to 1987. He reminisced on a number of topics but kept coming back to the terrible loss of output and increased unemployment in the first Thatcher government. It was obviously not his happiest period in the Civil Service. It was no intention of ours to go down that route, nor, I assured him, was there any need to do so. In this way I steered clear of the British Museum, about which it was clear the V&A had got a bee in its bonnet.

The Treasury eventually twigged that I was not keen on entrance charges and that I would not let the matter rest until I had a solution. But as usual it was necessary first to go through the motions of evaluating the pros and cons of charges. As always the Treasury view was straightforward enough. We had no money; the choice was between health and education on the one hand and museums on the other. Let ministers choose. Moreover the museums were elitist and stick-in-the-mud. They, like everyone else, needed a culture change. There was truth in the Treasury position on priorities, though it also played the same old refrain. In this instance it was reinforced by the reminder: why should the British tax payer subsidize rich tourists from countries where museum entrance is usually anything but free?

My problem was that we had no reliable figures as to what impact charging might have on attendance. The numbers put forward by the pro-museum lobby could not for the most part be accepted at face value. Most museums had until then only vague guesstimates as to the number of visitors. These were calculations assessed from video-camera recordings surveying the entrance area from a security point of view. At the V&A visitors had dropped steeply after the introduction of charging. But was that not just a temporary reaction? There was really no hard evidence to speak of, one way or the other. Common sense said that charging was bound to affect the less well-off and that if we were serious about improving access we should surely be moving in exactly the opposite direction. I fell back on my own background and instincts – the Chancellor's too, I think.

At the fourth time of asking the Treasury came up with a solution. I do not think they had been holding back. The solution came from Wilf White in the Treasury. The wheeze, as he gleefully called it – being on my side – was to change the accounting rules of the acceptance-in-lieu (AIL) scheme. The AIL arrangement allows the government to accept property of outstanding importance, including 'chattels, land and buildings' in satisfaction of inheritance tax. It was a sensible way to allow a wide variety of assets of the highest quality to pass from private ownership to public institutions all over the UK. As it had operated in the past the Inland Revenue was reimbursed from Heritage's (subsequently Culture, Media and Sport, DCMS) budget for the amount of tax satisfied under the AIL scheme. All we did in the July 1998 budget was to announce that the reimbursement arrangement would cease. This released £2 million extra for the budget of the DCMS, which itself promptly found, as usual, an extra £2 million which no one knew they had. The Heritage lottery fund agreed to complete the package from its new museums and access fund. These separate additional contributions were important, since in helping the four major galleries to retain free entry, we could also extend the package to make it a genuinely national one, giving help to other museums throughout the country, with the emphasis on widening access and providing educational initiatives to people of all backgrounds.

The £2 million we released simply by changing an accounting procedure amounted to 0.0005 per cent of government expenditure. It was tiny, but unlocked the situation. The £2 million did us more good with the luvvy community than anything else I can think of in our first three years. Its value for money in terms of the goodwill it created exceeded all our expectations. The success here made me very keen to help when the Tate brought me the problem of funding Tate Modern at Bankside.

The Strange Tale of the Serbs, the Turners and Tate Modern

I doubt that Sir Henry Tate, when he bequeathed his collection of nineteenth-century paintings to the nation and funded the building of the new gallery at Millbank, could have imagined the brilliant success it was to become. The Tate has in recent years opened new galleries in Liverpool and St Ives which have attracted visitors from all over the country. But one project had hitherto eluded it: the distinction of a major gallery dedicated to modern art. In the mid-thirties there was the possibility that Peggy Guggenheim might fund a gallery of modern art in London. But official indifference and the advent of war defeated that idea. A lack of official enthusiasm did not help Sir Herbert Read's attempt to revive the concept in the 1960s. During this time the Tate's collection was growing and is widely regarded as one of the three or four most important twentieth-century collections in the world.

The case for a gallery dedicated to twentieth-century art was stronger than ever. The number of pieces owned by the gallery rose from 1.1 million in 1959 to 2.3 million in 1996.

It was the advent of millennium funding that made Tate Modern at Bankside a reality. The Millennium Commission granted £50 million and English Partnerships provided £12 million to acquire the site of the former power station and pay for the removal of the huge turbines. Other funds were raised from charities and individuals. But in early 1998 there was still an awkward funding gap of £20 plus million. Dennis Stevenson, the chairman of the Tate trustees, put to me the proposition that the Treasury could release the insurance money that had been paid out for two Turner paintings stolen in 1994: *Light and Colour – Morning after the Deluge* and *Shade and Darkness – Evening of the Deluge.*

For the moment the Tate had neither the paintings nor the insurance money. There did not seem much chance of the paintings turning up and there could be an indeterminate wait for the money. And money was needed for the Bankside building.

The paintings had been stolen on the night of 28 July 1994 from the Schirn Kunsthalle in Frankfurt, where they were on loan from the Tate, by a group of particularly nasty Serbs. The German police had infiltrated the gang but then loused up on the recovery operation. After a short delay the Lloyd's syndicates coughed up and the money found its way to the Treasury, where it had quietly accumulated interest. The total was approaching £30 million in early 1997.

I was instinctively sympathetic to Dennis's approach. The money was serving no purpose at the Treasury. But there was no way the Treasury could release the funds, since in the event of the Turners being recovered the Tate would have to return the money, plus the accrued interest to the Lloyd's syndicates that had paid out under the insurance policy. This would be a direct call on Treasury funds.

A way had to be found to get round the problems if some money was to be released for the urgent requirements of Bankside. A different approach occurred to me. I was sure that the lead insurer and the syndicates would have written the money off. Moreover, after three years they probably had little hope of getting their money back and might well be amenable to a proposition that the Tate 'bought out' the rights to repayment that the syndicates still held under the terms of the policy. The alternative from their point of view could be an interminable wait with no guarantee of any payment at all. The alternative for the Tate was not much better. So long as the liability of repayment existed it could not get its hand on the money. For both parties, it seemed to me, a bird in the hand would be better than two in the bush. There would be a fight over who got the bigger bird – the usual haggling. It was worth trying to see if something could be worked out.

The Tate was led by an outstanding team of can-do people in Dennis, Nick Serota and Alex Beard, the finance director. The idea was pooh-poohed by the Treasury – even my private office were sceptical – but the Tate took up the running with resolve. I paved the way by speaking to Robert Hiscox, whose company were the lead underwriters with some 34 per cent of the total insured. He was very much on side from the start. By good fortune he was a member of the Museums and Galleries Commission. An urbane and cultured man himself, he warned us that we might not receive an altogether sympathetic hearing from the other underwriters to whom he had syndicated the debt.

Nick Serota followed up my call on 19 April 1998 when he explained to Robert Hiscox in more detail how the buyout might work. Robert explained that he would have to check out the likelihood of recovery before trying for a deal. He had had intermittent contact with the thieves about the terms on which the paintings could be returned, but he was unsure of the present situation. In these conversations with the Serbian gang he had variously posed as the chairman of the Tate or of Lloyd's. Nothing had emerged. I was not sure whether he would find it necessary to take up direct contact with the gang again. And I thought it better that the government should not be known to be involved.

The upshot of Robert Hiscox's inquiries was that the prospect of recovery was sufficiently remote for him to put a proposition to the other insurers. The proposal was the most basic of all deals: a fifty-fifty split. The Tate would scoop £12 million, plus the accrued interest. The syndicates would recover £12 million of their total payment of £24 million. It was not a bad deal for the Tate. But I felt we could do better. I told Nick Serota so when he put the proposal terms to me. We agreed to set up a meeting with the syndicates at the Treasury to see how the terms might be improved.

The meeting took place on 3 June 1998. The Paymaster General's room had seen many noisy battles over the past year, but nothing could quite equal the screaming match produced by this bunch of underwriters. Robert Hiscox and the representative of Nordstern – who by coincidence were the insurers to my own very modest collection – looked on in acute embarrassment as the motley crew fought with me and amongst themselves about what concessions could be made. It occurred to me that there really was more honour amongst thieves, perhaps even the Serbians.

We succeeded in splitting the payments into three stages of £4

million each. The first would be made on 29 July 1998, appropri-
ately the fifth anniversary of the theft, with a further payment on
1 January 1999 and a final payment, if the paintings were still not
found, on 28 July 1999. The first two payments were to be made
whether the Turners were found or not. If they were found before
the final payment was due, the amount paid would depend on the
condition of the paintings when returned. The paintings were not
returned in the agreed timescale, but the final payment was, in the
event, not made.

It was a good deal for the Tate. It would have access to £18
million straight away – and a further £4 million in July 1999. A
£22 million bonanza in all. A difficult funding headache had been
resolved. Dennis Stevenson, whose ten-year stint* as chairman of
the Tate had witnessed a tremendous expansion of the gallery's
popularity and experience, was kind enough to write to me in the
following terms:

I am writing formally to let you know how very, very appreciative I am
personally – and I know all the Trustees of the Tate together with
Nicholas Serota and Alex Beard – are at the key role you have played in
securing a favourable outcome in the matter of the Turners.

It embarrasses me to write that I should have seen the solution that
you saw a long time before! The fact is that amidst a very busy life –
within which the Tate, let's face it, is a very small dot on the PMG radar
screen – you saw a very ingenious way of securing a substantial benefit
for the public good.

Tate Modern opened on time and with a party such as only the
Tate knows how to throw. In its first two months more than 1
million people have visited. Not everyone liked the contents; but
I have hardly heard a bad word about the building.

Postscript. Since the deal went through there have been new twists
to the story. The Serbs, it seems, are desperate to offload at any

---

* Now Lord Stevenson; chairman of the Tate Gallery Trustees 1988–98.

price. They have sent Robert Hiscox a photograph of the paintings with a recent newspaper displaying its date to show they are still available. The Tate has passed a small amount of money to a German intermediary, who has come back for more. Time probably to call in Control Risks.

'We are All Film Buffs Now'

Labour's relationship with the arts world has always been a fractious love affair. New Labour has proved no exception. In some cases there seems to have been a personality clash involved, which is hardly surprising, given the sensitivities of the parties involved and their exposure to public opinion. For the world of arts, government support is emotionally vital. The Luvvies tend to be old Labour, and are generally speaking rather proud of it, as successful people can afford to be. Many successful businessmen become more hard-headed with success and less tolerant of the normal human requirements of others but creative-arts people – I only speak from my own experience – tend to mellow more with success and to indulge their fellow human beings. They wear their heart on their sleeve, too.

Someone who moved easily from Old to New Labour, but still retained the old ideals, was Dickie Attenborough. We knew what to expect when he came through the door soon after the election. The background to the meeting was as follows: Wilf Stevenson, the director of the British Film Institute, sensed there might be a chance, with the change of government, of encouraging an increased level of film production in the UK. I liked the idea and set up a meeting with the Inland Revenue. It was not a great success. All organizations have their *bête noire*. The Inland Revenue's was the film industry, and more particularly film stars, whose peripatetic work and huge remuneration make them attractive targets for their national tax administrations. Ingmar Bergman had terrible problems in Sweden. More recently, Laetitia Casta, the young French actress, has been castigated on French television for her domiciliary arrangements in England. We soon reached the expected impasse with the IR and I was reluctant to overcome it by issuing a ministerial diktat.

Wilf Stevenson had a better idea. Why not invite Sir Richard Attenborough to meet the Inland Revenue in person. For his film *Grey Owl*, Dickie apparently halted the flow of Niagara Falls for one scene, and in order to fit the requirements of the film's running time he accelerated the breeding cycle of a colony of beavers (which did not find favour with Dickie's brother, the distinguished naturalist Sir David Attenborough).

In full flow, Sir Richard is a difficult man to resist. He willingly agreed to the meeting. My office filled in anticipation of the great star's appearance. Inland Revenue staff, my private office and some advisers all crowded in. (It was rather like the excitement of the meetings with Sir Donald Gosling on the new royal yacht, especially when he spoke about who would go on the sea-proving trials!)

The Inland Revenue came in beaming sweetness and light. We were all film buffs now. I was enchanted by the change of tone and, much encouraged, inquired of our IR colleagues which films they had seen recently. There was a shuffling of feet and a clearing of throats. One official ventured that he liked the Ealing Studio productions starring Alec Guinness, notably *The Lavender Hill Mob* and *Kind Hearts and Coronets*. I tried to bring us somewhat more up to date and asked if anyone had seen any of Dickie's films. Yes indeed: a re-run of *Gandhi* on television (made in 1980–81).

As the mood changed, and after Dickie's departure, we got down to business. I offered the IR the choice. They could accept the repeal of paragraph 68 of the Capital Allowances Act of 1989 in its entirety – this is what the film industry wanted, as it would have left the tax treatment outwith the statutory framework – or they could accept a further amendment to paragraph 42 of the Finance Act 1992, which provided for accelerated depreciation for UK qualifying films. They sensibly chose the latter option, so that 100 per cent write-off was announced in the July budget of 1997 and incorporated in the Finance Act of that year. It was a major breakthrough.

The latest figures suggest that the measure has been a huge success. This year up to £50 million new money will have flowed into filming, mainly into independent productions. It is so successful that apparently the IR think it should be stopped. Sir Richard is standing by in the wings.

14. The ISA Man Cometh

I suppose it was my own fault that I got lumbered with designing and launching the Individual Savings Accounts. The taxation reforms we had prepared were going through so smoothly that I had quite a lot of time on my hands and I let it be known. Gordon hates underemployment and I got my just deserts when he asked me to devise the new personal savings scheme.

Our commitment to replacing PEPs and TESSAs was set out in the manifesto simply enough: 'We will introduce a new individual savings account.'

It was that dangerous animal: an unthought-out single-line commitment. I should have known better. No work had been done on it in opposition. Nor was it an area in which I had any personal expertise. I had neither a PEP nor a TESSA. My own 'savings' had been channelled into investments in property for our family use and into the manufacturing company I had built up as a family business.

It was this combination of no preparation in opposition and no direct personal experience, together with a surprising failure to follow my own instincts, that got us into a messy situation on policy and landed me in an embarrassing personal predicament.

Our opening position was not helped by the fact that neither the Treasury nor the Inland Revenue had done much work on what the new scheme might be. That was not surprising since there were no speeches or papers from our time in opposition that could have given guidance.

As far as officials were concerned, a principal aim of the new legislation was to cut back on the cost to the Exchequer of the present PEP and TESSA arrangements. We were informed that the tax 'lost' via the two schemes would rise to £2 billion within two years, and that, if unchecked, it would go still higher. We were even told by an Inland Revenue official that it was an 'open secret' that the Tories were planning to cut back on the level of tax breaks for savers. Remarkably, I think this was the only occasion on which I was told anything about the previous government's thinking.

It will already be clear that I consider we were well served by the Inland Revenue. It is in many ways a surprisingly swish outfit. The team put together for the new savings package was technically competent, but it suffered from a certain otherworldliness. I explained in one of the early meetings that we were seeking to expand the savings habit to the 50 per cent of the population that had no savings at all, to which one official remarked, 'Oh! To the hoi polloi, you mean.' At this my private secretary was overcome by a fit of the giggles and had to leave the room. The remark was not said in a snobbish or condescending way; it just reflected too many years cut off from the real world.

Certainly the two savings schemes, PEPs and TESSAs, had been very successful. There were estimated to be some six or seven million people with TESSAs and three million with PEPs. This was a large constituency and it would be difficult to push through measures to curb their growth without there being some losers. The sums involved were very large. TESSAs were straightforward savings accounts. The amount of money invested in them rose from £5 billion in March 1991 to over £30 billion in March 1999, a sixfold increase. The sums involved in PEPs were much larger: PEP investments rose from £2.6 billion in April 1990 to £92.5 in April 1999. They were already estimated at over £85 billion in 1997/98, when we were drafting the legislation.

Both were remarkable marketing successes for the City. It seemed that the tax-free tag prominently displayed on the promotional material, rather like duty free at airports, incited savers and spenders alike. Anything to beat the taxman. The success of the TESSAs was particularly surprising, since the actual tax saving was very small. And there was the considerable disadvantage for the smaller saver that the money in TESSAs was blocked for five years.

PEPs were understandably even more popular. Both dividend

income and capital gains made from a PEP investment were tax free. PEPs were often used as a quick route to the deposit on a mortgage, as I was indirectly reminded by ministers and political advisers who had interests at stake. In fact, I recalled that Peter Mandelson had used his own PEP when putting together the financing plan for his house. We were on sensitive territory.

Some investors had shown great financial acumen or had been unbelievably lucky. We knew of one PEP worth over £1 million and many in the hundreds of thousands range. The scheme had barely been running ten years so that these sums had been generated from an investment of no more than £50,000.

Nevertheless, the difficult questions had to be asked: were the two schemes generating additional savings? Or were they just dead weight: i.e. would the money have been saved anyway and were the tax breaks therefore not necessary? Nigel Lawson himself seemed to take a negative view on the incremental level of savings generated by the schemes. As far as PEPs were concerned, his view was that their main purpose was to encourage share ownership, not to increase savings.

The Treasury and Inland Revenue view was that the tax concessions were being given to no good effect; they were dead weight. Moreover, in the official view they were benefiting a narrow section of society – those in the higher income brackets, social groups A and B. This latter proved to be incorrect. In fact PEPs were more widely held among the lower income groups than was realized. When, belatedly, we had the research done it showed that over 30 per cent of PEP holders were found in social groups C and D; and that in addition they were very popular with working women – who were often single mothers too – as the basis for house purchase. Had we had this information at the start I do not believe we would have made the error of imposing the £50,000 cap on the amount which could be transferred from PEP schemes to ISAs. It proved a bad mistake from which we recovered with great difficulty.

However, while it was true that PEPs and TESSAs were more widely held than had been thought, it was also the case that more than half of the population did not save at all. It was fundamental to the ISA concept that it should be designed to spread the saving habit more widely.

The other basic principle to the reform was that the tax 'loss' should be contained at the present level, some £1.2 billion. This was a much lower figure than the £2 billion figure we would face within a couple of years if the schemes were left unchecked.

To achieve these twin objectives of spreading the saving habit and limiting the cost, the PEPs and TESSAs would have to be changed in a number of key respects.

As far as TESSAs were concerned, any proposals were aimed at an extension of the benefits. There should be immediate access to withdraw funds and there should be no minimum initial subscription. In addition, the marketing arrangements should be much more extensive – they should include supermarkets and other frequent points of contact for the non-savers we were reaching out to. That was all positive. On the negative side the annual limit I was proposing of £1,000 was considerably below the TESSA allowance of £9,000 over five years. But it was not difficult to justify the lower limit, which was comfortably in excess of what our target participants – the non-savers – were likely to be able to afford.

If we were to have more savers, then the amount per saver would have to be reduced in order to contain the costs. Moreover, even the most ardent advocates of the TESSA could hardly claim that the savings under the then arrangements were other than dead weight in the Treasury jargon. We judged that the new proposals – with no minimum level, the right to withdraw the funds at any time and accessibility at point of sale – should encourage new savers. Indeed the Inland Revenue calculated – I am still not sure how – that there should be some four million new savers under our ISA proposals. The Prime Minister emphatically made this claim at Question Time and so temporarily shut up the opposition, who were trying to mount a campaign on this issue.

Personally I do not like targets of this kind – for waiting lists, school class sizes or bringing criminals to justice. They become political footballs in a game of statistical definitions. But at least on the new ISAs I was confident we would meet our target, albeit for the wrong reasons. My own office in the Treasury – hardly our target audience – informed me they would be changing their current account to an ISA. It gave all the advantages of a normal account and allowed interest accruing to be free of tax. It was a 'no-brainer', really. The latest information I have is that there are some six million ISA savings accounts.

PEPs were altogether more tricky. They were by far the bigger fund. The cost to the Exchequer was nearly three quarters of the total package and, as we have seen, it was rising fast. Ministers and officials were rightly agreed that the increasing cost to the Exchequer had to be halted. A lower limit was inevitable and an easy point of agreement for the new package under the ISA umbrella.

The most thorny problem arose over what the transitional arrangements should be, from the old PEPs to the new ISA regime. In particular, at what level should the tax-relieved old PEPs scheme be brought over into the new ISA?

There were hawks and doves on the issue. The Treasury, as one would expect, were hawkish, recommending at one point that the cap should be as low as £10,000! This sat ill with the subsequent press briefing from the very top of the Treasury that I had not listened to the official advice, which was for a much higher level! Chris Wales was also in favour of a low cap. No one considered that there should be no cap at all. At £50,000, the mid-range figure for the losers, that is to say the number of people who had PEPs worth more than the £50,000 cap, was estimated at about 750,000. Under the new arrangements their savings over that level would no longer enjoy a tax break, since all dividends and capital gains made on PEP investments in excess of £50,000 would be taxed.

I have to confess that during the discussions on the transfer limit of PEPs I kept my feelings pretty much to myself. I was in an invidious position, since I owned neither PEPs nor TESSAs. There was also the issue of the family trust, which I will deal with fully in due course.

But my instincts told me that in tax reforms you should not take away from people a benefit they enjoyed – and one which was evidently an important part of their financial planning for their security and independence – except in circumstances where countervailing opportunities were being offered. We were offering no adequate alternative to 750,000 people who would feel they were being 'cheated'. In this sense the relief on savings was perceived differently from income tax, which everyone knew would be varied according to economic and indeed social priorities.

The public finances in 1997 could not allow us to be more generous on other relief. One route we could have taken would have been to leave existing PEPs as they were and cut back on future PEPs sufficiently to contain the cost of tax relief, as we had to do. We did not really consider this course. If we had pursued it no doubt we would also have ended up in an unholy row, as we did by setting the cap at £50,000.

The orthodox Treasury defence of the cap was that all the PEP literature made it clear that the scheme was subject to any changes introduced by government into legislation and in that sense the tax-exempt status was not guaranteed indefinitely. Indeed it was true that in the marketing literature which I asked to see a clear warning to this effect was given. But it was in the small print – very small print. It was not exactly a selling point and the City hucksters could hardly have been expected to draw much attention to it. The tax-exempt status by contrast was in large bold type.

The political reality was that people would feel that they were being penalized unfairly and that we would be taking on a vociferous and powerful lobby. That, unfortunately, did not put me off. In fact, anyone who works at the Treasury can rapidly develop a mindset that the louder the outcry, the more likely it is that the policy is right. Perhaps, I wondered, I was falling into this trap myself. In the event, and despite my misgivings, I settled for the cap, comforting myself that it was only one element in an otherwise good package and that the proposals were to be issued as a consultation document.

This was naive of me. I was soon to learn that any change to a consultation document is hyped in the press and Parliament as a

U-turn. Any change, therefore, is bitterly resisted by officials and politicians alike.

They are not meant as consultation documents at all. This is a pity, especially where complex issues are involved and where government has anything but a monopoly of wisdom or knowledge of the subject. Fortunately I took a relaxed view on changes to our proposals, which was just as well given the force-five hurricane we were sailing into.

The launch of the consultation document was scheduled for Monday, 1 December. The timing could not have been worse. On Sunday, 30 November 1997, the *Independent on Sunday* broke the story of the Robinson family trust, which stemmed from Joska Bourgeois' bequest and was based in Guernsey. I deal with this issue in Chapter 16, the chapter chronicling the events that led to my resignation. But since the charge of hypocrisy was and probably still is levelled at me, and since people no doubt still wonder why on earth I was in charge of working up the plans for the ISAs, I would like to put at least the following points on the record at this stage:

- The assets in the trust fund were never in the UK. They were not transferred out of the UK. They were a bequest to me and my family.
- The existence and nature of the trust were known to my colleagues in the Treasury, to the Treasury Permanent Secretary and to the Inland Revenue. No one at any time suggested I should not handle the ISA.
- Concurrently with dealing with the ISA I was working with officials on measures to limit the benefits of off-shore trusts.

All this is dealt with more fully later in this book. There may be legitimate questions as to whether my involvement was appropriate. The fact is I was asked to do it. Perhaps I should have refused. In all honesty it never occurred to me that I should not be involved – until the *Independent on Sunday* article appeared, the day before the launch was due to take place.

Under no circumstances did I want my involvement to prejudice the launch of the ISA. I therefore contacted Gordon and my senior official at the Inland Revenue first thing Monday morning. I explained that I was fully prepared to go ahead with the launch but considered that in the interests of getting the new scheme off to an uncontroversial start, it would be better for another minister to do the public launch. Neither was having any of it.

On reflection, from the government's point of view they were probably right. If I pulled out, the government would be seen to be running scared; my ducking the confrontation would create as many problems as it would solve. But from my own point of view, it promised nothing but further criticism from the press. Indeed press attacks became directly personal from this point on.

Resigned to my baptism of political fire I made my way warily to the QE II building in Westminster later in the day. My minders for the occasion took me on such a circuitous route through labyrinthine corridors on different levels of the building that to this day I cannot remember where the launch took place. But I do remember an awful sinking feeling as I read out the final phrase of the ministerial statement, 'for the many not the few'. I felt like dropping dead.

In the event the press conference itself passed without hostile questioning. But the next day the press went to town in a big way. However, despite the sustained press campaign the consultation on the document proceeded very constructively. I would occasionally allude to my current local difficulties which seemed to ease the tension, even if the laughter was nervous.

All the parties realized they would have to deal with me. The business was conducted in an expeditious manner and we introduced numerous changes to improve the package. There was, however, the one exception: the £50,000 limit on PEPs. On this there was no meeting of minds. I would have to make up my own. In doing so I was greatly influenced by many of the letters I received from individuals and families. I say many, not all, because some were just hate mail which I ignored, together with the worst of the press reporting. One letter from a gentleman in middle England summed up the situation for me. It read as follows:

I have studied the proposals which you are making, and under which you proposed to introduce ISAs. It seems to me that in most respects these are positive developments but in the lifetime limit of £50,000, I consider that you are introducing a major negative element into the savings regime.

My wife and I, and now our children, have been encouraged by PEPs to make prudent long-term provision: for many people these have also been associated with mortgages, and taken as alternatives to pension contributions. To limit PEPs now to £50,000, and here I should declare that my wife and I both hold in excess of this amount, is a penalizing act against us as prudent savers: it is a form of retrospective taxation. If you tax retrospectively, which is what the change would amount to, then you cause uncertainty for the future saver as he will never know where he stands.

I would ask you to reconsider the imposition of any overall limit: most importantly, to allow amounts already subscribed to remain within the system.

To that gentleman and to many other people who I fear did not receive a reply to their letters, may I take this opportunity of offering my belated apologies, if that is the case.

Part of the necessary Treasury function is to be hard-hearted even to the most deserving cases. I am not by nature terribly hard-hearted. And anyway I had come to the conclusion that on this one we had got it wrong.

As usual, it was Steve Robson who came to my aid. He had been discussing our proposals with various important PEP providers. It was clear that it would be impossible for the major financial institutions to adapt their computer systems to implementing and controlling the PEP transfer arrangements we had proposed. In simple terms, while it would be possible to exclude those PEPs that were currently worth more than £50,000, it would not be possible to exclude those that over the next few years would become worth more than £50,000. I did not press too heavily on the point, fearing I would find a way round it. It was too useful. We had a practical argument that killed the policy debate stone dead. Unless we were prepared to delay the ISA for a few years while new complex software systems were developed, there was no way our proposals in the consultation document could be made to work. It was precisely the sort of point that professional research work in opposition would have thrown up. It would have saved an awful lot of heartache and aggravation.

We were some two months into the three-month period set aside for consultation. It was gently suggested to me that our policy objectives at this stage could be met by continuing the PEPs and TESSAs with appropriate modifications. However, that would really have been a U-turn too many, even for my flexible turn of mind!

Moreover the ISA objective of spreading the savings habit and balancing the tax savings more widely required a new initiative.

I wrote up my own paper at the conclusion of the consultation period and circulated it to colleagues and officials. There was no response until, typically, a few days before the announcement of our post-consultation decision was due. Then in a flurry of last-minute activity further concessions were wrung from a battered Treasury and a compliant Inland Revenue.

The industry had timed its last push well. We badly needed their public support to restore credibility to the ISA.

The political advisers at No. 10 had also been thoroughly worked over. We were all anxious to get the new ISA off to a good start and we accommodated the life-insurance companies despite the considerable extra complexity this involved. We also set the first-year savings limit at £3,000, whereas previously we had proposed £1,000.

The ISA is now in its third year. The sometimes wimpish complaining has stopped. There are six million savings accounts and the sums in cash and equity ISAs now stand at £200 billion.

There seems sometimes no end to the goodwill – at least in the short term – that a few key concessions can be counted on to generate. In his budget in March 2000 the Chancellor extended the £3,000 limit for another year. I am completely in favour. No one is whining now. So why should I ask the Chancellor what the projected cost of the tax relief on the ISA will be; or how many of the six million savings accounts are accounts opened by those who were previously non-savers? Or even how much dead weight he thinks there is about the place? Sufficient to the day the labour thereof.

15. Wings and Wheels

Rolls-Royce

I have had a soft spot for Rolls-Royce ever since it crash-landed into my life in the late sixties. At that time I was working as a senior executive at the Industrial Reorganization Corporation (IRC). The IRC is generally judged to have been one of the successes of the Wilson government. Its principal role was to promote consolidation and rationalization in British industry with a view to achieving greater competitiveness. It also came to play a role as a trouble-shooter for the DTI in difficult industrial situations, as in the case of Rolls-Royce.

We got an early intimation of impending problems in 1968 via Lord Kearton, the then chairman of Courtaulds who was also chairman of the IRC. Rolls-Royce was developing the RB211 engine on the basis of revolutionary carbon-fire technology for the fan blades of the jet engine. The technology had gone wrong and all outstanding orders on Courtaulds for carbon fibre were abruptly cancelled. There would be huge cost overruns on the fixed-price contract with Lockheed and the money was running out.

The IRC was asked to look at the Rolls-Royce situation and to advise. There was much to criticize about the company: the lack of financial controls, not taking due account of the mounting cost of research and development and indeed the acceptance of a fixed-price contract in the first place. The criticisms were duly made. But in the end the executive report recommended financial support on grounds of the national interest. It was accepted by the government.

The outcome particularly pleased me since, with all its faults, Rolls-Royce was the premier British engineering company exploiting a British invention and competing with high technology in a very harsh world market place.

The IRC report was only intended as a holding operation until a longer-term basis for financial support was worked out. The incoming Tory government of Ted Heath in its initial macho phase refused to help further. Rolls-Royce went spectacularly bust. From that point I followed, with admiration tinged by constant apprehension, the company's progress from receivership into public ownership and thence into privatization and in more recent years in and out of bed with the US giant GE. There are few certainties in the aerospace jet-engine business.

Against this personal experience, as Paymaster General I faced with trepidation the request of Rolls-Royce in June 1997 for launch aid for the 100,000 lb plus engine. The official Treasury view was that the company did not need the money and that the request should be refused. It appeared a reassuring recommendation. Certainly Rolls's own financial forecasts did not show any need for the money.

At the first meeting with the company I explained to them that financial need was one of the criteria for launch aid and this was clearly not met. I also put it to them that their forecasting relied on a level of cost reductions which was much greater than they had achieved in the past. In effect they were impaling themselves on a hook of achieving hitherto unparalleled levels of performance, which in turn made any further government assistance unnecessary.

In my guts I felt that they would need launch aid and that we should find a way round the perfectly correct Treasury position that the need for assistance had not been demonstrated.

My proposal, therefore, was that we should have an accountant's investigation of the company's forecasts with a view to assessing how realistic they were. In the light of the report's findings we should be able to take a view on the company's eligibility for launch aid. Coming from where I did, I was also determined to avoid any nasty surprises.

The reaction of the company was one of some dismay – an accountant's review is the last thing any management wants when it is engaged in handling short-term problems and achieving long-term goals. It makes it worse when the company has to pay for it, as I insisted would be the case here. I went out of my way therefore to assure John Rose, the Rolls-Royce managing director, that the Treasury was prepared to help if a case was made, and that we would want a short, sharp report dealing with the main issues, particularly with the cost savings that were at the heart of their corporate plan.

We agreed that Touche Ross, Rolls-Royce's auditors, would do the review. It was led by John Rocques, the senior partner. He knew the company well and we could rely on the auditors to be quick and realistic.

The review was completed within the two months. The report was a model of conciseness and relevance. It confirmed that Rolls-Royce had to date made considerable progress in cost reduction. But it warned that the projected level of cost savings was very ambitious and noted that the company was currently achieving approximately 50 per cent of its target. The central conclusion was that the 50 per cent level of attainment would be a prudent basis for future financial calculations.

We reconvened our meeting with Rolls-Royce to discuss the Touche Ross review and I stressed to the management that there was no reason for them to accept the report's findings. It was their job to prove them wrong. For me, it confirmed my own thinking and provided the opening I had been looking for. The Treasury official who reviewed the report accepted the realism of its findings, and in doing so he accepted the case for launch aid. We agreed with colleagues in the DTI, who were naturally very pleased with the outcome, that terms for launch aid of up to £175 million should be negotiated with Rolls-Royce.

This gave me pleasure on several fronts. Rolls-Royce needed support and we gave it. They were competing in one of the toughest markets in the world against the US giants GE and Pratt and Witney. Many had felt that Rolls had behaved arrogantly when they unilaterally broke their partnership with GE in 1986. This partnership placed, in effect, a much too restrictive agreement on Rolls, preventing them from developing the engines in the 50,000 lb plus thrust range which would power the new generation of large wide-bodied jumbo jets. I knew the GE management quite well at the time, having sold some of TransTec's early control technology to them. They were disparaging of Rolls, both in personal terms of their management and in technical terms of their competence. Many, myself included, shared their doubts as to whether Rolls would break the 50,000 lb barrier or be broken by it. GE, feeling itself the injured party, was not going to make it easy for them. They threw everything into gaining the British Airways order to power its new fleet of Boeing wide-body aircraft. They won the order, worth over £200 million. Brian Rowe, a British ex-pat running GE aero-engines, gloated 'we didn't get mad, we got even'. One could only fear the worst and wonder why the government let it happen. On the other hand, some cynics commented, such were the terms of the order accepted by GE, that the government had done Rolls-Royce a favour.

In any event, Rolls fought back. Over the next five years they won order after order and were soon taking over 30 per cent of the total world market for jet engines. It was a fabulous achievement. And what is more, they tested their 100,000 lb thrust engine ahead of GE. Ironically, it was GE that ran into deep trouble and are still not out of the woods.

Rolls, on the other hand, with its latest range of Trent engines, has achieved a 43 per cent world-market share of both the Boeing and Airbus wide-body aircraft. It is another outstanding achievement. In 1999 Rolls spent £600 million on research and development, employed 15,000 people in well-paid jobs in the UK and contributed £8.5 billion to the balance of payments. All that sounds to some people very old-fashioned, I know. So let me add that the company also spends £250 million per annum on information technology.

In backing Rolls we were backing success. We had taken an indirect route to doing so. It needed an even more ingenious route to help British Aerospace, who came in hot on the heels of Rolls-Royce for their slice of the action.

British Aerospace

British Aerospace (BAe) operate in an intensely political world. They are extremely good at judging political sensitivities and exploiting them. They have to be.

BAe's was an improbable industrial success story. Rather like British Leyland, it was formed from a group of disparate entities lumped together by government in 1974 as the nationalized company British Aerospace. It had one big advantage over British Leyland: its principal customer was the government, not the consumer. The consumer gave the thumbs down on most of Leyland's products. The government could not do that to BAe without prejudicing the interest of the nation's defences.

However, the MoD was not in itself a sufficient condition of BAe's success. They had to rationalize and raise productivity. There was no alternative to cuts in overheads, plant closures and, in that wretched phrase, headcount reductions. These were all pushed through, much to the credit of management but inevitably at a great cost to the workforce.

Under the dynamic leadership of Sir Richard Evans, who took over in January 1990, the company's performance and productivity were dramatically improved. But it took time to convince the market. In the spring of 1992 the share price hit an all-time low of 98p, giving a market capitalization of a mere £440 million. The stock market was not registering the improvement in the company's performance. It was really the Gulf War and the consequent Saudi defence contract that changed the stock-market perception. Valued at over £25 billion and lasting for fifteen years, the Saudi contract was by far the largest export or national order ever won by a British company. The BAe leadership galvanized the company into action. The shares and profits rose steadily. By 1998 the share price had risen on a comparable basis to £21.80. The market capitalization was over £10 billion, matching that of GEC and encouraging BAe to seek a merger of the two companies as equals, some aspects of which I shall discuss in the section on defence restructuring.

It was by any standards a remarkable transformation in BAe's fortunes, which was not lost on the Treasury when the company came knocking on the door for £150 million launch aid for the European fighter. In their case the position was much more tricky than with Rolls-Royce. BAe were sitting on bank balances totalling £800 million. There was no financial case for assistance. We were in the politics of defence. Dick Evans had been very attentive to relations with No. 10 and the DTI. The plans for the major tripartite restructuring of the European defence and aerospace industry, and for the creation of a commercial Airbus industry, had been discussed in detail with the PM and Jonathan Powell. No. 10 and the DTI were fully informed and fully in support of these policies and of launch aid, which was in BAe's view an integral part of them.

What was not clear to the Treasury, however, was the link made between these apparently desirable developments at the pan-European level and the specific request for launch aid for which there was no discernible financial need. The Treasury position here was entirely defensible. No finance ministry could take a different attitude. We were in a period of severe restraint on public-sector spending: if £150 million were made available to BAe, there would be that much less available for health and education.

At first, BAe and Dick Evans personally seemed put out that the Treasury should even question the case for launch aid. This was perhaps not surprising, since he felt he had already agreed a deal with No. 10 and the DTI. Nonetheless, I tried to put Dick off the idea by explaining that, since there was no financial need for the case, the Treasury would expect any assistance to be on strictly commercial terms. Dick accepted this without demur, stressing that the support was important for two reasons unrelated to need. Firstly, from a psychological point of view it showed commitment from the British government to the Airbus project and to the reorganiz-ation of the inefficient consortium arrangement. The other European governments, Dick argued, had given support to their companies in the consortium and it would seem odd if the British government did not follow suit. I was not convinced by this line of argument. It was unclear what support was given by other governments and neither BAe nor anyone in government for that matter could quote chapter and verse. Moreover, no government was more clearly in support of the restructuring proposals than the British, who were recognized as the prime movers in the process — almost to the point of compromising our national interest.

The other argument alluded to, but not pressed, by BAe, was the special accounting treatment that launch aid made possible. Instead of being considered as a development cost and taken straight through the profit-and-loss account as expenditure, launch aid would be treated as an asset in the balance sheet of BAe's Airbus operations. This would have a double advantage. BAe's profits would be supported and its Airbus balance sheet strengthened. Their share of a single integrated Airbus company in the future would be potentially increased. Whatever the merits in terms of accounting principles, the argument had considerable force to BAe management, who were deeply committed to it. They continued to lobby hard at No. 10 and the DTI.

We were on the horns of the usual dilemma. I arranged to meet Dick privately at my flat to see if we could work our way out of it. One thing was for sure, given BAe's strong financial position: any new launch aid would have to meet strictly commercial terms. I asked Dick to bring with him the details of the financial return earned from earlier government assistance.

Dick came well prepared. He had details of the previous three launch-aid packages. They did not make happy reading. In one instance the capital of the original loan had not been repaid in full; in the others the return to the government had fallen far short of what would be expected on commercial terms.

We could not repeat such an arrangement now that BAe was in a much stronger financial position. In fairness, Dick readily agreed. Moreover, he stressed that, while the past flow of repayments of previous launch aid had been slow, the prospects over the next few years were promising.

The thought occurred to me that if these repayments could be underwritten and perhaps anticipated by BAe, and the timing of any new launch aid made to coincide with them, we could present a position where there would be no net outflow of government funds. If the package could be completed by a commercial rate of interest, say bank rate plus 2 per cent, this would be a deal that could be sold to the Treasury. Dick undertook to look at it and the next day confirmed that BAe could deliver on it.

I informed the Chancellor and No. 10, saying this was a good commercial deal and one whose terms I could live with.

Unfortunately, I had not reckoned with the principled objections of the Treasury, with which on reflection I could not disagree. My senior officials argued strenuously against the deal with the officials at No. 10, who liked the deal and wanted to do it. Moreover, the Chancellor, his office and special advisers all could not see why we were giving special treatment to a financially strong private-sector company. If there was to be a better-than-expected repayment of launch aid, so much the better. We had barely begun the two years of severe restraint on public spending and needed every penny we could get. Moreover, BAe's holding in Orange alone was thought to be worth £800 million at that time.★

There was nothing for it but to go back to Dick and explain my difficulties. Of course, Dick had his own difficulties with his colleagues, who could not see why the government was hesitating to accept so favourable a deal. It was clear that I would have to offer Dick a different proposal. There was not exactly a plentiful supply of alternatives. The best I came up with was that BAe would drop its present request for financial support on the Airbus A340, in exchange for a formal statement from the Treasury that it would positively consider an application from BAe for launch aid in relation to the future A3XX aircraft, a superjet carrying over seven hundred passengers. This was a principled position for the Treasury to adopt. We were not just putting off the decision. The development costs of the A3XX, a wholly new and much larger venture, would be enormous. BAe could be thought to be betting the company on such a project. The case for government support would not be

★ This was sold over 1998 and 1999 for £1.5 billion.

difficult to establish for such a project in a financial climate which, we were confident, would have considerably improved.

Over many years Dick had exercised his skills in easing difficult situations. He was the outstanding marketing man of his generation. He was anxious to ease tensions with the Treasury, whose support he knew he would need in the future. He faxed to us from an Airbus meeting in Paris his agreement to this holding arrangement, effectively withdrawing his request for assistance on the A340.

Unfortunately his colleagues on the BAe board took a dim view of what they considered a 'jam-tomorrow solution'. Mike Turner, BAe's Chief Operating Officer, came to see me to say there had been a misunderstanding. BAe stood by its original request. He was unbothered by Dick's acceptance of my plan. This had been obtained under duress!

There was little point in my trying to embarrass Dick, who had tried like myself to square the circle. I could see how things would pan out. No. 10 would back the company and the DTI would brief a victory over the Treasury. Accordingly I advised the Chancellor that we should give way gracefully, taking what credit we could for what was after all a very presentable deal. We duly negotiated a commercial deal, turning Her Majesty's Treasury, by a combination of the interest rate and the percentage return on further sales, into the most expensive bank in the country!

BAe knew the strength of their position and exploited it. They were right to do so. It was also right that they should have direct access to No. 10 and to the DTI. It is vital that they should feel free to explain their problems and their views of the national interest. There would be no return to the mistaken industrial policies of old Labour in the seventies – interfering with strategic stake holdings, planning agreements and all that ridiculous paraphernalia. Tony Blair in opposition and in government made it clear that New Labour was pro-business. The door to No. 10 was wide open. Quite right, too. No one rejoiced more than I did.

But where I could see this going wrong was that business was using this access, together with DTI support, to pre-empt the Treasury's position as the ultimate point of accountability. That is not acceptable. The DTI had no money in their budget for launch aid or major regional assistance. They tended to give indiscriminate and unconditional support to the companies and took a subliminal pleasure in screwing the Treasury, whose role was reduced to giving as little as possible when caught in this painful pincer movement.

Such was the uncomfortable position when BAe launched its offensive. So when, later, the headlines blazed Rover's financial problems, I determined in this instance to make the case for Treasury involvement clear and to set out our conditions for support from the start.

Postscript. BAe duly made their case for launch aid on the A3XX. They were successful there, too. They received £530 million from the Treasury. The public finances were by this time much stronger, as we had predicted. But all the same it was another coup for BAe.

Vauxhall

The motor industry is not much less political than defence. As a nation, though, we are not in world or even European terms a major player. Our industry is entirely foreign in ownership. Our role is to provide the best terms we can to attract overseas investment. The EU rules on state aid are very strict, and the UK plays very strictly to the rule book.

Even within these restrictions the sums involved can be quite large and competition between governments for inward investment projects is intense. We were to face this problem in the very near future with BMW, where I was determined the Treasury should play a constructive but rigorously exacting role. But first there was the threat of an imminent crisis at Vauxhall (owned by General Motors, the US giant).

The rumour mill out of No. 10 and from the unions was working overtime. The Vauxhall plant at Luton was under the threat of closure; and if that went it was only a matter of time before the factory at Ellesmere Port would go, too. It was part of General Motor's background thinking that Ford had been treated more kindly than themselves. They felt there was some sort of favouritism at work.

GM had been rebuffed in their attempt to take over Land Rover in 1991. They had been upbraided by Leon Brittan when Trade and Industry Secretary in 1985 for not being a good corporate citizen and they felt that Ford in its expansions both at Bridgend and at Jaguar had been more generously supported than GM.

Certain facts did, of course, make Ford a more prominent player in the UK. Ford employed more people and carried out more research and development in Britain than did GM. Ford probably played the GB card more successfully than GM, whose European management structure and manufacturing operations were more heavily concentrated in Germany. But such considerations in no way made a case for treating the two giant American corporations any differently. Nor was that so in fact, as would become clear. But it was how GM top management in Europe and most importantly the US felt. It was certainly true that relations with top US management at Ford were closer than at GM. I was not sure why this should be the case. After all, Ford had been prevented from taking over Austin Morris and felt pretty bad about that at the time. I made a mental note to check this out once we had passed the immediate crisis.

Such was the situation when Nick Riley, chairman of Vauxhall, was sent by the DTI to my office in early 1998. The DTI could help no further. There were no schemes or grants for which GM could qualify. It was a lost cause. Quite why the DTI should have passed the problem to the Treasury was a mystery – except that it would land us with the blame if the company proceeded with the closure of Luton. The sensible thing would have been to have refused a meeting. But that was not my style. There is usually something a government can do if it wants to and circumstances merit it.

I discussed the situation with Gordon Brown. There were seven thousand employed at Luton and seven thousand at Ellesmere Port. The threat to either one was something the government could not look on with indifference in the first year of government. The measures to stabilize the economy were beginning to be felt. Sterling was rising and we felt that it was only a matter of time before manufacturing went into recession. In this situation, one or two major closures might provoke a reaction in excess of any objective assessment of economic circumstances. Gordon was anxious the Treasury should help. I warned that we were probably just being set up by the DTI; but he asked me to try anyway.

The meeting took place on 12 March 1998. Nick patiently explained the background to the crisis. GM had settled wage and employment levels in their mainland European plants. They were confident of settling in the near future a new wages deal with their British plants. Their problem was excess assembly capacity throughout Europe. The focus as we feared was Luton, whose production could easily be supplied from Ghent in Belgium.

In his quiet matter-of-fact way Nick added that GM felt they were less favourably treated than Ford and that this was exacerbating an anti-British feeling. My reaction was to reassure him on this latter point. I took him through the history of regional assistance to GM, which showed a percentage of the total investment which compared well with what Ford had received and indeed was right at the limit of what was legal under the EU regime. He accepted this but said that while £18 million had been agreed for Luton, in fact only £9 million had changed hands. Certain discretionary targets of the investment had not been met and the grant was therefore withheld.

At this point I remembered that Ford had not in fact met the targeted employment levels for an investment at their Bridgend engine plant. The entire regional grant had, however, been paid out. This had taken place under the Tories. I was not sure how much of the detail had been made public and, if it had not, whether I would be able to gain access to it.

For the moment, it was enough to raise the point with Treasury officials. What occurred to me was that if such latitude could be shown to Ford, it must also be possible and indeed on the basis of precedent it would be correct to do the same for Vauxhall. Officials confirmed that there was indeed still £9 million outstanding that had not been paid to Vauxhall. The money had been provided in the government expenditure figures for regional support in that year. If the full grant was to be paid there would be no increase in government expenditure. There would be no accounting adjustment. Such a gesture would demonstrate at once an even-handedness on the part of government between the two American corporations, and send the signal to GM that the UK was serious about retaining and increasing its automotive manufacturing base in the UK.

I left it that officials would check out the feasibility of the proposal, which would have to be put through government legal counsel. Later I was told it had been cleared. The threat to Luton had been removed. Indeed, since then Vauxhall have introduced a Vectra model at Luton, reducing the plant's vulnerability as a one-model operation, and have transferred product development on all medium-range van models to the UK. More importantly, in mid-2000 Vauxhall announced investments, including the above, amounting to £190 million.

Had we not taken the steps to pay out the regional grant, it may well be that Luton would not have closed anyway. Who knows? What is clear is that we have gained significant extra investment at all Vauxhall plants and have a real opportunity of a new start in our relations with GM. Paying up on the regional grant was not a heroic solution. But it did prove that where there is a will, there is usually a way. What went wrong at Rover was a lack of will – to some extent the government's, but mainly BMW's.

BMW/Rover

The last time I discussed BMW at length was on Remembrance Day, 11 November 1998. As Paymaster General, I met Peter Mandelson, then the Secretary of State for Trade and Industry, in his office at the DTI. I had been pushing for the meeting for several weeks.

It has been public knowledge for some time that the situation at BMW's Rover plant was deteriorating seriously. The worse things got, the higher the price tag for necessary government support seemed to rise. From well-informed press reports, we were looking at a requirement of £250 million in regional aid.

The ostensible purpose for my meeting was to avoid the Treasury being squeezed by another DTI/No. 10 pincer movement into unconditional financial support. But beyond that, I was deeply concerned that the DTI was too laid-back about the situation. There seemed to be an inadequate sense of urgency in the department. I confided my thoughts to the private office at No. 10, which shared them and agreed that I should draft a letter for Mandelson to send to BMW. The letter was the basis of the meeting. It made the following observations:

- That BMW had given undertakings to the DTI about maintaining the Rover marque and the present size of its activities;
- That the DTI should insist that BMW hold to the undertakings;
- That the UK government would be prepared to make maximum support available, provided that, most importantly, BMW committed itself to a much deeper level of involvement in running the company to improve the productivity and quality standards that were so clearly at the root of Rover's problems.

The DTI officials were somewhat put out by the tone of the letter, which might have been considered a touch admonitory for their liking. But I was sure it was right to be concerned and to do everything possible to get BMW more deeply involved. The meeting ended on a positive note. We agreed that the two departments would work together. I even volunteered to visit BMW together with Lord (David) Simon, then minister both at the DTI and the Treasury, whose friendly personal relationship with Bernd Pischetsrieder, then BMW's executive chairman, might have been exploited to good effect.

This last idea seemed apposite to me in the light of the blazing public row that was raging between the top brass at BMW, with Pischetsrieder pro-Rover and Wolfgang Reitzle, another top director, anti-Rover. The visit did not take place. Peter and I went our separate ways a month later; and in a violent pas de deux, Pischetsrieder and Reitzle went their separate ways, too, exiting the BMW stage hot on our heels. Their departure resolved their personal stand-off, but did nothing to solve the ills of their 'English Patient', as Rover had become known at BMW.

BMW has since declared its patient terminally sick and cut off the life-support machine. Its declared reasons do not stand up; the exchange rate was first mentioned as the problem in an interview on the 'Today' programme given by a Rover spokesman in mid 1998. Gordon Brown moved quickly to shoot it down, declaring the problem to be Rover's low productivity. Without wishing to belittle the difficulties caused to British manufacturers by sterling's present level, I think the Chancellor had more than a point.

The pound, in fact, is worth no more today than it was in 1986; it is the Deutschmark/euro that has gone down by 29 per cent. But BMW can hardly be a stranger to an appreciating currency. Between 1967 and 1986, the Deutschmark revalued by 250 per cent against sterling. Over that period, BMW learnt to cope by improving quality and productivity.

On the issue of productivity the Chancellor was certainly right. There are two organizations that look at competitive productivity levels for the international motor industry. The most recent figures I saw from the study based at the Massachusetts Institute of Technology did not make happy reading for European companies as a whole. The Japanese and American manufacturers outperformed them across the board. But, within Europe, the worst – by a margin of about 40 per cent – was Rover. The same story was told of quality, where again Rover was ranged by authoritative experts as being right at the bottom.

I can accept that BMW may have inherited these problems when it took over Rover from British Aerospace back in January 1994. BAe recognized that it lacked professional management skills in the motor industry, and that was a main reason why it disposed of

Rover. But after six years of BMW ownership, how could this still be the case?

By the way of answer, some of our press, notably leader writers at the *Observer*, seem to be stuck in their own time warp: Britain is no good at making things, especially motor cars. That twaddle does not wash.

The Nissan plant in Sunderland is right at the top of the European league in productivity and quality. Ah, but that was a greenfield site, I can hear them object. Very well then, consider how Ford tackled Jaguar, even though it, like BMW, paid too high a purchase price. When Ford's Bill Hayden (to whom Britain owes an under-recognized debt) saw the Jaguar factory for the first time after Ford's acquisition, he observed that there was nothing wrong with it that a good bulldozer would not put right. But thanks to Hayden's sheer professional management as Jaguar's chairman and chief executive from 1990 to 1992, and to the equally good work of his successor Nick Scheele, Ford put Jaguar right. With a sustained commitment of management and technical support, as well as money, Ford sorted out the old Jaguar factory at Brown's Lane, launched the brilliantly successful S-type at Castle Bromwich in Birmingham and is bringing out the new baby Jaguar at Ellesmere Port, Liverpool. The effect? Jaguar will be tripling its sales and is making good profits.

So if the exchange-rate argument does not stand up, and if other automobile companies have successfully invested in the UK, what went wrong with BMW? The argument that BMW was put off by the Competition Commission inquiry into car prices and by ministerial talk of 'rip-off Britain' cannot be advanced with any level of seriousness. One might ask, though, how much profit BMW made on its exports of 71,000 vehicles to this country last year – there is always another side to the exchange-rate equation.

The bottom line must read that BMW grossly underestimated the size of the problem it had taken on, and never really put in the management resources to cope. Perhaps it was not able to do so: it is, after all, only a medium-sized German manufacturer. Perhaps there was an industrial a-literacy in the BMW management, which simply did not have the scale of operation or resources that Ford can bring. With hindsight, it would surely have been preferable to have allowed Ford to proceed with the acquisition of Rover in 1986 or to have left in place the successful Rover/Honda cooperation and shareholding arrangements that were gazumped by BMW.

But that is all history now. What are the lessons for the future? There will be little gained from beating BMW over the head. Certainly, the company seems to have behaved with breathtaking impudence, not to say downright deceit. Stephen Byers, Mandelson's successor at the DTI, had every right to feel let down. But the arrangements and conditions with BMW should have been more tightly tied down from day one, or not entered into at all. The danger is to pretend to a measure of control where, when the chips are down, you have not a fragment of influence. Governments cannot put their trust in a private-sector company's goodwill alone. Business situations change; managements and their attitudes are bound to change with them.

While this unhappy episode does not enhance the case either for or against early entry in the euro, it surely does try to teach us one lesson. Britain – brimming with inventive capacity, equipped with the English language, established with honest legal and accounting professions, served by a democratic Parliament, which has survived two world wars – cannot allow its future to depend on inward investment. Nor can our economic policy be determined by the need to attract it. Nothing gets up my nose more than to hear the argument for the entry into the euro being made first and foremost in terms of inward investment. The argument is injurious to the sensible political and economic reasons that exist for Britain's joining the euro and deleterious to our own national capability and pride.

It may be that sooner or later we shall join the euro. But let us do so at the right time for the right reasons and on the right conditions. Inward investment is a small part of the large equation.

Ménage à trois

Relationships between large-scale public and private organizations pose many problems. Rarely are they conducted successfully. There are difficulties of corporate and entrepreneurial culture, respective values and valuations and, not least, the characters of the powerful individuals at the top of the establishments attempting to put their activities under a single management.

In sensitive areas such as defence these problems were intensified and compounded by security and national-interest considerations. In the case of European-wide defence restructuring there were plenty of impediments blocking the way forward without my creating any more.

But I really did object to what I read in the official papers about European defence restructuring that arrived on my desk with ever-increasing frequency in the early months of 1998. I was not quite sure why they were copied to me and I suspect that the civil servants and advisers came to regret the fact that they were. I had three fundamental problems with our negotiating stance: we were positioning ourselves as the *demandeur*; we were exerting pressure on BAe, the British party to the negotiations, to make concessions against their better judgement; and we were in danger of cutting ourselves off from US technology.

After one really irritating Cabinet Office minute I felt I had to intervene. Having cleared my lines at official level in the Treasury, I set out my critique of the way the negotiations were being handled. I expected reactions amongst officials asking me to mind my own business since there was no money involved and therefore no direct Treasury interest.

This was very much in my thoughts when shortly after my memo went out I received an agitated call from Roger Liddle asking for a meeting.

I suggested that Roger came straight over. Roger was a special adviser on European affairs at No. 10 and was working very closely with the Cabinet Office and the MoD. In a tone of high drama he told me that it was imperative for Europe to be able to compete with the Americans in the defence industry and that the only way to achieve this was a tripartite merger between Britain, France and Germany for the creation of a single European Aerospace and Defence Company (EADC), to include Airbus as well. These plans were set out in the governmental tripartite declaration of December 1997. The negotiations were not going well. Roger's proposal was that I should be appointed minister in charge to push the merger through.

Roger was an idealist about Europe. Nothing mattered more to him, it often seemed, than achieving European integration across the board: industrial, monetary and political. This came over clearly in a Cabinet subcommittee meeting on the issue of landing slots at Heathrow. The UK policy was typically already much more open than the European. My proposal was that we should have a tougher policy that would oblige the European authorities to open more slots to non-national carriers. Roger's reaction was typical: 'What would our European partners think?' I retorted that they would think about their national interest. I did not object to that. It was what they were there for. And I shared that way of thinking. It was not anti-European, but pro one's own country. Roger's proposal would anyway be a nightmare of negotiation; I could see the prospect of interminable meetings getting nowhere – or not very far. The role proposed for the executive committee to promote the implementation of the letter of intent signed in 1998 to facilitate the restructuring of the European defence industry makes clear how matters of this kind are taken forward in Europe. The published text reads as follows:

The Executive Committee will be responsible for:

- Coordinating the drafting of any arrangements and agreements pursuant to this LoI;
- Monitoring the effectiveness of the implementation of any international instrument established pursuant to this LoI;
- Establishing ad hoc Working Groups to carry out tasks pursuant to this LoI;

- Coordinating, reviewing and evaluating tasks undertaken by the Working Groups;
- Preparing periodic reports to the Participants, as necessary.
- The Executive Committee will take its decisions by unanimous consent of its members. Where such consent cannot be reached, the matter in dispute will be referred to the Participants for resolution. Exceptionally, the Executive Committee may unanimously decide in advance that certain specific decisions may not require the unanimous consent of its members.

This was simply not for me. And I was not sure what authority Roger was speaking on anyway. My reply to his proposal was a firm no.

They do things differently in the States. The story is told that at a working dinner in 1993, Les Aspin, the US Defence Secretary, informed sixteen chief executive officers of the top US defence contractors that in his estimation the cutbacks in US defence expenditure would mean sufficient programmes to support only six major contractors. He also made it clear that industry was on its own.★ There would be no financial support from the federal government.

The US corporations reacted rapidly. The object of the exercise was higher productivity through rationalization, for which of course consolidation is a necessary precondition. An illustration of how they proceeded in America was Raytheon's programme of cutbacks for Texas Instruments: 8,700 job losses, twenty facilities closed – a 15 per cent overall cost reduction. By 1998, the procurement office of the US Defence Department was blocking the Lockheed Martin/Northrop Grumman merger as consolidation had gone too far!

McKinsey estimates that, by 1995, productivity in the US

★ In fact the Pentagon did aid the process in the US by the controversial practice of reimbursing military contractors for some of the costs of mergers and rationalization. Lockheed Martin alone apparently requested $1.7 billion on these grounds.

defence electronics sector had a 47 per cent advantage over European firms. This and other measures of productivity can only have got worse since then from a European point of view.

There can be no doubting, therefore, that a major improvement in European productivity levels from restructuring, accompanied by rationalization, is urgently needed. The problem is that those factors that make this possible in the US – private ownership, competition, entrepreneurial instincts and focus on shareholder values – are simply not there in the French nationalized structure and not sufficiently present in the German industrial culture either.★

Yet Britain was pushing for consolidation with no guarantee of rationalization other than what the German and particularly the French government would allow. It seemed to me from my discussions with the UK defence companies that they shared my doubts about the position of *demandeur* we were in danger of taking up.

The BAe position was perfectly understandable and the correct one: for rationalization to be carried through effectively, it would be necessary for the management to be able to get on with the job free from political constraints. This meant that Aerospatiale must be privatized and the 40 per cent block holding of Daimler Benz in DASA (Deutsche Aerospace) must be sold off. BAe knew from previous experience – shared by Marconi of GEC – that in European joint ventures when the requisite rationalization was carried out it was invariably the British plants and workforce that were expected to shoulder the burden. This prospect was particularly unacceptable to BAe since it had already carried through some severe rationalization measures within its own organization. The higher levels of productivity and profits reflected this. In BAe's view it was the European plants that had been cosseted from the harsh winds of the private-sector climate. BAe therefore were quite right to insist on their two prior conditions before entering any European Aerospace and Defence Company.

The short history of the Anglo-French joint venture on aircraft undercarriages is instructive. The UK side, TI–Dowty, were push-

★ Commodore R. G. J. Ward, Royal Navy, *Seaford House Papers 1998*.

ing for efficiency measures to achieve the same rate of return from the French factory as from the British one. The French would not play ball. Instead, the French government, which controlled their interest in the joint venture, bought out the TI holding for £200 million. This took place in 1999. It will be interesting to see how the rationalization takes place.

If BAe were rightly adamant about their two prior conditions, the Cabinet Office was anything but. The annoying memo that sparked my intervention was pressing a compromise position where the French made a vague statement about divesting a minority stake in Aerospatiale at some unspecified future date; and where Daimler Benz would retain its major holding in DASA subject to some unspecified limitations on voting rights. Our zeal for a deal seemed to know no bounds. This approach was no good at all.

I detailed my objections. We should require from the French a legally binding agreement with a specified timetable for the privatization of Aerospatiale; and Daimler Benz should proceed forthwith with the sale of their block holding, for which I understood there would be a ready market.

My memo seemed to have the effect of bringing some commercial reality into the situation. It was gratifying to see the language of my memo appearing in their subsequent documents and the Cabinet Secretary, Sir Richard Wilson, himself took an important initiative in establishing a ministerial subcommittee where these very important issues would be brought into a more formal decision-making process – not just left to a few individuals whose enthusiasm for an agreement risked compromising our national interest in an area of industry of which they had no experience.

I met Dick Evans, BAe's chairman, on a number of occasions during this period. In the early stages he was keen to get ahead with the restructuring and seemed optimistic. But as the entrenched nationalistic positions of the French and Germans seemed to harden, the realist in him understood that the sort of arrangement he wanted was not achievable in the short term. He asked to see me ahead of his meeting with the Prime Minister in June 1998. As he explained the position, it was clear he was unhappy about the pressure coming from the Cabinet Office, which he felt would compromise his negotiating position. I encouraged him to hold firm in his meeting at No. 10. He duly did and telephoned me later to say how well it had gone and how much better he felt BAe and the UK were now placed.

Dick's strong stance had done the trick. By July 1998 we had a clear-cut government policy, which the Prime Minister communicated in a firm letter to Jospin ahead of the forthcoming bilateral in that month. Privatization of the French companies was essential if progress on EADC was to be made.

There was another lesson to be learned from the American handling of defence restructuring. The Defence Department, having made clear its determination to see a rationalization take place and having put in place the incentives for it to happen, left the companies to sort out its implementation amongst themselves.

This was not the case with our approach. Such was the pressure in early 1998 on BAe to do the tripartite merger, it might well not have proceeded with the acquisition of Marconi from GEC. It was the second point of objection I made to our policy. We seemed to be forcing decisions on our companies. This was particularly so when a merger of the defence activities of BAe and GEC were discussed. Such a merger would obviously give rise to serious issues of competition policy. The Ministry of Defence was much inclined to make a meal of this. Their memos on it were quite as irritating as the Cabinet Office's on the politics of restructuring. It seemed so obvious that, if the European governments pulled off the tripartite restructuring and formed the EADC, they would be inextricably committed to putting their money into it: that is, placing orders with the European defence industry they had created. But all the MoD seemed concerned about was the reduction in competition that would occur if BAe and GEC–Marconi got together. The EADC on the other hand was acceptable because they liked it politically. I minuted out again in an attempt to get some coherence into our policy.

The point I stressed was that restructuring axiomatically meant fewer suppliers and less competition. It seemed to me that the national-interest case for a BAe–Marconi merger – if that is what the companies wanted to do – was twofold. It would strengthen the UK industry in the European negotiations. And it would keep open the strong UK links to American defence technology.

This was my third objection to the trend in our policy. Had we really thought through the implications of tying ourselves into EADC and what it would mean for our relations with US defence technology? It is widely known that the US military is deeply suspicious of the French government and defence industry, which, it seems to believe, had made attempts through industrial espionage to obtain access to American advanced technology. I have no idea about the rights and wrongs of the case. But a deep anti-French feeling does exist, as the disclosure recently of a Pentagon grading list made clear. This list categorizes countries according to their reliability in protecting US military technology. The UK was in the A category of reliable partners; Germany fell into the B category (with Japan), while France received a C rating. This grading meant that no French company can hope to take up with an American defence contractor involved in state-of-the-art technologies.

The official response seemed to be that collaborative programmes with the US could be ring-fenced within EADC to exclude the French. Inherently I thought this to be impossible from a practical point of view: it was unlikely to convince the Americans. And we might be cutting ourselves off from access to technology acknowledged to be ten years ahead of anything in Europe – especially aerospace and defence electronics. The risk did not seem worth taking without first securing very clear and written undertakings with the US Defence Department that our collaborative arrangements with them would continue. There was, for example, the memorandum of understanding signed between the US and UK governments whereby Britain is contributing £200 million towards the demonstration-phase cost of £2 billion for the joint strike fighter. Could our subsequent industrial prospects for contracts under the JSF programme be affected? No one seemed to know.

More than ever, as events in Kosovo and the Gulf War made clear, American technology will prevail. What is needed is a strengthening of NATO via transatlantic links. Surely the best step would be for France to privatize its defence industries, re-enter NATO and play a constructive political and industrial role in a North American/European alliance on which our best hopes for prosperity and security depend. There are some signs this cultural political change may have started in France. But there is a long way to go.

Developments since I left office seem to justify the view I took that a politically inspired EADC was not the best way forward and we did well to steer clear of it. It would, moreover, also certainly seem to be the case that Britain's capacity to continue its traditional role in military terms at the heart of the Atlantic Alliance has been much enhanced by the acquisition by BAe Systems, as it is now called, of GEC's defence business.

The situation in Europe has not improved very much. Daimler Chrysler, thwarted in its move for BAe Systems, bought at an inflated price CASA, the Spanish national aerospace company. Then Daimler Benz and Aerospatiale-Matra brought their activities together into a single company called European Aeronautics Defence and Space (EADS) which was based in Holland and which was the subject of an initial public offering of shares in July 2000. It was a sort of truncated EADC without British participation. It has unfortunately retained the worst features, the very ones which deterred BAe Systems from involvement in it. The French government, together with other French companies, have a 30 per cent stake; Daimler Chrysler has similarly retained a large block holding. There is a system of management aptly termed 'jobs by passport': the top sixty-eight posts being reserved on a national basis, to accommodate each country's pride, not to restructure the business. It will be interesting to see how it works out. The market is not yet impressed. The shares stand at about 17 euros, compared to the expected 23–24 euros at the initial public offering.

Interestingly the Germans do not seem wholly committed. Daimler Chrysler has a one-way put option on the French government which can be triggered under a number of circumstances whose occurrence it would not be too difficult to contrive. Unless the market value of the company improves, it would seem entirely possible that Daimler Chrysler would come under shareholder pressure to exercise the option. We would then have renationalization by the French. How would the German government react to that?

As for BAe Systems, it finds itself in a good situation. It has made two important acquisitions in the USA, bringing additional turnover of $2 billion and extending its competence in the most advanced American technology. All its links with European companies are intact, as is its position in Airbus Industrie, for which, moreover it has finally pushed through a more commercially oriented management structure reflected in its new name, Airbus Integrated Company. The outcome on any score seems to be a good one for the UK. I am pleased the companies were allowed to get on and do what they wanted. And pleased that I may have helped a bit in the process.

16. Resignation

The news that the *Independent on Sunday* was to run an article on 30 November 1997 revealing the existence of the Robinson family offshore trust reached the Treasury on the preceding Thursday. It came as a bolt out of the blue. The news reached me from my accountants, who had been contacted by the newspaper.

At first I could see no real cause for alarm. The existence of the trust was widely known at the time of my getting involved in Coventry City Football Club – indeed I seem to remember it being referred to in the newspapers and of course I had told colleagues about the trust's existence and its location. I had also made it clear that while my family and I could enjoy benefits from the trust, it was not an arrangement that I was in favour of prolonging and that I would willingly work in government to remove the tax reliefs that were involved. In a jocular vein I suggested that, knowing something about trusts, I was well placed to advise. And in government we had started work to enact the reforms of trust tax law in line with statements that both Tony Blair and Gordon Brown had made in opposition. In principle, there was nothing different in my position from that of most Labour supporters who take a life peerage while committing themselves to the abolition of the Lords if that was a Labour government's policy. The material considerations would be much greater, of course.

As far as the Treasury was concerned I had made meticulous preparation in the last months of opposition to meet the ministerial code of conduct, even to the point of having lunch in my flat with Sir Peter Gregson, a former Permanent Secretary at the DTI. Sir Peter, I had learned, exercised a coordinating role in respect of the ministerial code of conduct. He warned me with a wry smile that he had more trouble with ministerial interests than any policy issue.

A draft blind trust of my investments was drawn up before the election and was handed over to the Treasury Permanent Secretary, Sir Terence Burns, within days of my joining the government, as was required of all ministers with investments. It was signed by myself and the trustees on 7 May 1997. The advice I received prior to joining the government was that there was no need to include the family trust since I had already taken steps to exclude myself from it. Indeed, it was clearly understood with the Chancellor that there would be no benefits of any kind to me from the trust during my period in office.

The meeting at which the blind trust document was discussed with the Permanent Secretary took place on 21 May 1997. Both my personal lawyer and my accountant, who with some reluctance had agreed to act as trustees for the blind trust, came down from Coventry to attend this meeting, as I wanted matters as clearly and formally settled as possible. From my point of view we achieved those aims. I informed the Permanent Secretary of the existence of the offshore trust and of the reasons why it was not included in the blind trust. He seemed well satisfied.

Against this background I did not see that I had much to fear from the *Independent on Sunday* article. I met Gordon in his office early the next day to discuss how we should handle the matter. He stressed that I should get out a complete statement dealing with all aspects of the trust once and for all. Accordingly I ran through the situation with him. As was usually the case on matters of this kind Gordon went to his word processor and pounded out the first draft. It did not change much. The problem was not with the drafting but with getting the Permanent Secretary's approval for the wording and his agreement that I had adhered to the ministerial code. The apparent prevarication at official level seemed a bit odd after all the trouble I had taken to seek his advice and to ensure the fullest compliance.

I subsequently learned from overhearing a conversation in my private office that no note had been prepared by the Permanent Secretary's office of the meeting of 21 May, though one was hastily constructed later. The problem was not resolved until about 2.30 p.m. on Saturday afternoon, 29 November, when, just before

Queens Park Rangers kicked off against Wolves at Molineux, Charlie Whelan tracked down Sir Terence at the match and secured his agreement. It was 5.30 p.m. that evening when the statement went out on the Press Association tapes over my name. It read as follows:

It is well known I have substantial business interests. On being appointed a minister, in line with the past practice of businessmen in government, I sought the usual advice.

I have received and continue to receive much media interest in my financial position, including an inquiry this weekend which convinces me that there is a danger of misrepresentation. I am therefore making this statement today.

All my beneficial interests were declared in line with the Cabinet Office ministerial code and placed in a blind trust on 7 May. The blind trust was drawn up by my solicitors, Titmuss Sainer Dechert, and with advice from, as is established procedure, the Treasury's Permanent Secretary. I also informed him that I was a discretionary beneficiary under a trust established for my family. After advice from the Permanent Secretary and Titmuss Sainer Dechert I decided in accordance with their advice that there was no need to include this in the blind-trust arrangements since I was a discretionary beneficiary.

This trust, the Orion Trust, registered in Guernsey, was an offshore trust created by Madame Bourgeois, a long-standing family friend for twenty years. She was a frequent visitor to our home and regularly spent Christmas and new year with me and my family. She died in 1994. Madame Bourgeois was a Belgian national, resident in Switzerland. Therefore there was no, nor could there have been any, UK tax avoidance. Moreover, at no time have I transferred capital or other assets into the Orion Trust for tax or any other purpose.

The blind trust I set up on 7 May includes all my beneficial interests. They include nearly £18 million of shares in TransTec plc, the company I founded in 1981. All tax is paid on dividends received from these shares and, of course, income tax was paid on my salary when I was chairman of TransTec. The rights that arose for me from the TransTec rights issue in 1996 were bought by Orion Trust from Stenbell Limited, a company owned by me and to which I had sold them. These transactions were at the then market value and the transaction between Orion and Stenbell was on an arm's length basis. I was advised by my lawyers and Wilder Coe, my accountants, that this was a correct procedure. The capital gain for which I am liable will be taxed in the normal manner.*

I have not had occasion to retract anything from, or add anything of any material significance to, that statement. The press for the most part ignored it. So perhaps I can emphasize three additional points now, which readers of this book may wish to consider in an atmosphere of calm objectivity which certainly was not possible in the hectic weeks of December 1997, when I confidently estimate I featured in more pages of newsprint than the rest of the government combined.

Firstly, all my own holdings in TransTec and all my other assets were wholly declared to the Inland Revenue and open to their full tax liability. Anyone seriously interested in tax avoidance would have taken steps to change that position.

Secondly, I paid handsome taxes on all my income in each and every year, amounting to several million pounds in the last few years.

Thirdly, how many of us if beneficiaries, with our families, of a family trust – such as that settled for my family by Mme Bourgeois – would have taken the steps necessary to untangle perfectly legal arrangements in order to incur tax? Indeed, would all eight of the family agree? Perhaps some pious newspaper editors would. I wonder?

The fact is I did not. I made no secret of the existence of the trust. The first week's press was not too bad. All the papers ran the story. The *Independent* followed its sister paper's lead with a page-four story headlined 'MPs scent blood and hypocrisy over minister's £12 million trust'. Despite the headline, the story itself was remarkably balanced. It quoted Lord Parkinson as showing 'disdain for the attack on Mr Robinson on GMTV' and quoted Kenneth Clarke as saying on Sky TV's 'Sunday Programme': 'It's perfectly legal, I

---

* There was in fact no capital gain realized.

don't see any problems, no.' The most encouraging signal came ironically from the *Sun*, in its 'The Sun Says' column:

There is nothing wrong with being rich and taking care of your money. The fact is, a Labour government needs all the men and women with business acumen it can get. Perhaps Brown should put Robinson in charge of closing a few tax loopholes. **He seems the ideal man for the job** [the *Sun*'s bold type].

Fair enough. That is just what I had been doing.

Despite the fact that the Tories had started to make capital out of the situation – as any opposition would have done – it was the considered view of the Treasury team that we should and could ride out the storm. Gordon was very firm that I should not resign. For my part, though I had no intention of resigning, I made it crystal clear to Gordon that my resignation was unconditionally at his disposal if he wanted it.

The mood in the press changed dramatically after the launch of the ISA proposals on Tuesday, 2 December, though this was not fully reflected until the following week after some typically sensational 'revelations' in the *Sunday Times* of 7 December 1997. The headline blazoned: 'Robinson's Bermuda tax haven'. There was no truth in this at all. I have never had any money, trust or any other assets in Bermuda.

It was the first and last occasion on which I got angry. That was a mistake. I involved my lawyers and that was another mistake. We gave a statement to the editors of the *Sunday Times* and the *Observer* saying that I would issue libel proceedings if there were further untrue defamatory articles. And that was a mistake. If I had sued straight off that would have been a mistake, too. I would have had to resign.

It was a bad weekend. The *Sun* – very much a critical weather-vane for the government at this stage in its fortunes – seized the occasion of the 'Insight' article to change its mind. Trevor Kavanagh, the political editor, led the charge: 'The hypocrisy stinks. It won't do, Prime Minister.' The justification for this reassessment was that 'The new account in the tax haven of Bermuda is the last straw.' The *Sun* had swallowed the 'Insight' story. I felt I could have protested till I was blue in the face. It would have made no difference. But why? The so-called Bermuda affair was the occasion, not the cause.

Charlie Whelan took it on himself to speak to Kavanagh personally. The conversation in Charlie's words confirmed that 'we had a problem'. The pattern of attack in the press – the *Sunday Times* and *The Times* were intensifying their assault on me and the *Sun* had performed its volte-face – pointed clearly to a common policy line within the Murdoch group. I did not think then, nor even now, that there could be anything personal against me. They just wanted a 'head' at this still early stage in the government's life, with a view to showing who was the boss.

I had met Rupert Murdoch socially on a couple of occasions in his magnificent penthouse flat at St James's Place. In fact back in 1996 when TransTec shares were riding high and I wished to reduce my holding, I had contacted his private secretary in London to see if he would wish to sell the flat. Mr Murdoch is not often in the flat and I thought there might be a chance he would want to dispose of it. The answer came back to me personally from Miss Cousins: 'No.' It was a pity really, since the money would have been far better invested there than left in TransTec shares, which by the end of 1999 were worthless.

So if there was no *ad hominem* drive to get rid of me, it could only be that the Murdoch group had decided to embark on a trial of strength with the PM. That was our conclusion as we reviewed the press in the second week. The Prime Minister's office seemed to interpret it that way, too. The PM went on Channel 4 News on the evening of 8 December to mount a rigorous defence of myself and of his decision to keep me in the government. There were two central planks in his argument. I was in his words 'an extremely good minister', and 'the assets had never been taken outside this country'. He also made the point in passing that I did not take a salary, though that was not central to the question.

Naturally I was pleased that the PM had come out so sturdily for me. It had, however, no deterrent effect. The *Sun* returned to the fray three days later, probably with fresh instructions from on high. A new 'The Sun Says' leader appeared directed at the PM personally and headlined 'Friendly word. Sometimes only a good friend will say what has to be said.' The grounds of attack had shifted from the ridiculous Bermuda trust story (perhaps the libel letter had done some good after all?) to the fact that I was handling the ISA. The *Sun* referred to my having the 'bare-faced cheek to lecture the people who voted Labour that it's just their hard luck to be losing tax perks on their savings'. *The Times* continued in a big way with a negative piece from Lord Rees-Mogg on Thursday, 11 December, and with extensive coverage over five pages, including the front-page lead and a Peter Brookes cartoon on Saturday, 13 December.

I was mildly surprised at the Rees-Mogg article. Perhaps it was sparked off by the need to balance a similar opinion piece the previous day by Simon Jenkins, who mounted a robust defence on my behalf. It was unsolicited and the more appreciated because it was so. The headline and by-line ran: 'Here's to you, Mr Robinson. Politics and press need buccaneers such as the Paymaster General.'

In the article Jenkins suggested with Shakespearean overtones: 'There is too much envy in the world.' This is a sad but probably true reflection. As for being a buccaneer, my own view of myself is that I am too squeamish to be a real one. But if the choice was between being a buccaneer or a hypocrite it was not a difficult one to make.

The situation was discussed amongst the Treasury team regularly during that week – mostly over dinner in my flat. The consensus emerged that it was a concerted campaign; that it had turned into a trial of strength between the PM and the press; and that while my offer of resignation was at the Chancellor's disposal I would not put it at this stage at the disposal of the PM.

It was perhaps the most miserable week of my life. Throughout my career I had always been a problem solver. I hated the position I now quite unexpectedly found myself in of being a problem creator. I felt I was letting the side down. There was nothing I could do about it. Gordon was adamant I should not resign and I felt the same way. I just had to get on with it, buttressed by my own determination not to give in.

We knew that the *Sunday Times* was planning a renewed onslaught for the next weekend. We decided that we should follow up Tony's Channel 4 interview with more positive coverage in some of the less hostile weekend papers. We needed to go on the offensive. Interviews were arranged with the *Sunday Express* and the *Sunday Telegraph*, and Ed Balls involved himself in what seemed a hopeful bridge-building exercise with the *Observer*. The *Express* and *Telegraph* sessions went off all right, not doing much harm nor good. The *Observer* interview was a fiasco.

It was partly that we had not prepared well enough, but mainly, it soon became apparent, that the *Observer* had its own agenda. From the start their top team – Will Hutton, Patrick Wintour and Ben Laurance – were overtly hostile. The coverage was harshly negative and included remarks that I had stressed were to be off the record concerning work I had been doing on the reform of trust taxation, remarks which I had made in order to demonstrate the integrity I brought to the Treasury job. The *Observer* wrote the story it wanted to. It was on the front page, the lead editorial, and splashed across the centre pages with an eight-feature cartoon. In addition to its three most senior journalists, the *Observer* had deployed eight others in London, Paris and Siena. With this gargantuan effort, I reflected, they had just about reached the levels of the *Sunday Times* Insight team.

The weekend press enabled the opposition to step up the pressure for my resignation. The PM held firm. The following Tuesday, Philip Webster, political editor of *The Times*, caught the mood with an article headlined: 'Robinson's fate becomes test of Blair's authority'. This piece quoted a senior minister as saying 'provided that Geoffrey has done nothing wrong . . . Tony will stand with him'. The Prime Minister's spokesman, Alastair Campbell, asserted the PM's authority: 'The first principle is that the Prime Minister – nobody else – will decide who is in his government.'

Charlie telephoned me that Sunday morning, 14 December, with his summary that 'there was acres of newsprint, but none had really said anything'. Gordon, Ed and Charlie were in despair at the press we had got – or not got, whichever way you looked at it. In varying degrees, each blamed me. But as is always the case in those situations no one blamed me as much as I blamed them, Ed and Charlie, especially for the *Observer* debacle! Suffice to say that Treasury relations with Hutton went into deep-freeze. (No one seemed to mind when Hutton, in due course, moved on from the *Observer* to head the Industrial Society.)

For my part I had had enough of reading the press. I was determined not to make the same mistake as John Major, who according to his private secretary, Stephen Wall,★ could not *not* read the newspapers. From that fateful weekend onwards I only read the sports pages.

But I ran no danger of becoming isolated. Despite repeated protestations from myself, solicitous friends and relatives faxed through every article they came across just in case I had not seen it. The *Mail* papers were clear favourites!

Of course, once the PM had declared his support for me, my position became a live issue at Question Time. It was understood from the start that only in so far as my answers to the questions raised by the press proved satisfactory would I be able to retain the PM's confidence. Quite right too. There was an unending stream of questions from No. 10. My private office performed miracles in getting the information out. At times the information requested of me seemed to go beyond the requirements of the question at hand. It was a small price to pay for the PM's confidence. He was under intense pressure. For PM's Questions on 18 December the Tories had prearranged their questions to concentrate solely on myself. Hague at that time had not perfected his formidable techniques of interrogation. The PM dealt easily enough with the supplementaries. I watched that particular Question Time in my office alone with my private secretary. Harold Macmillan used to say that he felt sick ahead of PM's questions. I felt sick *after* this one.

There was no let-up in the last days of December. We took no

★ Now Sir Stephen Wall, UK's top representative to the European Union.

calls at home over Christmas, but were bombarded with calls over the New Year in Venice. Heaven knows how the press obtained the information that we were staying at the Daniele Hotel, but they did.

Back in the office in January, I enjoyed a comparatively calm few weeks awaiting Sir Gordon Downey's ruling on whether or not I should have declared the trust in the Common's register of members' interests. The Tories, having failed to make the trust an issue from a ministerial point of view, had referred the matter to the commissioner of standards for the Commons. It was the first time the position of trusts had been considered in this way. To the best of my knowledge no trust had ever been the subject of a declaration. And I think that was, to the best of my recollection, one of the reasons why I did not challenge the view of my advisers that registration was not required.

In the light of the Downey inquiry, however, I judged that a high-level legal opinion should be sought. For this purpose I turned once more to Michael Beloff. The two key clauses in the MPs' code of conduct are 9 and 10. Lord Beloff summed up his judgement: 'In my clear view . . . [Mr Robinson] had no obligation to register under category 9; or under category 10.' Sir Gordon's judgement came on 21 January 1998. He unequivocally cleared me of any breach of the rules: 'There is no case for saying that Mr Robinson has breached a rule of the House on registration.'

The story led on most of that evening's TV and radio news bulletins. We were at the flat for the BBC news. I was still a bit morose at having myself dragged through the mill in this way. Gordon was very pleased. 'But Geoffrey, you're cleared. What more do you want?' My reply was to echo through my mind on several occasions in the following months: 'I'd rather not be in this position.'

The press coverage was predictably less positive than the broadcast media. The headlines in particular concentrated on the fact that Sir Gordon had also said that, had he been consulted, he, unlike my own advisers, would have recommended registration. That was OK by me. But surely I was not the only person in this situation? And, if not, since there were no similar trusts declared at that time, some new registrations could be expected to come out of the woodwork. Quite amusingly, within a few days, the Tory member for Guildford, who had been one of my most vociferous critics on the issue, felt obliged to register a number of family trusts, one of which was offshore.

The opening salvo fired by the Tories had missed its mark. But they had reloaded their magazine and more was on its way. In professional terms it was an impressive attack: well coordinated and extensively researched. I had learned from my alert PPS, Ian Pearson, in early October, that the opposition had a team working on me. Ian had overheard a conversation at the Tory Party conference. Apparently, the centre of operations was an accountants' office in Dover, where David Shaw, the former Tory member for Dover, was involved. He had lost his seat in the '97 Labour landslide. It seems the ammunition to Peter Lilley, David Heathcoat-Amory and Francis Maude came from there. These attacks, I would like to emphasize, were and still are for me an expected and acceptable part of the adversarial system on which our political democracy is based. I bear no ill feelings to those involved. We would have been at least as relentless ourselves. If you do not like it, do not go into politics.

The Tory attacks covered the whole range of our family interests. Nigel Evans, the MP for Ribble Valley, seemed to draw the short straw. He took up the question of our olive trees and fields in San Gimignano. It is a lovely property, and we are very lucky to enjoy some 200 acres there. My wife values her privacy, and intensely resented the journalists who clambered all over the buildings and the grounds. One managed to leave the gate swinging half off its hinges! The journalists had inspected the fields and reported back that crops and olives were growing there. This was a traditional – quite civilized – arrangement whereby the farmers worked the fields and kept the produce. It suited both parties. Sir Gordon Downey, of course, supported my position. Francis Maude was to return later in the year on a separate issue relating to the same property. He, too, got nowhere.

But amongst the complaints lodged by the opposition, it was pointed out that there were some omissions in my declaration dating back as far as 1983. I explained to Sir Gordon they were just that. He was – as I had found out on the Hollis question – a wise and decent person. He remarked that it was a long time ago, attitudes were different then and the whole business really amounted to a vendetta.

Although it took an immense amount of time and cost quite a bit of money replying to all the detailed and mostly irrelevant questions, the work in the department went ahead very well. In particular the committee stage of the March 1998 budget progressed smoothly despite some tricky technical problems. As with the previous budget, I took about half of the committee work myself. We finished the corporate tax reform. The Tories hardly laid a glove on me and my colleagues were kindly complimentary about my performance.

In the run-up to the second Downey report, which was expected towards the end of July 1998, Derek Draper, a former aide to Peter Mandelson, created a minor furore which was not without its comic aspects. He was making no doubt mildly exaggerated claims about the influence that he and Roger Liddle could exert on ministers to the benefit of their clients. Quite ludicrous really. He listed amongst other pretensions to high-level access that 'he could have tea with Geoffrey Robinson at the Treasury'. No one, for once, pursued my apparent involvement in the story. Draper, who was not exactly cut out to be a Trappist monk, concluded his cameo appearance in the headlines with an interview to *The Times*: 'I am disappointed that my big mouth has caused trouble, not just for the party and the government, but for the people I admire and respect.'

The committee's second report was published on 15 July 1998. The report accepted that I had not received the Hollis payment, a position later endorsed by the DTI inquiry, and in the words of *The Times* I was 'mildly rebuked over the failure to declare two paid directorships in the MPs' register in the 1980s'. I still contend that there was only one omission, my sole point of disagreement with Sir Gordon over the twelve-month period and a very insignificant one in any event. As *The Times* rightly reported, echoing Sir Gordon, the rules were 'vaguer' then.

I was cleared again and in good shape in mid-July. There were just two problems on the horizon: the July reshuffle and my impending operation. My mother had suffered from diverticulitis and it was my bad luck to inherit it. I informed Gordon in May that I would be undergoing major abdominal surgery, which the doctor said could wait a couple of months, though he was not too happy about my staying on antibiotics for that long.

During July Gordon pressed me to go ahead with the operation. I remonstrated that I thought it better to stick around until after the reshuffle. But the nearer the reshuffle got, the more emphatic Gordon became that I would not be involved. 'I've told you, Geoffrey, the reshuffle will not affect you,' he informed me as late as Thursday, 23 July, at a meeting in his office. The reshuffle was to take place on the next Tuesday.

It was a surprise, therefore, when he phoned me at my home at about nine o'clock on the Sunday evening, 26 July. We were discussing a few outstanding items of Treasury business when he incidentally dropped into the conversation a question about my receiving personal cheques from Maxwell. In a flash I remembered a conversation around the fireplace in his office a few weeks earlier, when he had caught my eye and asked a similar question even more pointedly: 'Is there anything in this story about you and a Maxwell cheque?' I did not then, and have not since, asked Gordon where these inquiries came from.* At the time, July 1998, I was unaware of this mysterious cheque. On the Sunday evening I assured him again that I knew nothing of any cheques and that my relations with Maxwell were always correct. He himself had remarked on the significance of the fact that I was not one of the people interviewed by the DTI inspectors in the wake of the Maxwell collapse.

Gordon's call perplexed me and I was expecting trouble when I arrived early from the country on Monday, 27 July. The first hint of it was when Ed Balls called in about 11 a.m. He said they had

---

* By the time I learned there was an issue at all I was no longer a minister. A DTI inspector had been appointed and it would have been improper for me to discuss the matter with the Chancellor.

had problems with Tony about the reshuffle. He reassured me that it was now 'sorted', a favourite word of his. However, the pendulum was swinging back in Downing Street and just before lunchtime No. 10 came on the phone to ask if I would see Tony in his office in the Commons at 3.30 p.m. My office immediately smelled a rat and alerted the Chancellor's office. Gordon killed the meeting. Instead, to my astonishment, I was told that he and I were to expect a visitation from Sir Richard Wilson, the Cabinet Secretary, the country's top civil servant, later that day.

Gordon came straight round to my office. He asked me to provide him with a written rebuttal of all the points in an article in the February 1998 edition of *Business Age* which purported to outline my relations with Maxwell. The article was made up of fantastic lies. Even the newspapers most hostile to me did not pick up on it. The few points of fact on which it was correct were harmless. I wrote a note and passed back along the corridor to the Chancellor.

The Cabinet Secretary went first to the Chancellor. I heard subsequently that Gordon was requested to ask for my resignation to avoid any further awkwardness. Gordon asked why and was told that the press campaign was an embarrassment to the government. He said that I had been cleared twice by Downey. Ah yes, but there is all that stuff out in the press, particularly the *Business Age* article. Gordon was well prepared and went through the article point by point. Having drawn a blank there, Sir Richard came down to my office. It was by now late afternoon.

He was all sweetness and light, very old boyish. 'Rough old game, politics,' was his opening gambit, as he walked in through the door. He went on to the Maxwell affair and cited the *Business Age* article despite his conversation just a few minutes earlier with the Chancellor. Icily but as politely as I could, I told him it was a pack of lies. He replied blithely, 'But it is all out there.' 'Are they the grounds for my leaving the government?' 'Yes,' he replied. 'And it's rather more dignified to resign than to be sacked.' I thanked him and said I would think about it as I showed him to the door. He was visibly shaken as he left. In the doorway he turned to impart his final disarming shot: 'I like you.'

In fact our relationship since he had taken up the post in January that year had been a constructive one. He had been instrumental in setting up the ministerial subcommittee on defence matters which helped restrict what could have been too much political influence from the Cabinet Office (see Chapter 15). As part of the Comprehensive Spending Review, I had conducted at ministerial level an assessment of the public service side of the Cabinet Office. It was one of the biggest shambles I have seen in or outside politics. I was intent on a reduction in its budget by 30 per cent, redeploying capable officials to more productive employment elsewhere in Whitehall. Sir Richard pointed out that, as he had only been a few months on the job, he could hardly be blamed. After fencing around for a bit he blurted out, 'I need the money.' His aim was to make the Cabinet Office an effective force in government for setting and delivering priority objectives.* It was plausible and, though I had my doubts, I agreed there would only be a minor reduction in the budget. He had been unusually straightforward about it – not trying to defend the mess that was there, as the department itself had done earlier in the Comprehensive Spending Review. I appreciated that. He was also upfront about the coal debate in which we were embroiled at the time. He had served in energy in various capacities between 1974 and 1986 and must have had some knowledge of the area. He thought the Interconnector arrangement with France was a good business deal: in fact it must rank as one of the worst commercial arrangements this country has ever entered into. That did not matter. He said he would be helpful and I appreciated that, too, though in the event staff at No. 10 were anything but. I had also met Lady Wilson and himself socially at various receptions. They were quite charming.

It was not difficult, therefore, to reciprocate Richard's goodwill, though the occasion when he demanded my resignation in my

---

* Sir Richard Wilson's report was published in December 1998, entitled *Civil Service Reform*. Annex D to the report set out sixty-five key tasks to be achieved progressively by September 2002. It seems, I am afraid to say, that Sir Humphrey still rules.

office in the Treasury was not the most propitious moment for me to do so. What I could not understand was why he had embarked on this unorthodox – dare I say it, unconventional – mission in the first place. If he had been asked to do it, he should have refused. If he volunteered, as I am reliably informed he did, it was an act of hubris. Either way it was a manner of proceeding I could not accept. In recording the incident I hope a repetition can be avoided. When a senior minister is to be sacked, the PM must do it.

The outcome of the Wilson démarche was that I decided, after one quiet moment of reflection on my own in the office, not to resign. I was fortified in this decision when I learned two further pieces of intelligence later that evening. First, that a colleague had already been invited to become Paymaster, and, moreover, that his prospective appointment had already been leaked to a national newspaper. Neither item of information did much to lighten my mood or weaken my resistance.

We met early that evening in Gordon's flat to review the situation. Gordon was distraught. We had worked together very closely for over four years. It had been the best of relationships at the working and personal levels. He had given me unstinting support throughout the turbulence. Now he was desperate for a face-saving arrangement for both our sakes. In his discussions with Tony he had put forward the idea that I should become a PFI supremo: the chairman of the PFI task force. Tony had agreed to this. It would bring with it an office in the Treasury, from which, Gordon suggested, we could continue to work together as before. He stressed that I had been a competent minister and he did not want the Treasury to lose me. Ed Balls, who was very upset at developments, interjected. 'He's been a f— brilliant minister.' I was very touched. I sensed strongly that Ed, though he had made only the one expostulatory remark during the meeting, was against my entering any sort of deal that smacked of plea bargaining.

At this point I took up the running myself. My first line of resistance to Gordon was the same as that I would put to the PM later in the evening: I could not accept a situation where I was leaving the government under a cloud. No one, not even my severest critics, had ever suggested that I was less than competent. To leave now after being cleared would be inexplicable. Moreover, the way it had all blown up overnight left me mystified. After weeks when it was all meant to have been settled and I was not to be involved in the reshuffle, I was suddenly confronted by the Cabinet Secretary with an ultimatum – resign or be sacked – commuted now to a quango-type job, thanks to Gordon's eleventh-hour intervention.

I thanked Gordon for his efforts on my behalf. I apologized for the problems I had caused. But politely refused any involvement in the PFI chairmanship. I had throughout my life – starting with my resignation from Jaguar in 1975 – refused face-saving compromises of that kind for myself. Just into my sixtieth year I was not about to change.

The conversation jumped around to no good effect. I suggested that the only way forward was for me to see the PM personally and have it out with him. Gordon went straight to the phone on the desk in the middle of the room to arrange it. I turned up at No. 10 at 8 p.m. on the dot.

I had not been to see the PM at No. 10 since he had moved into the more commodious office just round the corner from the Cabinet Office. The principal private secretary sat sentinel-like on the right-hand side of the entrance door. He had seen quite a traffic of people over the last few days. As I walked by him to go through to the PM's office, he encouragingly said to me, 'You'll be all right.' I retorted over my shoulder, 'I'm not taking that job,' referring to the PFI position.

The PM looked tired, the strains of the wretched job of reshuffling showing through. We got straight down to business.

Tony began the meeting by thanking me for the work I had done at the Treasury. He was desperately sorry about the press campaign, which he thought was most unfair and totally misrepresented me personally. He felt it would be better for me from my own point of view to resign, since I had now been cleared by Downey. He was to return to this point after we had gone upstairs for a drink, which I declined, since – unusually – I did not feel like one.

It was a good idea of his to retire to the sitting-room. It was more informal and we both relaxed. He was frank enough to tell me that he was in a very uncomfortable position, since the Cabinet Secretary had put it in writing to him that I had to go. This appeared to explain the change that had occurred overnight and I found it distasteful to learn that the Cabinet Secretary had involved himself in this way.

The PM talked in encouraging terms of the new PFI position. It seems that Gordon had gone to some lengths to explain my particular skills in stitching together deals. I was even 'a superb wheeler-dealer', I remember the PM saying. I recalled my daughter warning me, when the Maxwell stories started appearing, that I was stuck with that tag and would have to live with it. Gordon no doubt felt that extolling this particular skill was the best way to sell the PM the idea of giving me the PFI position. He had done a good job.

At various stages in the conversation I suggested that being a fixer – if I was one at all – was one of the lesser ways in which I could serve the government. I had a way of finding solutions to problems – as Gordon kindly remarked after the 1998 budget – but that was different. Anyway, the essence of my position was that having been cleared twice by Downey there was no reason for me to resign. To leave now would be to do so under a cloud. Bluntly, I told the PM I would not do that, pointing out that if I were to resign now no one would understand why, since I had been cleared. He reflected an instant and said, 'Well, that is correct actually. And I went right out there to defend you.' It was a good moment for me to put another point to him, with some feeling. Surely he would agree that the way we were handling the matter did no one any justice. For weeks I had been telling Gordon that if I was to resign in the reshuffle, which I was quite prepared to do, then I would like to plan it properly. I was always conscious of Francis Pym's resignation speech to the Commons, in which he made plain that he did not object to being sacked, but the manner of it, with persistent briefings from No. 10, he found offensive. The PM interjected that Alastair would not brief against me. I resumed and told him that I was going in for surgery that Thursday and we could easily have built the resignation around doubts about my health. We could proceed with it in September on those grounds. What I could not accept was to go now in circumstances that would be humiliating and prejudicial.

We were not getting anywhere, though the atmosphere was friendly throughout and replete with mutual respect. It was in this vein that I brought Gordon into the conversation. Tony seemed anxious to talk about his Chancellor. He was disarmingly frank. He considered Gordon 'the most brilliant brain in British politics'. He had advised him to go for the leadership in 1992. It was right for him then, just as it had not been right for him in 1994. This seemed an appropriate point for me to reassure him that whatever had or had not been agreed between them before 1994, Gordon accepted in 1994 that Tony was the right choice. Looking to the future, the PM was sure that if anything should happen to him, Gordon would certainly be the party's overwhelming choice. He also added that he was sure Gordon would have his chance in due course anyway.

We had been chatting for about an hour. I felt that, before leaving, I should clarify the position between myself and some senior officials. In general terms I explained my view that a strong-minded minister, though effective, would not always be popular with officials. This was certainly the case when I killed the GOGGS project and when I faced down the whole of officialdom on the energy policy. Tony indicated that he was aware of that, but tended to agree with the officials that I was 'unconventional'. Hence the title of this book. My rejoinder was perhaps uncalled for. Gordon would hardly be called 'conventional'. Nor, really, could the PM himself. I would never have worked as he did for the first months of his premiership out of a poky little office tucked away on the ground floor. The small two-seater settee would have killed my back. At the time I had admired the simple arrangements. But they were not exactly *comme il faut*. I could not see that it mattered whether any of us was conventional or not. What mattered was how effective we were. Sensing that the criticism would have been made by Sir Richard Wilson, I mentioned the Spending Review encounter, reassuring him, however, that I had been probably too accommodating to the Cabinet Office.

We both sensed there was not much more to say and we agreed to sleep on it. I told him that if in the morning he felt the same way, then I would put out my statement and he would put out his. Whatever happened he and his government would have my full support. I phoned Gordon at about 10.30 p.m. He had spoken to Tony, who, he said, was feeling better about the situation.

We met the next morning, as agreed, at No. 10. The PM told me straight out that he had slept on it – though badly – and had decided I should stay. He said it had been a difficult decision and one that he had reached out of deference to Gordon and me. Anyone else would have been out on their ear. But he added two things rather ominously: that I was a target and the government could do without one; and that he was reliably informed there was still more trouble to come. This reference had probably come from Alastair Campbell, who had close links with Anthony Bevins, the chief political correspondent of the *Daily Express*. This newspaper was now leading the pack against me.

It was no time to remonstrate. I thanked him and assured him that my resignation was at his disposal any time he should request it. He thanked me for that, saying he did not want to go through all this hassle again, as he sensed it would come sooner or later. Neither of us guessed how soon. As for hassle, I thought on balance I had had more than my full share.

Though he did not say so, the PM had clearly talked the matter over with Alastair, from whom the reiterated dire warnings had emanated. He also told me that I was bitter about things. This was the first time this word had crept into our conversations. It appeared frequently in subsequent lurid press stories leading up to the publication of this book. I trust there is no trace of it in my writing. Certainly I feel none. Perhaps too much pride. But no bitterness or envy. So I picked him up on this and said there was no reason to feel bitter. He had offered me a very good alternative at the PFI where I could use my talents. 'Yes,' he replied, 'that offer still remains open.' Pity, I teased him, that it came up right at the last minute. He smiled that wide, irresistible smile of his – how could anyone not like and admire the guy. 'Good luck with the op,' he called out. And off I went.

On the following day, 29 July, I received a Labour Party delegation from Coventry which Gordon kindly hosted at No. 11. I left late in the afternoon for the Royal Surrey Hospital at Guildford where my operation was scheduled for 9 a.m. the next day. It came almost as a relief to face the surgeon's knife after the last forty-eight hours.

The surgery was a success. I was out of hospital in five days and back in the Treasury on Monday, 10 August. Gordon had invited me to stay with him at Cape Cod, but I did not fancy the journey. I felt good in the office. Just a year earlier I had also spent August on my own.

My thoughts turned to the new areas of work for the next session of Parliament. On my own front we still had to complete on capital-gains tax, which would require primary legislation. Having started the major reform here I was keen to finish it off. Now that most of the corporate-tax legislative programme was out of the way, I was looking to expand the work of the Growth Unit. We had started the process of adding real-world considerations to the Treasury thought process. There was still some way to go. Government purchasing is appallingly inefficient, locked in the era of pencils, rubbers and requisition notes. It needed to be opened up to the best modern practices in the private sector. A team of the most hard-headed businessmen would have a job on their hands to modernize the ancient practices. Given that there was over £10 billions' worth of purchases on civil procurement of goods and services carried out each year, it was well worth a major effort to improve the system. On the productivity front there was still a lot to do. We had run a series of successful seminars on increasing efficiency in the economy. It was about time we looked at the government itself. I could feel the official resistance at the mere thought of it.

The London stock exchange was a target in my sights. Talks were already under way with the Frankfurt exchange. There was no doubt who would have ended up top-dog in that merger – it would not be London. I had had discussions with NASDAQ, which had established itself as a real competitor to the New York Stock Exchange and was keen to establish a base in London, with the idea of repeating its success in Europe. My aim was to secure them a listing in London, concentrating, as they had done in the USA, initially on high-tech, small-company stocks. The discussions had gone well in New York. Their top executive had visited me in the Treasury. They were as keen as mustard. This was another project pregnant with possibilities, despite the imprecations of the governor of the Bank of England against it.

We had to devise a successor organization for the PFI unit, which was due to be wound up the following July. My aim here was to get the body into the private sector with some government equity capital. It would still be available to advise the Treasury and other departments, but it would have more freedom of action, subject to the disciplines of the market, to get things done.

Indeed there was plenty to do all round. I had the outline work programme ready for the Chancellor on his return from holiday. He was in great form, bursting with energy. He liked the ideas. But I was not to be given the chance of realizing them.

On 22 September 1998, the letter arrived from the DTI informing me that they were opening an inquiry into possible false accounting by the Maxwell business with which I had been involved, Hollis Industries. The Mandelson loan crisis was to arise three months later. In between I faced the third Downey report. The issues that had been raised by the Tories were fourfold. Sir Gordon Downey found for me on three of them, but rightly judged that I had not registered a shareholding. One complaint was therefore upheld.

A word about Sir Gordon is in order. It is likely that I have had more extensive dealings with Sir Gordon than any other Member of Parliament. He handled in all three reports on myself. Through-out he was as decent and sensible a person as one could hope for. He might be called 'old school', but there was nothing wrong that I could see in that. He seemed to me to develop a fastidious distaste for the Tories and their vendetta, as he called it, against me. His view was that 'they were really scraping the barrel'. Perhaps I was lulled into a sense of false confidence. I should not have allowed that to happen. But it was in that frame of mind that I confronted my peers in the committee room, where, at my suggestion, the Standards and Privileges Committee met to discuss my situation.

The Tories took no part in the proceedings. They left the Labour members to make the running. Rereading the minutes does not evoke pleasant memories. Of my interrogators, Shona McIsaac was most to the point: 'It seems to me you are getting the breach of the advocacy rule mixed up with non-declaration?' I was not, but I was trying unsuccessfully to make the point that there was no intention on my part to conceal any wrong action behind my non-registration. It was a genuine oversight. Dale Campbell-Savours adopted a friendly approach and in passing referred to the good work I had been doing in rebuilding the New Statesman. However, towards the end of the meeting we seemed to be getting bogged down in the technical aspects of the TransTec rights issue, the details of which I could not remember and the relevance of which escaped me. I left the meeting feeling frustrated that I had not got over sufficiently well to the committee the differences between mistakes of omission and those of commission.

Any initial doubts I might have had about how the committee were thinking were dispelled when I bumped into Bob Sheldon* that night in the gents in the Commons. 'How did it go?' I asked him. 'Oh, you'll be all right,' he replied. 'I expect they'll want a personal statement?' I posed the question in a rhetorical sort of way. 'I wouldn't like to comment on that,' was his parting remark. No further comment was required. I went back to the flat and drafted the statement which I knew I should have to make.

The committee's report was duly published the next day, Wednesday, 18 November, embargoed for 11 a.m. They recommended that I should 'make an apology to the House by means of a personal

*Robert Sheldon, chairman of the Standards Committee. Sheldon himself became the subject of a ridiculous attack by the press and the Tories in July 2000.

statement'. I showed the draft to Gordon after the publication of the report. He suggested small changes. The statement was short and to the point. It ran as follows:

Madam Speaker, I am taking the earliest opportunity available to me to apologize to the House for the late registration of my ownership of Stenbell Limited and the directorships of Agie UK between 1984 and 1987 and TransTec plc between 1987 and 1990. I have apologized in writing to the Committee on Standards and Privileges and have amended my entry in the register to include Roll Center Inc., which I owned between February 1988 and January 1992.

The House will want to be assured that these shareholdings and directorships were matters of public record. No attempt was made by me at any time to use my position in this House to advance any commercial interest. The oversight concerning registration, for which I apologize, is entirely my responsibility.

I could not think there was much more to add. There were no motives to explain. There were no brown envelopes, no cash for questions, no surreptitious advocacy, no hidden agenda. I had over-looked in a period of more than twenty years two – though I would contend only one – registerable directorships and one shareholding.

That is all the most intensive and sustained examination of my affairs had raised. My colleagues were genuinely, I think, complimentary about the tone of the statement and the manner of my delivery. No one seemed to think anything more was required. The press took umbrage. The *Daily Express* ran an absurd front page devoted to just a photograph of myself with the caption 'Who does he think he is?' I was way beyond caring.

I have on occasions reflected on the Standards Committee's decision. One such occasion was when the new commissioner, Elizabeth Filkin, reported that a colleague 'had breached the standards of conduct expected of members'. No apology had been required then, and shortly after the publication of that report Bob Sheldon was kind enough to remark to me, 'Geoffrey, you have been hard done by.' I made no reply. Sir Gordon, Elizabeth Filkin's predecessor, had told me that in my case the committee were into 'totting up'. Perhaps a geometric progression had crept into their calculations.

Whatever the reason for their recommendation the committee's decision marked a real setback for me. My PPS, Ian Pearson, came to see me the following week. For the first time colleagues in the parliamentary party were critical. Until this point it had been one of the great strengths of my position that I enjoyed wide support throughout the Labour ranks in the Commons. Only Paul Flynn had been fleetingly critical. Now Ian reported there was some loss of confidence. Remarkably perhaps there was no call from the PM. But within a few weeks the Mandelson loan story broke and the rest is history.

My resignation was something of an anticlimax subsumed in the high drama of Peter's departure from office earlier in the day. In my own office there was sadness. Sue Nye came down from Gordon's office and threw her arms around me in support. She had seen many such events and I much appreciated the warmth of her gesture. Steve Field, my private secretary, kindly authorized the use of the official car to take me to my flat.

As we said goodbye at the Treasury side entrance, Steve in his laid-back, dispassionate way remarked, 'It was only bad admin, you know really, Geoffrey.' I thanked him for that remark and for all he had done. I looked once more at the dilapidated Treasury building, where the PFI project is now well under way, and bade it farewell. I felt in my heart that as a Treasury minister it was not au revoir.

Back at the flat I could not help but reflect that despite how strongly truncated my period of office had been, the last four to five years had been extremely eventful and productive ones. And I determined there and then to write a book about them.

I knew I should have to face up to the complicated problems that were brought into my political life by my business relations with Robert Maxwell, which, though they were not the direct cause of my resignation, were grossly exaggerated and distorted in much of the press. For this reason if no other I want to set the record straight.

17. An Inspector Calls

It was in 1967 that as a young researcher at Transport House I was sent on an urgent mission to deliver Labour Party briefing papers to Robert Maxwell, who was flying out to a Council of Europe meeting in Strasbourg. He was rapporteur of the council's scientific committee. I vividly recall this brief encounter. He was travelling on a private jet. I met him on the runway in front of the plane. He asked me for a verbal summary of the brief, which I gave him on the spot. Handing the brief over, I added that I had not written it myself and I thought it too negative on the prospects for European cooperation. He might wish therefore to go a bit further, I suggested. I knew his inclinations lay in that direction. He beamed at me – 'Very good'. (He loved intrigue at any level.) I was pleased, since I was myself in my early political life briefly caught up in the grand concept of European technological cooperation. Harold Wilson was to play this card in the then Labour government's abortive attempt to negotiate entry into the EEC in 1967.

As I accompanied Maxwell to board the plane I inquired whether this was not an expensive way to travel. He replied, 'Money is the only problem I haven't got!' He had it to come though, I am afraid.

I am not a particularly impressionable person. But it was hard not to be in some awe of Robert Maxwell. Looks, stature, voice, brains, money, languages – he had the lot. Many people from the start of his public career have affected to see through Robert Maxwell. Not many, though, have refused to do business with him. Indeed, whole firms of bankers, lawyers and accountants in the City of London virtually lived off him in the later years! And, like him or hate him, he inevitably engendered a reaction. From the start, to be truthful, I have to say when I first met him I liked him. His evident gargantuan vanity and gigantic ego did not really bother me. I was mildly amused by them. Many years later, when

Maxwell was at his business prime, the *New Yorker* magazine ran an article on the battle of the egos between Maxwell and Donald Trump. Maxwell was given the edge, much to his pleasure.

But that was a long way ahead. During the four years I was working as a researcher for the Labour government the airplane meeting was the only contact I can remember having with Robert Maxwell. He was fiendishly busy in Parliament. I moved on to the IRC★ in 1968, disillusioned over Vietnam and the handling of the sterling devaluation.

It was not really until the 1986 Labour Party Conference at Blackpool that I renewed my acquaintance with Maxwell. We had, of course, come across each other at meetings and conferences from time to time. He was always flatteringly friendly towards me.

During 1986 I had followed with keen interest his attempts to establish a medium technology manufacturing empire with Sir John Collyear, and envied the vast sums he could apparently make readily available for this purpose. I was struggling to get my own high-tech start-up venture off the ground. In the event, his ambition for manufacturing never really got going and when he lost the bid for AE – a major engineering company in Rugby – the manufacturing venture was put on hold.

There remained within the Maxwell empire, however, two manufacturing companies of which I had a good knowledge from my motor-industry background. Moreover, they were both in Coventry, adjacent to my constituency and very near to Coleshill, where I had located my own business. These Maxwell businesses were Coventry Apex and A. L. Dunn.

When I bumped into him in Blackpool I mentioned to him the proximity of these companies to my own and that I felt that, given more management attention, they could be successfully developed. He was sufficiently interested in the idea to suggest a meeting in the New Year.

Kevin Maxwell was present when we met in due course. Bob

★ The Industrial Reorganization Corporation was set up during the 1964–70 Wilson government to effect the restructuring of British industry.

made it clear that he would be pleased for me to be involved with Apex and Dunn and that the sensible way forward would be for me to join the board of Central & Sheerwood plc, the holding company. Central & Sheerwood was a publicly quoted company in which the Maxwells had a large stake. Bob Maxwell hinted that in due course he would also consider appointing me to the board of Hollis Industries if all went well at Central & Sheerwood. I could tell he rather regarded a directorship of Hollis as a great prize – a reward I might aspire to and gain by good works. In due course, some eighteen months later, I become non-executive chairman of Hollis, which, far from being a reward, became a curse.

For the moment I was pleased enough to become involved at C&S. It was a typical penny stock languishing unloved and unattended to. But given its quotation, I could see potential development in the engineering sector, with links in due course to my own company, TransTec, as well. I told him about TransTec and my plans for it. He seemed interested and gave a positive response to my inquiry as to whether he would be interested in backing the enterprise if we needed funds for expansion. He nodded his approval, rather world-wearily I thought. No doubt many people were seeking his support.

For the moment I was keen to get started with Apex and Dunn, where the line management responded positively to my involvement. However, it was not long after I had joined the board of C&S that I became aware of quite different plans to develop the business into a major property company. These were put forward by the Robert Fraser Group, led by Colin Emson. The plans were duly put in place the next year. My role from then on became not just to run the car companies but also to seek buyers for them, as obviously they would not fit into the new scheme of things, to be based on property. I was somewhat disappointed, since a potential route for the development of TransTec had been blocked – at least temporarily.

My objectives were to increase the size and profitability of the companies, get a good price for them and, for me the most important, to find the right home for them. It was a growth period for the motor industry and the companies prospered. But finding the right buyer and getting the right price were anything but easy. I got quite close twice – on each occasion with US companies. Both were brought to water; but neither, in the event, would drink.

Time and the collapse of the property market caused fortune to smile on me. Barely was the ink dry on the Robert Fraser deal formalizing its commitment to property development than the market headed due south. The peak of prices for commercial sites coincided almost exactly with the date, September 1988, of the Robert Fraser agreement. Thereafter it dropped 40 per cent within a couple of years! Timing in business, as in politics, is key. The C&S move into property had not got it quite right. I did not regret this. One door closed, another opened.

I seized the opportunity and by mid-1990 had worked up an alternative plan for the development of the company, which would involve an alliance between C&S and my own company TransTec, and which would include two subsidiaries of Hollis Industries. The plan found favour with the board. If feasible, the move would successfully resolve at a stroke the future of my own company and that of the engineering companies of C&S and of the two manufacturing companies of Hollis Industries.

At this stage, I should explain the Hollis situation, which became the bane of my life some seven years later – in 1998, when I was serving as Paymaster General.

The Hollis story began at my first business meeting with Maxwell in early 1987. What was offered as a great prize turned out to be a running sore from the moment when he sold it to a management buyout group in June 1988 and when at his request I became its non-executive chairman. He wanted me to keep an eye on his remaining interests in the company, which were made up of subordinated loans and preference shares.

The management buyout group paid too high a price. The new company was too heavily geared and could not service the interest on the debt or repay the capital. Within eighteen months Maxwell bought it back, with my full support as chairman, in order to safeguard both bank and trade creditors.

By this time I had had pretty well enough of Hollis. It had been an uncomfortable period. There were two successive recapitalizations in 1989 aimed at avoiding the show going belly up. Relations with the MBO team had been uncooperative and confrontational. There was one blazing row after another between them and Robert Maxwell. So after the buy-back I was keen to call it a day. But Maxwell wanted me to carry on. I reluctantly acceded, but made it clear that I wanted to bring two of the companies into the new group we were preparing to launch – and that at that point I would leave. This was June 1990. By the following May the plan I had outlined to the C&S board was successfully implemented. C&S, the quoted company, acquired the two Hollis companies and my own TransTec. The company was under my management control and renamed Transfer Technology Group plc. Robert Fraser sold their shares at once – Robert Maxwell followed suit in September 1991.

Against the background of the wild allegations that, nearly ten years later, were to be made about my deep and extensive involvement with Robert Maxwell, it puts matters into perspective to see just what my involvement actually was.

At no point did the assets or turnover for which I was responsible represent more than 3 per cent of the total of Maxwell interests. Moreover, the areas with which I was involved were peripheral activities in the engineering sector – just about as far removed as possible from the mainstream public or private businesses of Maxwell. For none of the positions I occupied did I have any contract for remuneration. There was no more than an undertaking between Maxwell and myself that any emoluments would depend on the commitment required of me and the success achieved.

The success varied with the companies. Coventry Apex and A. L. Dunn both did very well under me. After three and a half years without remuneration or expenses I was voted a £150,000 payment by the board. The directorship was registered in my House of Commons declaration as soon as this board resolution had been signed.

For the period of my non-executive chairmanship of Hollis

Industries, including the management buyout, I neither requested nor received any compensation as non-executive chairman, nor was any payment made to me, despite an erroneous entry in the 1988/89 accounts showing the chairman, myself, receiving £200,000 – a mystery to which I shall return after making three further points that underline the limited nature of my involvement with Maxwell.

The first point is that I was not invited to any of his flamboyant birthday parties. (I would certainly have gone if I had been invited.) But there was no question of pique. I was not close or important enough. This is further borne out by the scant references to me personally or to the Maxwell companies I managed in Tom Bower's book *Maxwell*, the most detailed and best researched exposé of the Maxwell financial scandals. There is a single and inconsequential mention of Hollis amongst the companies and there is a single mention of myself.

It is not, however, the Bower book that, by its total disregard of my dealings with Maxwell, best demonstrates how peripheral they were. There is the plain fact that the DTI inspectors appointed after the collapse of the Maxwell empire did not consider it necessary to interview me or communicate with me in any way whatsoever. They had no interest in a few engineering businesses on the outskirts of the empire.

The Tories, however, discovered a new-found interest in Maxwell and me in the course of their investigation into my business activities in 1998. They brought to light the 1988/89 accounts for Hollis, in which the payment of £200,000 was recorded as the chairman's remuneration. They drew this to the attention of Sir Gordon Downey, the Registrar of Members' interests at the House of Commons and asked him to investigate it. They had a point: I had not registered Hollis as a remunerated directorship, as it appeared I should have done. What the Tories did not know was that I had not declared the payment to the Inland Revenue either – I had never had it!

How then did I not spot this error in the accounts? At a distance of eight very busy years, I do not remember seeing these accounts.

My feeling is that if I had seen them I would have looked at the details of the directors' remuneration and seen the £200,000 entry. It would have stuck out like a sore thumb. What I have discovered since the Downey inquiry has convinced me I never saw these accounts. I was never shown them and, of course, did not sign them.

Readers of this book will probably find it in some measure reprehensible that I did not demand to see the Hollis accounts. No doubt I was not as attentive as I should have been. In my defence I can plead the extreme pressure of work at that time. That may indeed have played a role. But it is never an adequate reason. More to the point, I think, is the reality of the Hollis situation at that time. It was a company of no interest to anyone. Its assets and liabilities belonged exclusively to Robert Maxwell. There were no external shareholders. Its accounts were signed off with those of dozens of other subsidiaries subsumed in the myriad of companies that Maxwell had assembled. There is nothing unusual in this. In many publicly quoted companies there is often a quite large number of small non-trading companies where accounts are signed off without scrutiny by the officers of the company.

It was nevertheless quite right that I should have to explain the situation. Sir Gordon Downey is a decent and sensible man. A gentleman in fact. I demonstrated to his satisfaction, from my own bank statements, which we had fortunately kept, that I had not received this payment. It was also possible to show that neither Hollis nor its holding company Pergamon had made such a payment. Sir Gordon concluded in his report: 'On the basis of the evidence we have seen, the relevant entry in the published accounts is false, and we do not uphold the complaint.'

It was a balanced and correct judgement subsequently confirmed by a DTI investigation instigated by the Tories. Having taken the lead, David Heathcoat-Amory remarked to me outside the members' entrance, 'Nothing personal, Geoffrey.' I smiled. In politics, as in the boxing ring, the last thing you do when hurt is to show it.

The inquiry got under way in January 1999. I offered and gave it my fullest cooperation, as I had done with Sir Gordon Downey. I was anxious above all to demonstrate that there was no secret account in my name, or in the names of any of my family or for that matter any of my companies, to which the supposed fee of £200,000 had been paid.

This meant my family and TransTec signing up to reveal all accounts held in the period from mid-1990 to mid-1991. I knew that no such secret account existed. But my efforts to prove this had in retrospect their comic aspects.

My lawyers came through with bad news. National Westminster had found previously unknown accounts at Colmore Row, Birmingham (the very branch at which my family and I and my companies held our accounts) in the name of a certain Geoffrey Robinson and his wife, Pauline. The spelling of this Geoffrey was the same as my own; Pauline was the first name of my stepmother, my father's third wife. I had acted briefly as a trustee for certain assets in which Pauline's children had a beneficial interest after my father's death in 1994. This had been the subject of an earlier abortive attack on me by the Tories.

For the moment I was bemused. How on earth would I find out who this Geoffrey and Pauline Robinson were? The only clue I had was that the Geoffrey Robinson in question had been involved in a fork-lift truck business in Coventry. It was not much to go on. Despite a deep sense of despair I set to work to see what I could find out. I remembered that in 1991 or thereabouts we had done a deal at TransTec with a small Coventry-based company for the supply and maintenance of all our fork-lift trucks. I remember predicting they would go bust, but I could not for the life of me remember the name. I made two unsuccessful calls to ex-colleagues at Dunn and Apex, the Coventry-based TransTec companies. Neither could recall the name of the company we had done business with. One made the helpful suggestion that I might ask John Stubbs, the former supply manager at Dunns, and he did remember the company we had dealt with. It was called Prestige. (He confirmed in passing that they had indeed gone bust!) By a stroke of luck he also knew another fork-lift truck company called Truman King.

This company, he thought, had also failed and had been picked up by Fiat, who had relocated it with its own operations in the Black Country. He did not recall the name, but I guessed it would be under OM – Officina Meccanica, the named used by Fiat for these activities. I soon ascertained that the company still operated out of Walsall under the same name. I reached a Mr Khan there. He told me that he did remember a Geoffrey Robinson who had been the managing director of Truman King. Mr Robinson had moved with the company to Walsall but had then left to start up his own business near Knutsford in Cheshire.

Mr Khan had no forwarding address for him, but remembered the name of his accountants. Through them, having acceptably proved my bona fides, I was finally able to reach the object of my search. By coincidence, I was just about to phone Geoffrey Robinson when my lawyer came through on the other line. I invited him to listen in as I cold-called my namesake.

I introduced myself to Geoffrey Robinson and explained the purpose of my call. Would he mind answering a few questions for me? It would be of great assistance since people were mistaking him for me. He took the approach in good part, remembering me from my Jaguar days and passing me nice compliments about them. I put my questions to him. Yes, he was called Geoffrey Robinson. Yes, he had been a director of Truman King in Coventry. Yes, he did bank at National Westminster, Colmore Row, in Birmingham. And yes, he did know Pauline Robinson, from whom he had been divorced for two years but with whom he remained on good terms. I could hear audible sighs of relief from my solicitor on the other phone. By the end of the conversation, which he had heard live, he needed no written confirmation. We had at least caught that red herring before it escaped the net. There were no other apparently undisclosed accounts in my or my family's name.

However, for the most part, the course of the DTI inquiries during the fourteen months of their duration, was much less entertaining. So it was with a sense of satisfaction that I read, on 29 December 1999, the DTI press statement vindicating my position: 'There have been thorough inquiries in line with the department's normal procedures in these matters . . . and the department does not propose to take any further action.' It had been a long year. My friends were delighted. The Tories were deflated. I started to put in place my plans for the future. Two days later, the DTI launched a full-scale inquiry into TransTec's receivership. The company I had formed nearly twenty years before, and which had grown to have a turnover of over £300 million and profits of £18 million in 1998, had collapsed in strange circumstances surrounding a major contract with the Ford Motor Company. Any person who had been a director during the last three years would be involved in the inquiry. My resignation from the board had occurred two years and eight months prior to the relevant events. I had played no role whatsoever in the fatal period of the company's affairs. The family trust and I myself had lost over £30 million. Was that not enough? Apparently not. As this goes to print the DTI inspector is back on the job.

Index

ACT (advance corporation tax) 83–8, 91, 94
Advent 64n
AE 235
Aerospatiale 203, 204
Aerospatiale-Matra 207
Agie UK 232
AIL (acceptance-in-lieu) scheme 164
Aims of Industry 78
Ainsworth, Bob 147
Airbus 188–91, 201, 208
Andersen, Arthur 68, 70, 71, 80–81, 84, 87–91, 94, 95
Annual Spending Review 60
Archer, Jeffrey 75
Armstrong, Hilary 103
Armstrong, Lord 162–3
Aspin, Les 202
Atkinson, Ron 143, 145
Atlantic Alliance 207
Attenborough, Sir David 170
Attenborough, Lord 169–71
Attlee, Clement 140
Austin 12, 16
Austin Morris 18, 193

Balls, Ed 9, 32, 34, 56, 67, 74–5, 76, 90, 93, 144, 216
  and Bank independence 35–41
  and Europe 124, 125, 127, 131, 134
  Fiscal Policy document 57–8
  Fiscal Stability Code 58–9
  and the reshuffle 221–2
Bank of Credit and Commerce International (BCCI) 39
Bank of England 33, 35–9, 55n, 56, 57
Bank of England Bill 53
Barings Bank 39, 44

Bates, Malcolm 99–100, 101
Bates report 103
Beard, Alex 166, 168
Beckett, Margaret 152, 157, 158
Belgian Motor Company 17, 18, 22
Bell, Wedlake 75
Beloff, Michael 75, 78–9, 218
Benefits Agency 105, 106
Benn, Tony 19
Bergman, Ingmar 169–70
Bermuda affair 214
Bevins, Anthony 127, 228
BG 70, 72–3
Billiton 91, 92
Birt, Sir John 5
Blair, Cherie 75
Blair, Tony
  the 1997 election 34
  the Airbus project 188
  and the coal industry 152, 157–8
  decides that Robinson should stay 228
  and defence restructuring 205
  defends Robinson 214
  and Europe 122, 128, 131, 137
  in Japan 106
  the Mandelson affair 11–14
  Prime Minister's Question Time 93, 152, 175, 217
  pro-Bank independence 38
  pro-busines 191
  relations with Brown 138–9
  relations with Robinson 30
  and the reshuffle 221–2, 225
BMW/Rover 8, 16, 18, 19, 192, 195–9

Booth, Albert 2
Bosman ruling 76, 146
Bourgeois, Joska 16–26, 178, 211, 212
Bourgeois, Micheline 21
Bower, Tom: Maxwell 230
Britannia 108–21
Britannia building society 11
British Aerospace (BAe) 186, 187–92, 197, 200, 203–8
British Airports Authority 70
British Broadcasting Corporation (BBC) 5, 15, 56, 59, 66, 162, 218
British Film Institute 169
British Gas 72, 82
British Leyland (BL) 16, 17, 18, 22, 187
British Museum 161, 162, 163
Brittan, Leon 193
Brookes, Peter 215
Brown, Gordon
  the 1997 election 34
  ambition of 47
  his approach 60–61
  and BAe 190, 191
  the Bank independence 35–7, 41, 42–3, 45
  and BMW/Rover 197
  and Britannia 109, 120, 121
  and the budget 93
  and the coal industry 151–4
  and Europe 122–3, 127–8, 129, 131–2, 134–5
  GOGGS project 50
  'Iron Chancellor' 57
  and ISAs 179, 181
  the Mandelson affair 11, 12, 13
  relationship with Blair 138–9
  speech-writing 132–3

supports Robinson over
   his resignation 224
his team 30–33
and Vauxhall 193, 194
watches football 144
windfall tax idea 66
Browns Lane factory,
   Coventry 27
Bruce, Malcolm 129
BT 70, 72, 81
Budd, Alan 44n
Budge, R. J. (coal company)
   150, 151, 152
Budge, Richard 150
Budget 52, 54, 59, 93
Buiter, William 44n, 45
Burns, Sir Terence 40,
   46–51, 210–11
Business Age 222
Butler, Sir Robin 108, 109,
   115
Buydendyk, George 22,
   23
Byatt, Ian 82
Byers, Stephen 199

Cabinet Office 51, 61, 62,
   102, 153, 154, 157, 158,
   200, 201, 204, 205, 211,
   223, 228
Caborn, Richard 152
Callaghan, James (later Baron
   Callaghan of Cardiff)
   29, 62
Campbell, Alastair 109, 125,
   127, 130, 132, 133, 139,
   216, 228
Campbell-Savours, Dale 231
Capital Allowances Act
   (1989) 170
Casson, Sir Hugh 110, 114
Casta, Laetitia 169
Cayley, Michael 53, 90–91
CBI (Conferation of British
   Industy) 39, 42, 89, 92,
   93, 125, 129, 135
CEGB 159
Central & Sheerwood plc
   (C&S) 236, 237, 238
Central Intelligence Agency
   (CIA) 44
Centrica 82
Channel 4 News 214
Channel Tunnel rail link
   (CTRL) 104–5,
   107

Charles, HRH The Prince
   of Wales 110, 120
Civil Service 54, 106, 158,
   163
Clark, Lord 162
Clarke, Kenneth 43, 45, 66,
   67, 73, 84, 124, 212
Clementi, David 44
Clinton, Bill 133
coal industry 14, 150–60
Code of Fiscal Responsibility
   39
Collyear, Sir John 235
Competition Commission 63
Comprehensive Spending
   Review 60, 223, 227–8
Confederation of British
   Industry *see* CBI
Cook, Robin 125–6
Cooksey, Sir David 64
Cooper, Tony 151
Cooper, Yvette 54, 144
Council of Europe 77
Courtaulds 183
Cousins, Miss 214
Coventry Apex 235, 236,
   238, 241
Coventry City Football Club
   141–9
Cranston, Ross 54
Cruickshank, Donald 63, 82
Cunningham, Jack 61
Curwen, Peter 134

Daily Express 10, 228, 232
Daily Mail 10, 127, 128, 135
Daily Mirror 10, 13, 109, 145
Daily Telegraph 10, 79,
   135–6, 141, 144
Daimler Benz 203, 204, 207
Daimler Chrysler 207–8
Darling, Alistair 55
DASA (Deutsche Aerospace)
   203, 204
Davies, Howard 42–3, 44n
Davis, Sir Peter 90
De Lorean 69
defence restructuring
   200–208
Department of Culture,
   Media and Sport 164
Department of Economic
   Affairs 62
Department of Employment
   61
Department of the

Environment 148, 157
Department of Trade and
   Industry (DTI) 10, 18,
   63, 105, 106, 137, 155,
   156, 158, 183, 185, 188,
   191, 192, 193, 196, 199,
   220, 221, 230, 239, 240,
   242–3
Deutsch Kleinwort Benson
   44, 102
Devonport Royal Dockyard
   114–15, 118, 119
Diana, Princess 110, 120–21
Dobson, Frank 130
Downey, Sir Gordon 218,
   219–20, 222, 225, 226,
   230, 232, 239, 240–41
Draper, Derek 220
Drummond, Maldwin 113
DSS 105
Dunn, A. L. 235, 236, 238,
   241
Dyall, Robina 53
Dyke, Greg 56

Eastern Electricity 75, 159
Eastham, Paul 127
EC law 76–7, 78
Ecofin 131
Edelman, Maurice 19, 27
Edwardes, Sir Michael 19
Elizabeth II, Queen 108,
   109–10, 116, 117, 121
Emson, Colin 236
EMU 57, 122–8, 131, 132,
   133, 136
English Partnerships 165
ERM 47, 48, 56, 57, 126, 136
European Aeronautics
   Defence and Space
   (EADS) 207
European Aerospace and
   Defence Company
   (EADC) 201, 203, 205,
   206, 207
European Communities Bill
   122
European Community (EC)
   80, 234
European Convention on
   Human Rights 74, 76,
   77, 78
European Court of Human
   Rights 74
European Union (EU) 30,
   124, 192, 194

Evans, Nigel 219
Evans, Sir Richard 187–81
Evans, Trevor 54
Eversholt Leasing 81–82

Falconer, Charlie 8, 9, 10
Fanning, Peter 32
Fellowes, Sir Robert 116,
    120, 121
Fiat 242
FIDS (Foreign Income
    Dividends Scheme) 85,
    91
Field, Steve 53, 233
Filkin, Dame Elizabeth
    232
films 169–71
Finance Bills 54–5, 81, 171
Financial Service Bill 55
Financial Services Authority
    53, 55n
Financial Times (FT) 124,
    135
Fleming, Roddie 92
Flynn, Paul 233
Football Association 149
Ford Motor Company 22,
    23, 193, 194, 195, 198,
    198, 243
Foreign Office 50, 51, 137
Frankfurt stock exchange
    229
FTSE 71–4, 93
Fujitsu 105

G8 158
Gardiner, John 183
Gaulle, Charles De 122
GE 184, 185, 186
GEC 100, 187, 203, 205
General Motors (GM) 22–3,
    192–5
George, Eddie 36, 40, 41, 43,
    44
Getty, John 115
Gilbertson, Brian 92
GOGGS project 49, 50, 52,
    227
Goobey, Alastair Ross 100
Goodhart, Charles 44n
Goodyear 23
Gosling, Sir Donald 112–13,
    116, 118, 119, 121, 170
Graham, Sir Peter 80
Greenspan, Alan 36, 37, 124
Gregson, Sir Peter 209

Growth Unit 53, 62, 63, 65,
    97, 229
Guardian 9–12, 79, 90, 109,
    135
Guinness, Sir Alec 170

Hague, William 136, 217
Hailey, Stephen 69
Hartlepool 2
Hayden, Bill 198
Heath, Sir Edward 81, 122,
    184
Heathcoat-Amory, David 54,
    219, 240
Heathrow Airport 201
Heritage Department 164
Heseltine, Michael 79, 104,
    155
Heywood, Jeremy 14, 48–9
Higgs, Derek 107, 146, 147
Hill, Jimmy 141, 142, 145
Hiscox, Robert 166–7,
    168
Hobson, Ron 113
Hollis Industries 219, 220,
    236–40
Holmes, John 133
Home Office 3
Honda 199
House of Commons
    Standards and Privilege
    Select Committee 11n,
    231, 232–3
House of Commons
    Treasury Select
    Committee 44
Hover, Graham 142
Howe, Sir Geoffrey 66, 71
Huckerby, Darren 145
Hughes, Philip 162
Hunter, Anji 4–5
Hutton, Will 216, 217

ICL 105, 106
Inchcape Group 24
Independent 10, 121, 128, 135,
    212
Independent on Sunday 34,
    47n, 123, 150, 178, 209,
    210
Industrial Reorganization
    Corporation (IRC)
    183, 235
Industrial Society 217
Inland Revenue (IR) 52, 53,
    89, 90, 95, 96, 97, 161,

    164, 169, 170, 171, 212,
    239
    and ISAs 172–5, 178, 179,
    181
Institute of Actuaries 88
International Monetary Fund
    (IMF) 36, 47, 131
IPO (initial public offering)
    207
Irvine, Derry 41, 101, 132
ISAs (Individual Savings
    Accounts) 96, 172–82,
    215

Jack, Michael 49
Jaguar 16–20, 22, 27, 28,
    114, 193, 198, 225,
    242
Jay, Peter 59, 80
Jenkins, Christopher 80
Jenkins, Roy 136
Jenkins, Simon 215
Jospin 205
JSF programme 206
Julius, DeAnne 44n

K, Mlle 170
Kavanagh, Trevor 213, 214
Keane, Robbie 145
Kearton, Lord 183
Kemp, Fraser 4
Keswick, Henry 162
Khan, Mr 242
King, Mervyn 44n
Kingman, John 62, 63
Kinnock, Neil 29–30, 68
Kleinwort Benson 102
KPMG 43

Lamont, Norman 87, 98
Land Rover 193
Laurance, Ben 216
Lawson, Nigel 36, 48, 93
Liddell, Helen 54
Liddle, Roger 200–201, 220
Littlechild, Prof. Stephen 82
Lloyds syndicates 166
Lockheed 183
Lockheed Martin/Northrop
    Grumman merger 202
London Stock Exchange 106,
    229–30

McGinnity, Michael 143
McGuigan, John 147
MacGregor, Neil 162

McIsaac, Shona 231
Macintyre, Donald:
    Mandelson 7
Macmillan, Harold 122, 217
Maguire, Kevin 145
Mail group 125, 217
Major, John 34, 122, 123,
    134, 162, 217
Mandelson, Peter 1–6, 30,
    199
    and BMW 195–6
    and *Britannia* 120
    and the coal industry 154
    and Europe 125, 126, 128,
        130, 132, 137–8
    the loan issue 6–15, 174,
        230
    role in the government
        138–40
Mandelson, Peter and Roger
    Liddle: *The Blair
    Revolution: Can New
    Labour Deliver?* 139
Marconi 203, 205, 206
Marshall, Sir Colin (later
    Lord) 135
Masters, Dame Sheila 43–4,
    100
Matheson, Steve 53
Maude, Francis 219
Maxwell, Kevin 235, 236
Maxwell, Robert 10, 16,
    221, 222, 226, 230, 233,
    235–40
Menem, Carlos 42–3
Miliband, Ed 33, 35
Militant 30
Millennium Commission 165
Ministry of Defence 108,
    109, 112, 113, 115–19,
    187, 205
Monetary Policy Committee
    (MPC) 37, 38, 42, 44,
    45
Monopolies and Mergers
    Commission 63
Montague, Adrian 102–3,
    107, 111
Morris 16
Morrison, Herbert 140
Mottram, Sir Richard 108
Mounier, Jacques 17, 18, 22,
    23, 24, 26
Mowlam, Mo 61
Murdoch, Rupert 30, 34,
    125, 214

museums 161–5
Museums and Galleries
    Commission 167

NASDAQ 230
National Audit Office 57
National Gallery 162
National Grid 70, 81, 82,
    155–6, 159
National Health Service
    (NHS) 56, 83, 103
National Portrait Gallery
    161, 162
National Power 70, 159
National Union of
    Railwaymen 2
National Westminster 241,
    242
NATO 207
Neal, Phil 143
New Deal 52, 61, 75, 83, 96,
    120
New Statesman 10, 130
New Yorker 235
News of the World 34
NIESR model 90
Nissan 22
Nolan Committee 102
Nordstern 167
Nye, Sue 4, 33, 233

Oakley, Robin 15
Observer 123–4, 135, 198,
    213, 216, 217
Office of Fair Trading 63
Oftel 82
OM (Officina Meccanica)
    242
Orion Trust 211
Osborne, Chris 69

P&O 111, 112, 119
Parkinson, Lord 212
Partnership UK 64, 107,
    240–45
PAYE 86
Pearson, Ian 219, 233
pension funds 87
PEPs 96, 172–7, 179–81
Pergamon 240
Peston, Robert 124–5, 126,
    127
PFI 50, 53, 64, 98, 99, 101,
    102, 103, 107, 109, 121,
    224, 225, 226, 228, 233
Philip, HRH Prince, Duke

of Edinburgh 110, 115,
    121
Pinin Farina 114
Pischetsrieder, Bernd 196,
    197
Plenderleith, Ian 44n
POCOL project 104, 105,
    107
Porterbrook 81–2
Portillo, Michael 109, 113,
    114
Powell, Jonathan 188
Powergen 70, 152, 159
Pratt and Witney 185
Prescott, John 2, 112, 152
Press Association 211
Prestige 241
Price, Lance 9, 12
Primarolo, Dawn 55, 111
Private Finance Initiative 32,
    108
Prudential 90
Pryor, Tony 114–15, 119,
    121
PSBR 57–8
PSP (pool selling price) 159
Pym, Francis 226

Railtrack 70
Raytheon 202
REC 70, 72
Redwood, John 113–14
Read, Sir Herbert 165
Rees-Mogg, William 215
Reitzle, Wolfgang 197
Renwick, Robin 92
Richardson, Bryan 142–8
Richardson, Dick 143
Richardson, Peter 143
Riddell, Peter 157
Riley, Nick 193, 194
Robert Fleming 91
Robert Fraser Group 236,
    237
Robertson, George 121
Robins, Derrick 142, 146–7
Robinson, Cayley 5
Robinson, Geoffrey
    (author's namesake)
    241–2
Robinson, Pauline 241, 242
Robinson family trust 178,
    209
Robson, Sir Steve 41–2,
    52–3, 62, 92, 100, 103,
    106, 180

Rocques, John 185
Roll Center Inc. 232
Rolls-Royce 183–6, 188
ROSCO 70, 81, 82
Rose, John 185
Routledge, Paul 13, 123
Rover *see* BMW/Rover
Rowe, Brian 186
Royal Mail 105, 106
Royal Navy 110, 112, 116
Ryder Report 18, 27

Sanger, Chris 69
Saumarez Smith, Charles 162
Scargill, Arthur 152
Scarman dictum 77
Scheele, Nick 198
SCOTSCO 70, 72
Scott, Derek 45, 125
Scottish Electricity
    Companies 70
Serota, Nick 161, 166, 167,
    168
Shaw, David 219
Shearer, Alan 146
Sheldon, Robert 231, 232
Shephard, Gillian 148
Shrum, Bob 133
Silicon Valley 63
Simon, Lord (David) 196
Singh, Rabinder 75, 78
Smith, John 3, 4, 29–30, 31,
    68, 69, 123
Sopel, Jon 5
Spottiswoode, Clare 82
Stenbell Limited 211, 232
Sterling, Jeffrey 111–12, 119
Stevenson, Dennis (later
    Lord) 165, 166, 168
Stevenson, Wilf 169, 170
Steward, James 107
Stokes, Donald 19
Stubbs, John 241
Sun 10–11, 12, 213–15
Sunday Express 216
Sunday Telegraph 216
Sunday Times, The 80, 82,
    213, 216

Tate, the 161, 162, 165–9
Tate Modern 55, 162, 168
Taxation of Chargeable
    Gains Act (1992) 73n
Taylor, Stewart 61

Tescos 148
TESSAs 172–6, 181
Texas Instruments 202
Thatcher, Margaret (later
    Baroness Thatcher) 31,
    45, 51, 111, 122, 162,
    163
Thompson, Ruth 61
Thomson, Richard 48
TI-Dowty 203–4
Times, The 10, 48, 122, 128,
    133, 137, 149, 157, 215,
    216, 220
Titmuss Sainer Dechert 211
Tomlinson, John 28–9
Touche Ross 185
Toussaint, Willy 21
Toyota 17, 19, 22, 23
Transco 82
Transfer Technology Group
    plc 238
Transport Act (1983) 2
Transport and General
    Workers' Union 2
Transport House, London
    27, 28, 234
TransTec plc 142, 186, 211,
    212, 214, 232, 236, 237,
    238, 241, 243
Treasury 5, 6, 10, 36, 41, 44,
    86, 90
    and BAe 188, 190, 191,
        192
    and BMW 192
    and the coal industry 154,
        155, 156
    duty-free goods policy 111
    and Europe 126, 127, 130,
        131, 132
    and ISAs 172, 174–8, 180,
        181
    life at the 46–85
    and museums 163, 166,
        167
    and Rolls-Royce 184, 185
    shadow 27
    and Vauxhall 193, 194
Triumph Meriden
    Motorcycle cooperative
    16, 18, 19, 29
Truman King 241–2
Trump, Donald 235
Truss, Lynne 149
TUC 98, 129

Turnbull, Sir Andrew 47, 51
Turner, Adair 92
Turner, J. M. W. 165–6,
    168
Turner, Mike, 191

US Defence Department
    202, 205, 206

Vallance, Sir Iain 181
VAT on fuel 82
Vauxhall 192–5
Victoria and Albert Museum
    (V&A) 163–4

Wales, Chris 69, 73, 74, 176
Walker, Anna 154
Walker, Peter 44
Wall, Stephen (later Sir
    Stephen Wall) 217
Wallace Gallery 161n
Wallis, Ed 152
Ward, Commodore R. G. J.
    203n
WASC 70, 72
Webster, Philip 128, 216
Weinstock, Lord 100
Welfare to Work programme
    52
Wellcome Foundation 64n
Wellcome Trust 64
Whelan, Charlie 5, 6, 9,
    12–13, 14, 32–3, 39,
    120, 125–6, 129, 130,
    134, 139, 145–6,
    211–22, 214
Whelan, Noel 144
White, Wilf 164
Wicks, Sir Nigel 131, 133,
    134
Wilder Coe 212
Williams, Michael 53
Wilson, Harold (later Baron
    Wilson) 19, 28, 29, 122,
    234, 235n
Wilson, Lady 223
Wilson, Sir Richard 51,
    204–5, 222, 223–4, 227
Wintour, Patrick 216
Work Incentives and Poverty
    Analysis team 62

Yorkshire Electricity 75
Young, Robin 153